PRINCIPLES OF
MACROECONOMICS
UNDERSTANDING OUR MATERIAL WORLD

SECOND EDITION

Fred Newbury
Dave Shorow
Richland College
DCCCD

Gus Herring
Brookhaven College
DCCCD

Kendall Hunt
publishing company

Kendall Hunt
publishing company

www.kendallhunt.com
Send all inquiries to:
4050 Westmark Drive
Dubuque, IA 52004-1840

Copyright © 2009, 2010 by Fred Newbury, Dave Shorow, and Gus Herring

ISBN 978-0-7575-8049-9

Printed in the United States of America
10 9 8 7 6 5 4 3 2

An Important Note from Your Authors

Welcome to the study of macroeconomics. You have already seen quite a bit of information about this learning program. The purpose of this preface is to give you some background about the development of this material and suggestions on how it may best be used.

In considering the overall learning/teaching process, everyone has their own preferred learning style—the way that we learn "best." A student's optimum learning style may be reading the printed word. This has been the primary mode of teaching and learning for many generations and printed textbooks the vehicle that has been used to communicate information. On the other hand, you may learn best by listening to the spoken word. This would certainly be characterized by the lecture method in classrooms. Or, you may learn best by being actively involved in a process. This "hands-on" participation calls for students to make decisions, apply information, and reach conclusions. This learning-by-doing has become an increasingly preferred learning style.

Fred Newbury

No doubt that all of these modes are important methods of gaining information—learning. However, nearly all students have one primary learning style that is most efficient for them. More and more, research indicates that students are moving away from the reading or listening mode as their primary method of gaining information and toward the active, "doing" approach to learning. We can debate whether these changes are positive or negative but our world is changing. Certainly computers have contributed to this change and will, undoubtedly, continue to influence the way that we learn and the way that we live.

How does all of this relate to you and to this course? First, the material for this course is designed to be multi-modal in delivery. That means you will be utilizing a number of different learning aids—not just a textbook. This text is intended to be a concise overview of the basic fundamentals of macroeconomics. **It is only a part of the total learning system**—you will be utilizing a number of on-line, inter-active elements which will expand these basic concepts.

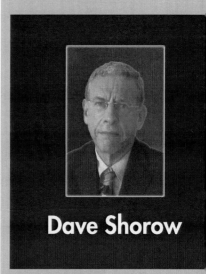

Dave Shorow

This development of this learning system is based upon the following conclusions:

- Learning materials should be multi-modal in design and function and not focus on just one learning style, such as reading.

- It is important to encourage as much active student interaction as possible—learning by doing.

- The computer can be a valuable and efficient tool to expedite learning, encourage active participation and reduce costs.

- More active student involvement can increase understanding, mastery of concepts and course completion.

Please log-in as soon as you can to the site (INSTRUCTONS ARE ON THE ACCESS CARD) and begin to familiarize yourself with the program. You should find answers to most of your questions. We hope that you will have a productive and beneficial semester.

Gus Herring

Lesson One
Fundamentals of a Market Economy

Introduction

In this lesson, we will focus on some of the basic ideas that describe economics. As with any survey course, the learning objectives provide the basic foundation. Definitions, as well as an understanding of the methods used for analysis, are also important components.

LEARNING OBJECTIVES

Please note the listed objectives. As you will see, the course materials are all objective driven. This provides you with a constant way to direct and monitor your progress throughout the course. Each objective is color-coded and corresponds to that particular section in the text.

OBJECTIVE ONE | 1

Define Economics.
Describe how economists define Human Behavior. Why is this important in today's world?

OBJECTIVE TWO | 2

Describe the difference between Macroeconomics and Microeconomics.

OBJECTIVE THREE | 3

Describe the use of the Scientific Approach to economics.
What are the tools and terms associated with the Scientific Approach?

OBJECTIVE FOUR | 4

Identify the Goals of Economics.
Demonstrate an understanding of the related Terms and Concepts.

OBJECTIVE FIVE | 5

Describe the difference between Positive Economics and Normative Economics.

INTERACTIVE EXERCISE

Demonstrate an understanding of the Basic Circular Flow Model.

WHAT IS ECONOMICS?

It is important to understand that economics inevitably involves some type of system—a system that is used to allocate resources. In more simple terms, an economic system helps determine "what is produced" and "who gets what."

DEFINITION

While there are several elements to consider when attempting to define economics, the simplest definition focuses on economics as a study of the allocation of resources. Specifically, economics is the study of the choices, methods and systems used by societies to allocate scarce resources.

"To allocate" our scarce resources (our productive assets) implies that we would like to divide them so they could be used in the best possible way. The idea that resources are "scarce" implies that we have limited amounts of these assets compared to our desire to have more of the things that those resources can produce. As individuals as well as a society, we continue to desire more — our wants seem to be insatiable (unable to be fully satisfied).

In short, then, the study of economics seeks to help us improve the choices, methods and systems by which we allocate our scarce resources. In doing so, we strive to better satisfy the basic needs (and hopefully some portion of the wants) that people have. We will study the behavior of the economy at the societal level as well as the economic behavior of individuals and organizations within our society.

MACRO VS. MICRO

The discipline of economics is divided into two major areas of study: Macroeconomics and Microeconomics.

Macroeconomics is the study of the overall allocation of resources within a society; it is the study of the overall national economy. Macroeconomics analyzes how resources are used at the aggregate level (the total supply and demand for goods and services). This includes measures of performance, such as the growth rate of the economy, inflation, unemployment, government expenditures and total investment expenditures by business.

Microeconomics is the study of resource allocation from the perspective of smaller units in the economy, such as the individual consumer and the individual business unit or firm. Microeconomics analyzes how resource allocation is influenced by consumers seeking "utility" (satisfaction of their needs and wants) and by businesses seeking "profits." Microeconomics includes measures of behavior and performance, such as consumer utility patterns as well as business revenues, costs and profits.

Both branches of economics seek to measure and analyze something called economic "efficiency."

AN ECONOMIC WAY OF THINKING

Economists are social scientists who try to measure the attainment of economic "efficiency." In concept, economic "efficiency" is maximized when the most utility is obtained for the most people. Economists, then, are social scientists who analyze the choices, methods and systems that seek "efficiency" in the allocation of limited resources. A number of different realities and considerations influence the quest for an "efficient" allocation of resources. These will be explored as we move through the course.

One of the skills required for economists is the ability to reason critically. Critical reasoning in economics is the ability to analyze the allocation process logically and evaluate the expected outcomes and uncertainties of various courses of action. Critical reasoning in economics is an activity that considers alternative courses of action and expected results relative to the costs and risks of each action.

The Principles of Economics are the generally accepted concepts and theories that relate to the overall allocation of resources. These principles are derived from the observation of human behaviors that occur over and over as people attempt to meet their material needs and wants. This body of knowledge evolves as we develop an even better and deeper understanding of basic economic relationships.

Policy Economics is the application of economic principles when a government is attempting to formulate an approach that will contribute to an efficient and growing economy, yet one that is also reasonably stable and equitable (fair). A strong insight into basic economic relationships is critical to understanding how the government attempts to manage parts of our economic system in trying to reach these objectives.

WHY STUDY ECONOMICS?

There are widely divergent reasons why people study economics, but for a student the answer is often very simple — it is a required subject or part of a core area of study. The most common reason for this requirement is to promote an understanding of how a society can best use its resources and how as a society we must make rational choices in seeking a better standard of living. In a free market society based on capitalism, an informed electorate is a necessity for social and economic development. A better understanding of our economic system is essential for all citizens in order for good choices to be made in our ongoing roles as business people, consumers, savers/investors, taxpayers and voters. In all these roles, critical reasoning skills are extremely important.

ANALYTIC TOOLS

WHAT ARE THE TOOLS OF ECONOMICS?

TOOL 1 - RATIONAL ANALYSIS:

The study of Economics involves the use of a logical pattern of thinking as well as the use of a number of analytical tools. Economists assume that people make rational choices by being able to understand what they want and that people consider the benefits, costs, uncertainties and risks involved in a particular path of action.

TOOL 2 - MARGINAL ANALYSIS:

When studying different possible paths of action, the results of inputs vs. outputs are considered. An application of this concept would be involved in making the choice of whether to go to another (or your first) country music concert this month . . . or not. The marginal cost (the additional cost of an additional event) is considered relative to the marginal benefit (additional amount of satisfaction expected). When deciding whether or not to undertake the action, a rational person considers the marginal cost relative to the marginal benefit.

The benefit of an action is simply the "utility" that the action creates (recall that "utility" is simply "satisfaction"). Total utility is the total amount of satisfaction gained from all allocations of resources, whereas marginal utility is the additional amount of pleasure gained from the allocation of one additional unit of resource. In the example above, marginal utility is the benefit gained from going to the additional (or first) concert. The choice to attend one more concert this month is economically justified if the marginal benefit is greater than the marginal cost (i.e., if the utility gained is greater than the utility that had to be given up). This leads us to a discussion of our next tool: opportunity cost analysis.

TOOL 3 - OPPORTUNITY COST ANALYSIS:

Anytime we receive a benefit from the use of a resource, it comes at a cost because we could have used that resource for a different opportunity. All our resource allocations come at a cost and this cost is compared to the benefit we receive in deciding if we should undertake the action. In the above illustration of going to a concert, an individual must certainly consider the monetary costs of going to the concert, such as the ticket price and transportation, but she must also consider what had to be forgone (given up) in order to attend. Perhaps the person could have caught up on her sleep, or worked and made additional income. These opportunities are lost if she chooses to attend the concert.

The overall cost of the choice to attend the additional concert includes not only the out-of-pocket costs but also the opportunity cost (lost sleep or lost wages . . . whichever might have provided the greatest utility at the time). Every activity that we undertake requires us to not do other activities. The total cost of a choice is the out-of-pocket costs plus the opportunity cost (the most desirable alternative that was given up). The overall cost of this course includes the direct dollar expenditures plus the wages you could have earned during the time allocated to the course.

TOOL 4 - VARIABLE ANALYSIS:

In an analysis of any situation, economists carefully consider the relationships among all the interacting variables. However, special emphasis is placed on considering changes in only one variable at a time. This is called "ceteris paribus" (Latin translation: "with other things remaining the same").

Any one variable is evaluated for its affect on a situation rather than in combination with many other variables. This concept is illustrated when an economist seeks to find the main factor determining individual income in the United States.

Many variables determine how much income individuals are able to earn during their career, but a major variable is level of education. Variable analysis reveals that college graduates as a group make considerably more money than high school graduates over the course of their careers. Once again, a number of variables are involved in this type of study . . . but they must be considered one at a time. Economists use the "ceteris paribus" approach to help identify cause and effect relationships. It is important to note here that the correlation between two variables (for example, education and income) does not always mean that one variable is actually causing the other variable to change.

ECONOMIC GOALS

A number of different goals in our economy are constantly being pursued. For example, one goal of the consumer is to maximize utility. One goal of the business firm is to maximize profit (this may or may not be accomplished by maximizing the consumer's utility). In the case of the business firm, there are actually many participants whose goals must be recognized, including workers, management, stockholders, bondholders and even the government.

At the macroeconomic level, we strive to improve the allocation of resources in order to produce a better standard of living for everyone. The following are generally accepted national goals for our economy:

MACROECONOMICS GOALS

Growth is the goal that seeks an increase in the amount of goods and services being produced. The amount of goods and services produced is measured as Gross Domestic Product (GDP). The goal is to increase the real value (value without inflation) of goods and services and to create new jobs in that growing economy.

Efficiency is the goal to produce a maximum output of the most desirable items with a given input of resources (more on this in Lesson Two).

Full Employment is a goal strongly related to "growth" and seeks the full use of workers who are willing and able to be productive. Attainment of this goal is often reported in the media as the "unemployment rate." Since an unemployment rate of "0%" is not realistic (or desirable, as we shall see later), the actual goal is to have a reasonably low level of unemployment in a growing economy with low inflation.

Stability is a constant concern as we attempt to achieve a balance between a low rate of inflation and a low rate of unemployment in a growing economy. This is an extremely important macro concept and will be discussed in much more detail.

Ecological Balance emphasizes the need to maintain a sustainable global environment. Ecological balance assumes that the global economy can achieve its other economic goals while maintaining a healthy, living planet.

Freedom for citizens is a goal of economics within capitalism. The freedom to make purchases as desired and to work and live independent of extensive controls by government is a basic and fundamental principle of free markets and free people.

Social Balance is when we seek a reasonable balance within our social structure and between our public sector (local, state and federal government) and our private sector (households and business firms). A reasonable balance within the social structure and among the economic sectors requires responsible actions on the part of all participants.

Equity (or fairness) in the distribution of income is essential to the health and survival of a free society. It is important to note here that an "equitable" distribution of the economic pie does not mean an "equal" piece of pie for everybody. It does mean that every person should have an equal opportunity to *earn* a larger piece of the pie and that no person should be left to suffer in unreasonable poverty.

A **Balance of Trade** within the **international markets** is an increasingly important goal. Over time, a nation must balance its position within the global markets in order to achieve and maintain prosperity.

DEBATES IN ECONOMIC POLICY

The variation in the amount of emphasis placed on each of the goals above is determined by the cultural values of a society. It is a reality, however, that some goals will have to take priority over other goals. Although human nature desires maximum attainment of every goal, some of our goals are conflicting (as progress is attained on one, progress on the other may be sacrificed). Some goals are actually complementary (progress on one can be made at the same time as progress on the other).

Growth and Full Employment tend to be "complementary" goals, while Growth and Stability tend to be "conflicting." When growth is strong, full employment is likely. But when growth is strong, it is also likely (although not a certainty) that there will be inflation. If inflation does occur, that is definitely in conflict with the goal of stability.

Vigorous debates are likely when macroeconomic goals and changes in government policy are discussed. There is much agreement among economists about the basic principles (generalizations) of how an economy "works." However, there is considerable disagreement about which goals should be emphasized, how to pursue these goals and how much emphasis should be given to government policy. An understanding of the possible roles that the government sector might play (in relation to the private sector and foreign sector) is critical in developing an overall understanding of our material world.

The two macroeconomic goals that tend to be emphasized the most by the government sector are Stability (trying to keep both unemployment and inflation low) and Equity. Two goals that tend to be emphasized the most in the private sector by microeconomic actions are Efficiency and Growth. At this point, it is very important to understand that there will be "trade-offs" when attempts are made toward progress on any of these four goals. This means that gains in Stability or Equity will often lead to short-run, or possibly long-run, losses in Growth or Efficiency and vice versa. Even within the goal of Stability, an improvement in the unemployment rate can in the longer run result in a worse inflation rate and, once again, vice versa. The ongoing challenge in any society is to understand the reality of "trade-offs" and then try to make good choices that lead to a reasonable balance in the attainment of its economic goals.

POSITIVE VS. NORMATIVE ECONOMICS

Positive Economics is the description of an economy by stating facts or objective data. The inflation rate or unemployment rate as measured by a government agency would be considered an example of positive economics. If we say, "the current unemployment rate is 5 percent," it would be positive economics because it is a statement of fact — no opinion is stated or implied.

Normative Economics is the statement of an opinion about the economy. It is a subjective view. Normative economics describes many of the disagreements among economists relating to what goals should be emphasized or what the economic policies of the government should be. If we say, "the unemployment rate has not risen above 5 percent because of the government's aggressive fiscal policy," that is quite different from simply stating, "The current unemployment rate is 5 percent." Now we see that an opinion has been expressed and, yes, the "scientific testing" of opinions and theories opens additional areas for discussion and disagreement.

Debates within economics are expected to be rationally based on widely accepted economic principles and well-tested (or at least testable) theories. As we consider the scientific testing (and real-world application) of economic theories, we will see how much "normative economics" can enter into debates about which government policies should be used. Biased opinions without any probable economic merit can be very destructive. Societies without bias in their economic debates appear to make better choices about how to efficiently use their resources.

Another difficulty that sometimes occurs within economic debates is called the **fallacy of composition**. A fallacy of composition exists when we conclude that something that is beneficial for an individual person or an individual business is also beneficial for society as whole. An example of this concept would be if you concluded that your pollution of the creek behind your house or business is beneficial since it saves you the hassle of hauling your trash to the dump. What if all the people along the creek (including those "upstream" from your place) do what is "beneficial" for each of them individually? What is beneficial for each person individually is not necessarily beneficial for society as a whole.

> Positive vs. Normative
>
> **Positive statements** assert facts and objective data.
>
> **Normative statements** assert how things ought to be. Opinions.

THE CIRCULAR FLOW MODEL OF ECONOMICS

The **Circular Flow Model** is used in our course to illustrate the basic relationships that exist between the household sector and business sector in a market-based economy. The government sector (whose responsibilities include developing policies to deal with the pollution problem mentioned above) will be added to the model in a later lesson along with the foreign sector.

In a market-based system, the household sector usually owns the four basic economic resources. In concept, the land, labor, capital and entrepreneurship are provided to the business sector in exchange for the products and services produced by the business sector. This exchange is facilitated by two markets — the product market and the factor market.

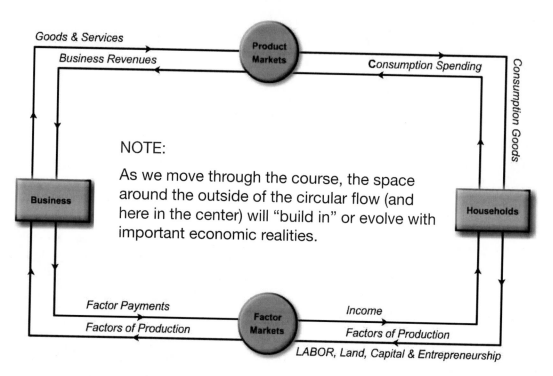

In the factor (or resource market) located on the underside of the model, the households supply the land, labor, capital and entrepreneurship to the businesses in exchange for four different types of income. Landholders (the owners of natural resource) receive rent. Labor (the owners of productive time and talent) receives wages. Capital holders (the owners of productive tools and equipment) receive interest. Entrepreneurs (the owners of business building skills) receive profits.

The product market is the exchange located on the topside of the circular flow. Businesses supply the goods and services which are desired by the households. In turn the households pay for the goods and services with the income which they have received from the businesses. These payments become revenues back to the businesses which, in turn, they use to make the factor payments to the households. Yes, it is very much a circular flow.

Where is the actual starting point of this circular flow? In a market-based economy, the answer is that it starts with the entrepreneur. It is the entrepreneur who has a new idea and takes the risk to start a business. The entrepreneur then employs some combination of the other three resources from the factor market to create a good or service and then tries to sell that item in the product market. If the entrepreneur is successful, then the circular flow will continue and grow.

If not, then the circular flow will cease (at least for that particular entrepreneur in that particular business).

The Circular Flow Model is one of the most important concepts in all of economics. It provides an improved understanding of the microeconomic foundations of our society and it provides important insights into many of our macroeconomic problems, such as recession and inflation. Pay very close attention to the circular flow examples in the "Animations & Interactives" component of the course. In each new lesson, important "economic realities" will be added to this model.

You have now reviewed the Preview Questions and Learning Objectives for Lesson One **and** you have completed the video, PowerPoint and E-text components. Now use the **ANIMATIONS & INTERACTIVES** button to apply what you have learned.

Real-World Economics

IS A COLLEGE DEGREE WORTH THE COST?

For many years, the answer to this question was an automatic "yes." However, with rapidly rising costs in higher education (tuition at some private schools is more than $30,000 per year), that question has been receiving closer attention. Is a college degree really worth the dollar cost and the opportunity cost? Is the marginal (extra) benefit greater than the marginal (extra) cost?

According to ongoing research by the College Board, the answer is still yes—especially when you look at the lifetime earnings of a high school graduate compared with someone with a bachelor's degree. The college graduate will earn (on average) 60% more than those with a high school diploma. Over a lifetime, that amounts to more than $800,000. It certainly appears that the marginal benefit is still greater than the marginal cost — which makes earning a college degree a sound decision.

Key Terms

Economics: Economics is the study of the choices, methods and systems used by societies to allocate scarce resources.

Fallacy of Composition: The fallacy of composition exists when we conclude that something that is appropriate for an individual also must be appropriate for society. Example: If it is good for the individual to save more, it must be good for the overall economy.

Macroeconomics: Macroeconomics is a study of the allocation of resources relative to the overall national economy or large sectors within it.

Marginal Analysis: Comparing the marginal (extra) costs to the marginal (extra) benefits as an aid to decision making. Example: Is the extra (marginal) benefit of a college degree greater than the marginal cost?

Microeconomics: Microeconomics is a study of the allocation of resources in smaller units, specifically the individual consumer and the individual business unit or firm.

Normative Economics: The description of the economy where opinion is used and value judgments are made. Example: Because of government's effective use of fiscal policy, unemployment has fallen to only 5%.

Opportunity Cost Analysis: Anytime we receive a benefit from the use of a resource, it comes at a cost because we could have used that resource for a different opportunity. All our decisions come at a cost and this cost is compared to the benefit we receive in deciding if we should undertake the action.

Positive Economics: The description of an economy by stating facts or using specific data. No opinion is involved. Example: The unemployment rate is 5%.

Policy Economics: The application of the principles of economics to government policy actions. Government seeks to understand economic activities in order to influence economic activity.

Rational Analysis: The study of Economics involves the use of a logical pattern of thinking as well as analytical tools for analysis.

Variable Analysis: Economists consider the variable relationships in their analysis with an emphasis on considering the relationship of one variable at a time. This is called ceteris paribus (Latin translated as meaning one at a time). Each variable is evaluated relative to itself rather than in combination with many other variables.

Applied Exercises

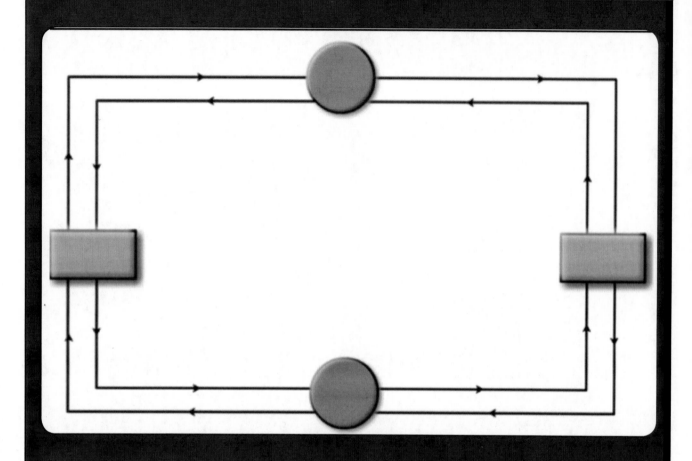

Exercise One:

A. Complete the circular flow chart above.

B. The exchange flows in the top of the model are called the
    _____ market.

    The exchange flows in the bottom of the model are called the
    _____ market.

Applied Exercises

Exercise Two:

Consider each of the following costs and benefits and find the marginal cost and marginal benefit of each.

Project	Cost	Benefit	Marginal Cost	Marginal Benefit
A	$1,000	100		
B	$2,000	300		
C	$5,000	500		
D	$10,000	650		

Exercise Three:

Consider the cost of each of the actions and relate whether or not you should undertake each given the data.

	Cost	Benefit	Action
Vacation A	$500	$1,400	
Vacation B	$1,000	$3,250	
Vacation C	$750	$2,300	
Vacation D	$1,250	$3,750	

If you have $1,250 to spend, how should you allocate your funds and why?

Applied Exercises: Answers

Exercise One:

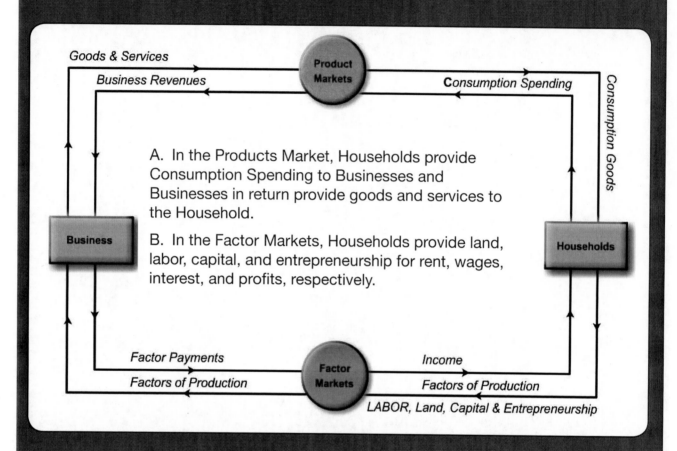

Goods & Services

Business Revenues

Product Markets

Consumption Spending

Consumption Goods

A. In the Products Market, Households provide Consumption Spending to Businesses and Businesses in return provide goods and services to the Household.

B. In the Factor Markets, Households provide land, labor, capital, and entrepreneurship for rent, wages, interest, and profits, respectively.

Business

Households

Factor Payments

Factors of Production

Factor Markets

Income

Factors of Production

LABOR, Land, Capital & Entrepreneurship

Exercise Two:

Project	Cost	Benefit	Marginal Cost	Marginal Benefit
A	$1,000	100	$1,000	100
B	$2,000	300	$1,000	200
C	$5,000	500	$3,000	200
D	$10,000	650	$5,000	150

Exercise Three:

The largest benefit from spending $1,250 would be Vacation D because no other combination is within the income limits and provides more benefits.

Lesson **Two**
The Economic Problem

Introduction

In this lesson, we will focus on some of the basic ideas that describe the **Economic Problem** and the beginnings of a market economy. As with any survey course, the objectives provide the basic foundations. The questions posed by the Economic Problem give rise to the need for a system that will help allocate scarce resources.

LEARNING OBJECTIVES

Please note the listed objectives. As you will see, the course materials are all objective driven. This provides you with a constant way to direct and monitor your progress throughout the course. Each objective is color-coded and corresponds to that particular section in the text.

OBJECTIVE ONE · 1

Define the Economic Problem and describe the three Economic Systems that have been employed down through history to address this problem.

OBJECTIVE TWO · 2

Identify the four Basic Economic Questions that every Economic System must answer.

OBJECTIVE THREE · 3

Identify the four Basic Economic Resources (the Factors of Production) that every Economic System has available to help answer those four Basic Economic Questions.

OBJECTIVE FOUR · 4

Describe the historical evolution of the Market System and describe the contributions of five prominent economists to this evolution.

OBJECTIVE FIVE · 5

Use the Production Possibilities Model to explain the Economic Problem and the related concepts of Efficiency, Equity, Stability and Growth.

OBJECTIVE SIX · 6

Use the Production Possibilities Model to explain Trade-offs and Opportunity Cost.

THE ECONOMIC PROBLEM?

The Economic Problem is an idea that is very basic to our study. The problem centers on the contrast between unlimited human wants and the relative scarcity of all resources. The questions posed by this problem give rise to the need for a system that will help allocate scarce resources.

There are two parts to the Economic Problem. First, human wants are insatiable (unable to be fully satisfied). As a group, humans desire to have more goods and services than are available. This tends to be a natural state of the human condition. We always seem to want more. Second, resources are finite and limited in nature. There are fixed amounts of resources available at any one time, and these resources can only be directed toward satisfying a limited number of human wants. The conclusion is that, taken as a whole, our wants exceed our limited resources. Therein lies the nature of the Economic Problem.

While the Economic Problem is as old as society itself, the systems developed to answer it are relatively new. Macroeconomics has become a study of these large systems, while microeconomics has become a study of business behavior and consumer behavior within these systems. Economics is the study of how these behaviors and systems interact to allocate scarce resources toward the satisfaction of unlimited wants.

The Economic Problem focuses our attention on the efficient use of our scarce resources. Economic efficiency is gaining the most output to maximize consumer utility (or satisfaction) from a given amount of input. Productive efficiency is simply gaining the most output of certain items with a given amount of input, but not relating that output to consumer utility. A maximum of output of certain items, even if efficiently produced, is not desirable if consumers do not really want the items produced. Throughout history, however, the goal of some powerful entities has been to emphasize the production of certain items regardless of whether or not those particular items were actually "wanted" by the citizens in that society. Do any examples come to mind? Perhaps pyramids or missiles or "the Edsel" (try that in a search engine) would be examples? But we should be careful to consider these examples (and any others) in the context of their time and culture.

ALLOCATION

Four questions of allocation must be addressed by any economic system striving for economic efficiency and responding to the Economic Problem.

THE FOUR QUESTIONS OF ALLOCATION

What to Produce?

We must determine what specific items will be produced and how much to produce of each item. Within a market-based system, the process of responding to these questions is driven by consumers. Market-based systems are driven by consumer wants.

How to Produce?

In a market-based system, this question is answered primarily by the businesses. In trying to produce what consumers want, an individual firm will try to use the most efficient combination of resources. This approach keeps the firms production costs down and its profits up.

Who to Produce For?

This is the question of how the items will be distributed among the population or what approach to "income distribution" is considered fair and equitable. This question is largely answered in a market economy by individual productivity. Individuals who produce the largest quantities of those items that are considered most desirable will be rewarded with the highest income. This raises several interesting issues that will be addressed as we proceed through the course.

Efficiency and Power?

The fourth question of economic allocation is answered in a market economy by competition. The goal of efficiency is to produce the maximum output of desirable items with a given input. For a business, this will lead to a gain in market share that, in turn, creates market power. Every modern society has choices in how resources are allocated. But cultural values are still a very strong influence in determining this allocation process. Pay close attention to the "market mechanisms" as presented in the PowerPoint section.

THE STANDARD OF LIVING

The standard of living in a society is ultimately determined by the amount of resources that are available and how efficiently they are used. There is a complex economic process involved in determining what is produced as well as how much of each item is produced (and whether it is produced by national or international sources). This economic process begins with the four factors of production.

FACTORS OF PRODUCTION

The factors of production are simply the four basic categories of economic resources used for creating goods and services.

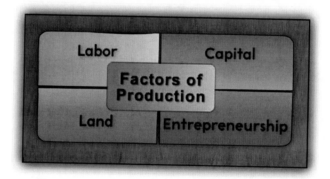

LAND

The first factor of production is Land. In order to produce and deliver any economic good or service, there must be some use of natural resources. The basic economic term encompassing all natural resources is "Land." Regardless of whether the item is wheat or the World Wide Web (or anything in between), "Land" will be a necessary factor of production. It is obvious that wheat production requires "dirt," but it is equally apparent that services delivered over "the web" require such basic natural resources as silicone (for computer chips), coal (to generate the electricity) and even air (to carry the waves of wireless information).

LABOR

The second factor of production is Labor. All production involves some amount of human effort. The time and talent of humans (Labor) must be mixed with the other factors of production to create goods and services. Labor is a highly valued factor of production because it is closely tied to increasing a society's standard of living. The efficiency and effectiveness of Labor is determined by peoples' skill and knowledge as well as their attitude and use of economic Capital.

CAPITAL

The third factor of production is Capital. The term economic (or "real") capital describes the tools, facilities and equipment that aid in the production of all products and services. In this sense, the term Capital is not money but rather is used to describe the man-made tools used in the production process. The term Capital includes computers and office buildings as well as shovels and dump trucks. Capital, then, describes any tool that aids in production—regardless of how simple or complex. Capital is also referred to as the "manufactured resource" and must be created by human effort before it in turn can be used to create other products.

We normally use the term financial capital (or business investment) to describe the money used to purchase the "real" (or economic) capital. The funds for business investment must come from corporate earnings that are retained for that purpose or from household savings borrowed by businesses. Business investment is critical for economic growth. Investment by businesses in better economic capital means that our productive capacity, and our economy, will have greater efficiency as well as increased opportunities for growth in the future.

ENTREPRENEURIAL SKILL

The fourth factor of production is Entrepreneurial Skill. Entrepreneurial Skill is the ability of a person: 1) to conceive a business idea (to innovate); 2) to take the risk involved in implementing the idea; and 3) to bring together the other three resources in an efficient combination. Entrepreneurial Skill tends to be the most highly valued resource in a market-based economy. Entrepreneurs are well compensated with profits if they provide high utility to consumers at a relatively low cost. While land, labor and capital are used by all economic systems, the entrepreneur is unique to the market-based economy.

HISTORY

The history of economics describes how the basis for choice has changed over time with different allocation systems. This has been an evolutionary process and has followed changing social and political values as well as technological innovation. The human response to the Economic Problem (limited resources and unlimited wants) has over time produced three basic types of economic systems.

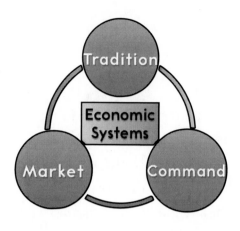

TRADITION

The first system was Tradition. In a traditional economic system the basic resources were allocated by the customs and folkways long used by a particular society or culture. These systems were often primitive, but they also provided relative stability for that society. A difficulty with this approach was that any type of suggested change or improvement was often met with strong resistance.

COMMAND

The second system was Command (or authority), which involved a strong central government or leader making all decisions relative to resource allocation. This system was controlled by only a few people who made all the fundamental economic choices for that society. It allowed for very little, if any, private ownership of resources.

MARKET

The third system is the Market. Within this system, the choices of producers and consumers interact to determine the allocation of the four basic resources. What is produced and how much is produced of each item is determined by market supply and demand. The Market allows the free interaction of buyers and sellers and also provides for the private ownership of most resources.

The transition away from Traditional and Command systems gained momentum as the manor life of Europe yielded in the 17th and 18th centuries to the beginning of the Industrial Revolution. This was a gradual process as economic markets evolved and adapted to new technologies and the need for different types of skilled labor. Not only was the economic system changing but the very nature of society itself, for better or worse, was being changed forever.

The direct underpinning of today's modern market-based economic system can be found in 18th century Britain. The prevailing philosophy of the time was logical order and natural law. An idea was taking shape that states of nature, such as the standard of living, could be logically explained and enhanced by applying several fundamental laws of economics. The condition of resource allocation was first considered in a comprehensive manner by Adam Smith.

THE FATHER OF ECONOMICS

Adam Smith, remembered as the "Father of Economics," was actually a professor of moral philosophy in Scotland. His best-known work, *An Inquiry into the Nature and Causes of the Wealth of Nations*, was published in 1776 and provided the theoretical foundation of free-market economics. Within this text a number of economic issues were addressed. The most basic question in economics regarding "what to produce" was answered by "consumer sovereignty." For Adam Smith the answer was clear—the demands of consumers should direct the supply processes of producers.

In *The Wealth of Nations* (the book's popular title), the question of how income and wealth should be distributed was answered by **productivity**: the volume and utility of a worker's output. The more "**utility**" that an individual created for society, the greater the income and wealth to which that person was entitled. The overall market process was called the "invisible hand" and this is a phrase we often use to describe the benefits of competition within the market. The final element discussed by Smith was a **laissez faire** role for government. He explained that the purpose of government was to facilitate the market and, thereby, the government should have a very **limited role** in an efficient market system.

THE WORLDLY PHILOSOPHERS

Beginning with Adam Smith, the "Worldly Philosophers" of 18th and 19th century economics held widely varied but influential views on markets and governments. David Ricardo was an economist of note in the early 1800s. During his career in the London stock market, he shared many of Smith's views and also advocated a free and open economy, unencumbered by government restrictions. His most significant theory was comparative advantage, which argued that a nation will gain through trade by specializing in the good which it produces most efficiently. According to this theory a nation will gain from trade by specializing in that product where its opportunity costs are lowest.

After Ricardo's writings, Thomas Malthus became well known for his economic views that population grew geometrically (i.e., 2, 4, 8, 16, etc.) while food production grew only arithmetically (i.e., 1, 2, 3, 4, etc.). Thus, he predicted that economic activity would evolve in cycles of misery and catastrophe. His theory did not take into account advancements in technology or in the economic systems themselves, but it did suggest that there were some limits to economic growth.

Robert Owen, a successful industrialist of this period, also had influence on the prevailing economic perspectives in England. The world of economics was in the romantic period of history, which argued that industrialization had many negative consequences and a more society-based system (less centered on the individual) would be better for everyone. Owen was a Welsh utopian socialist who believed that socialism was a remedy for the poverty of the period.

He viewed social systems as primary in determining economic activity and demanded that technology be subordinated to human interests through government intervention.

Another economic philosopher of the period was Karl Marx. Within his Communist Manifesto, published in 1848, he argued that capitalism itself would lead to socialism and then to communism as armies of unemployed workers would force economic change and a complete takeover of the economic system by the government. Marxian economics led to the creation of the communist state in Russia and influenced many other parts of the world. Marx was a prolific writer and had a profound impact on political and social systems in the 19th and 20th centuries.

Since the United States is considerably younger than the countries in Europe, it did not follow exactly the same evolution but these theories did affect the development of the United States. The classical economic views of Smith and Ricardo had considerable impact as the market economy began to grow in this country.

A Brief History of the American Economy

Financial as well as economic capital was secured from Europe to advance the American economy as it began to grow and prosper and we moved into the 1800s. Railroads became instrumental in bringing American businesses together. But this era also marked the beginning of a concentration of economic power in several sectors of the economy, including railroads, steel and banking. The Sherman Anti-Trust Act was passed in 1890 to restrain the monopoly power that had been created in these economic sectors. This legislation was, in fact, designed to return competition to these markets.

During the early 1900s, labor unions became an economic force. Workers demanded recognition of their fundamental role in the process of economic growth. Natural resources were abundant but in order to gain output, increasing numbers of workers were necessary.

The living standard of workers was very low at this time, and many began to question the distribution of income within the economy. Workers formed unions to constitute a force with the system. After much strife, unions were eventually recognized as a legal entity with the right to collective bargaining.

The depression of the 1930s caused many people to lose confidence in what had become known as the "classical theories" of economics. As unemployment increased, a new theory was emerging. This new theory, from John M. Keynes, unfolded during the 1930s and 1940s and became know as Keynesian Economics. This Keynesian approach became widely accepted in the 1950s and 1960s, only to be challenged in the 1970s by the Monetarist Theory and other related new classical theories.

The change in social attitudes that emerged in the 1960s, with an emphasis on greater equality of opportunity and income, resulted in much conflict with traditional values. During this same period, the Vietnam War added to the social turmoil.

Since the onset of the Industrial Revolution, accelerating change has been one of the major characteristics of our world. But our economic, political and social systems have evolved and responded to many challenges over the years. Change has been the only constant in this evolution, and it will, undoubtedly, continue.

As you can see from the historical material outlined above, economic theories have evolved substantially since the 1770s. One of the challenges in modern economics is to describe in simple terms the sometimes complex human choices that we encounter in today's world. During this course, we will examine several different "models" (pictures of economic behavior and human choices) that will provide important insights.

In the Animations & Interactives component of Lesson One, you had a brief introduction to two of these models—the Circular Flow Model and the Production Possibilities Model (PPM). We will now take a deeper look at the PPM.

THE PRODUCTION POSSIBILITIES MODEL

The PPM (or "PPF" for Production Possibilities Frontier) illustrates the maximum potential output of a society at a point in time. Because many different variables affect economic output, we need to note the three simplifying assumptions used with this model. Initially, we will assume that: 1) the society produces only two goods and these are graphed in various combinations using the x and y axis; 2) the factors of production remain constant in time and are fully used; 3) technology remains constant in time and is fully used. The resulting green concave curve, labeled the Production Frontier, describes the various output combinations that are possible. By producing at any point on the curve, maximum output or *production efficiency* is obtained. Recall that *economic*

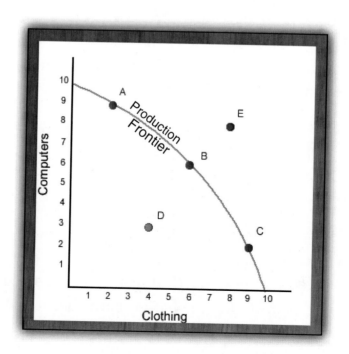

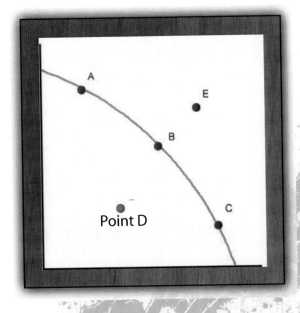

Point D

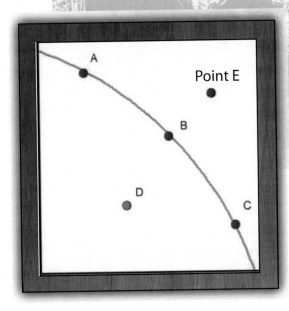

Point E

efficiency requires the production of that one specific output that consumers find most desirable.

Point D: Any point inside the frontier (curve) describes an economy with unemployment of resources or under employment of resources. Under employment is when a resource is not efficiently and fully used. This occurs when a worker (labor) is not able to work at his highest skill level or when a manufacturing plant (capital) is only being used at a portion of its capacity. Unemployment is when some resources are totally unused, such as some workers being unable to find any job at all or some manufacturing plants being totally shut down.

Point E: Any point that is slightly outside the frontier (curve) describes an economy in which the resources are working overtime or are being overused. An example of "overused" would be if a significant amount of labor is working 12-hour days, seven days a week. Point E is attainable (doable) in the short run, but in the longer run it is not sustainable. A point that is more than "slightly outside" the frontier is simply unattainable given the current amount of resources available and the current levels of technology.

Frontier Shift: This represents an overall increase (or decrease) in the potential amount of output. When the entire curve shifts outward (or inward), this would indicate that either the amounts of resources available have either increased (or decreased) or that the level of technology has changed. The widespread business use of Internet technology has certainly moved the production frontier outward. In times past, the increased availability of oil (a "Land" resource) moved the frontier outward. Certainly, the destruction of a country's productive resources in a time of war or widespread natural disaster moves the frontier inward in a very dramatic way.

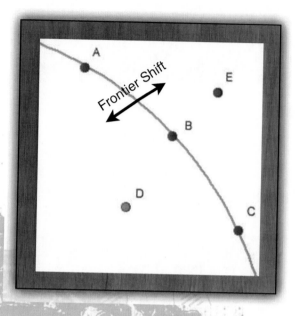

Growth: For the long run, it is important to focus on the idea of an outward shift in the frontier. Growth in the Production Possibilities Curve is possible when we loosen our assumptions about resources and technology always being fixed. Increases in technology and in the availability of resources are both possible over time if people have the incentive to be creative. If either one or some combination of these increases can be encouraged in a society, a better standard of living

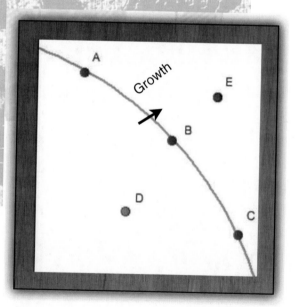

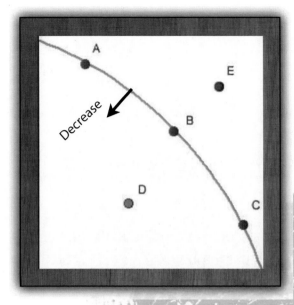

and improved quality of life can be shared by all.

The Production Possibilities Curve may decrease or shift left with a decrease in available resources. When forces of nature decrease resources, the frontier will decrease.

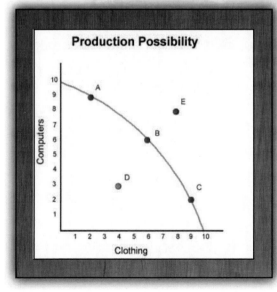

See page 30 for the larger version of this graph.

Once again, we note that the points in the graph at left are labeled A through E. All of these points are very important to understand. By reviewing the numerical values at each point (by going horizontally across from each point as well as down to find the numerical values), one can better understand the basic production possibilities concepts. We will be using these production possibilities concepts in each and every lesson throughout the course.

Point	Units of Computers	Units of Clothing
A	9	2
B	6	6
C	2	9
D	3	4
E	8	8

Point B represents the production of 6 computers in combination with 6 units of clothing. Since Point B is on the frontier, this represents an economy that has "full employment" and "production efficiency." We do not, however, have enough information to know if this point represents "allocative efficiency" and, therefore, "economic efficiency" for this society.

Point D represents the production of only 3 computers in combination with only 4 units of clothing. This represents an unemployment or under-employment situation within the model (note that Point D lies inside the frontier).

Point E represents the production of 8 computers in combination with 8 units of clothing. This represents an unsustainable (or possibly unattainable) situation (note that Point E lies outside the frontier).

Now let's explore the two other points (A and C) that are actually on the frontier along with Point B. All three points (A, B and C) represent "full employment" and "production efficiency" (since they are all on the frontier). Question: What is the **benefit** and what is the **cost** of moving from Point B to Point C?

The "benefit" and "cost" of moving from Point B to Point C are found by taking the numerical values at B and subtracting those from the values at C. At Point B, there are 6 units of clothing produced along with 6 computers. At Point C, there are 9 units of clothing produced, but only 2 computers. In a nutshell, then, to have the benefit of 3 more units of clothing (9 minus 6), there would be a cost of 4 computers (2 minus 6). Four computers would be "given up" to obtain three units of clothing if this society moved from Point B to Point C.

Would the move described above from Point B to Point C be a good choice for this society? This is a deeper question than we can fully explore in this lesson.

This goes to the question of allocative and economic efficiency for this society and the utility of clothing vs. the utility of computers at this moment in time and in the future. Looking quickly at the issue, here are some questions to consider: 1) What if it is very cold outside at the moment and there is no electricity? Would Point B be a better choice for this society than Point C? 2) What if we have plenty of electricity and no real need for extra clothing at the moment, but in the future we would like a better variety of both clothing and computers? Would Point A be an even better choice for the future than either Point B or Point C? At Point A, perhaps we could even "export" those 2 units of clothing and "import" some food from the country next door? These kinds of questions about benefits, costs and "allocative efficiency" (present and future) might be explored further in a discussion board or perhaps in a classroom discussion.

OPPORTUNITY COST IN THE PPF

The basic opportunity cost of a choice is illustrated by moving from one point on the PPF curve to another point on the curve (as we introduced in the discussion above). To determine the basic "cost" of the change (as well as the basic "benefit"), we must examine the coordinates of the points on each axis to find the amount of gain and loss from the former position. If the numerical gain from one position to another is the same as the numerical loss, then the graphical relationship is a straight line and is referred to as constant cost.

If one must give up more units of one item to gain a smaller number of units of the other item, then there is an increasing cost relationship. Increasing costs are present when resources are not perfectly shiftable; when resources are not as good at producing one thing as they are at producing the other. This is usually the case in most "real-world" situations. We must also keep in mind the reality that one unit of clothing at a certain point in time may or may not be more highly desired in the society than one computer.

For another example of the "increasing cost" concept, let's consider a situation where a nation can produce both wine and beef. However, in order to produce more wine beyond some point the nation must give up larger and larger amounts of beef output. Land used for beef production is usually not equally well suited for wine production. If another equivalent increase in wine production is desired, then even more land will need to be taken from beef production than in the last round of resource shifting. This would be just to obtain the same increase in wine output as we obtained with the previous resource shift.

In summary, if a nation's goal was to increase wine output, the nation would typically have to sacrifice more and more of its beef production. This is because the land resource is not equally suited for the production of both products. Can you think of a similar example for the labor resource? What if (following up on an example from Lesson One) we wanted to increase the output of country music concerts? Or the output of professional sports entertainment? Are we all equally well talented to produce "an equivalent level" of those entertainment services? Some of us are probably not perfectly "shiftable resources" in those examples.

The Production Possibilities Model is an important tool and one that you will see again and again as we move through the course. The PPM introduces a graphical method of analysis and emphasizes the two realities that are an inescapable part of economics—scarcity necessitates choice and every choice has a cost. If scarcity did not exist and we did not have to make choices that have costs, then we would have no real need for economics. It is very important that you spend time with the Interactive Exercises in this lesson to deepen your understanding of these important concepts and the graphical analysis that is used.

You have now reviewed the Preview Questions and Learning Objectives for Lesson Two and you have completed the video, PowerPoint and E-text components. To begin applying what you have learned, you should pay close attention to the **Animations&Interactives** component.

Authority or Command System: An economic system that is controlled by a central authority that owns and allocates resources.

Capital: The manufactured resource. The tools and equipment that aid in production.

Economic Efficiency: Gaining the most output to maximize consumer utility with a given amount of input.

The Economic Problem: The contrast between virtually unlimited human wants and the limited availability of resources.

Entrepreneurial Skill: The entity in a market economy that combines land, labor and capital into a finished product or service.

Factors of Production: The basic economic resources required in production—land, labor, capital and entrepreneurial skill.

Insatiable: A human condition where wants are incapable of complete satisfaction.

Increasing Costs: As the productivity of a factor of production decreases due to increasing production, the cost of successive units produced must increase.

Labor: The human resource. A certain amount of labor is required to produce any product.

Land: The natural resources required to produce any product.

Market Economy: System that allows free interaction between buyer and seller in the marketplace. It is characterized by private ownership of resources.

Opportunity Cost: Due to scarcity, the choice of one product means giving up something else. It is the alternative not chosen.

Production Possibilities Curve: A model that shows the trade-off that exists between two goods or services that could potentially be produced by a full-employment, full-output economy, assuming that all resources are fixed.

Traditional Economic System: A system that allows prevailing customs to determine the allocation of resources.

Applied Exercises

Exercise One: Production Possibilities Curve

Types of Production	Product Alternatives				
	A	B	C	D	E
Computers	0	2	4	6	10
Cell Phones	30	27	21	12	0

A: What do the points on the curve indicate? How does the curve reflect the law of increasing opportunity costs? Explain. If the economy is currently at Point C, what is the cost of 2 million more computers in terms cell phones? Of 6 million more cell phones in terms of computers?

B: Upon what specific assumptions is the Production Possibilities Curve based?

Applied Exercises

Exercise Two: Production Possibilities Curve

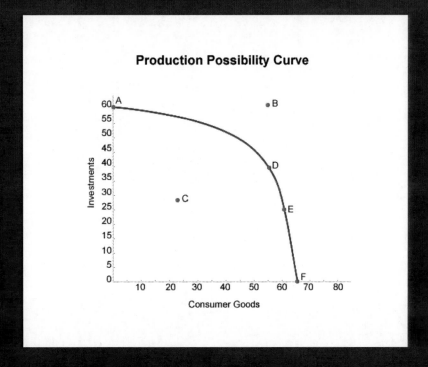

Production Possibility Curve

A: Describe the economic implications of Points A–F?

B: Upon what specific assumptions is the Production Possibilities Curve based?

C: Which allocations will lead to greater future growth?

Applied Exercises: Answers

Exercise One:

A: What do the points on the curve indicate? How does the curve reflect the law of increasing opportunity costs? Explain. If the economy is currently at Point C, what is the cost of 2 million more computers in terms of cell phones? What is the cost of 6 million more cell phones in terms of computers?

The points on the matrix illustrate the trade-off between computers and cell phones. The Law of Increasing Costs is present because as more of either is produced from Point C, the costs increase. From Point C, the cost of 2 million more computers is 9 million cell phones that have to be given up. From Point C, the cost of 6 million more cell phones is 2 million computers.

B: Upon what specific assumptions is the Production Possibilities Curve based?

The assumption of the Production Possibilities Curve is that there is a constant state of technology and resource use. Since resources are not perfectly shiftable, to obtain more of one will require an increasing sacrifice of the other past the mid-point of the curve.

Exercise Two:

A: Describe the economic implications of Points A–F

	Investments	Consumer Goods
Point A	60	0
Point B	Unattainable	
Point C	Unemployment	
Point D	40	55
Point E	25	60
Point F	65	0

Applied Exercises: Answers

Exercise Two:

B: What is the cost of moving from Point D to Point E?

To gain 5 more goods, one must give up 15 (40-25) investments.

C: Which allocations will lead to greater future growth?

Generally, investments lead to more capital goods and therefore more growth in the future. However, when an economy is in recession, more spending on goods can be beneficial.

Lesson **Three**
Market Allocation of Supply and Demand

Introduction

The allocation of resources within a capitalistic system is accomplished through a market approach. This is the seemingly simple idea that a buyer can trade money for goods or services provided by a seller. According to economic theory, then, the allocation of resources is accomplished through this basic demand and supply process. This theory assumes that no single buyer or any individual seller can actually have an impact on the market situation. The theory further assumes that demand behaviors and supply behaviors are shaped and positioned through the pricing system.

LEARNING OBJECTIVES

Please note the listed objectives. As you will see, the course materials are all objective driven. This provides you with a constant way to direct and monitor your progress throughout the course. Each objective is color-coded and corresponds to that particular section in the text.

OBJECTIVE ONE 1

Explain the overall role of Demand and Supply in the process of Market allocation.

OBJECTIVE TWO 2

Describe in detail the nature of Demand and the two essential types of change that occur with Demand behavior.

OBJECTIVE THREE 3

Describe in detail the nature of Supply and the two essential types of change that occur with Supply behavior.

OBJECTIVE FOUR 4

Describe in detail how the interactions between Demand and Supply behaviors move a Market toward equilibrium and how price functions as an allocation mechanism.

OBJECTIVE FIVE 5

Explain how Government Interventions in a Market can create Shortages and Surpluses.

INTERACTIVE EXERCISE

Use the Major Economic Models to demonstrate an understanding of the chain reactions resulting from human choices and how they move through an economy. Demonstrate an understanding of the Tradeoffs that result.

MARKETS

Supply and demand are the two primary forces in market _allocation_. Supply is provided by producers and demand is created by consumers. The market is the interaction of these forces. A market system is most efficient if there is perfect (or pure) competition. Perfect competition is characterized by a very large number of both independent buyers and independent sellers. Two examples (although not "perfect" examples) are the stock market and an international bazaar.

In the 1920s, Alfred Marshall addressed the relative importance of the supply side vs. the demand side of the market. He compared supply and demand to the actions of a pair of scissors. Both blades of the scissors are equally important. The market is cleared (cut) by finding a price where producers are willing and able to supply (one blade) and consumers are willing and able to buy (the other blade).

SUPPLY

Supply is created to satisfy consumer demand. Producers are continually seeking new opportunities to satisfy the needs of consumers. Supply is the response to the dollar votes of these consumers. Ultimately, then, it is the consumer who drives the allocation process. If a larger quantity of a particular item is demanded by consumers, then suppliers will increase their production of that item and will try to raise the price of that item.

A series of prices and individual quantities that producers are willing and able to produce at a particular point in time.

DEMAND

Demand is determined by the sovereign (independent) consumer. When a consumer purchases a product, a demand is created for this item to be re-stocked by the merchant. This idea is the origin of the saying, "the dollar votes when an item is purchased." Ultimately, consumer sovereignty determines what is produced in a market-based economy.

A series of prices and individual quantities that consumers are willing and able to buy at a particular point in time.

Demand, then, is the relationship between the possible prices of a product and the quantities of that product that would be demanded by the consumers. Stated a bit differently, Demand is the series of prices and the related quantities that consumers are willing and able to buy at a particular point in time.

LAW OF DEMAND

The Law of Demand assumes there is an inverse relationship between price and the quantity demanded. The amount of a product that consumers are willing and able to purchase at a particular price is called the **quantity demanded**. When price increases, the **quantity demanded** by consumers <u>decreases</u>. When price decreases, the quantity demanded by consumers increases if all other influences remain the same. For example, a consumer might purchase only 3 units of a product at $8, but actually buy 5 units of the product at $6. Thus, as price decreases the **quantity demanded** increases.

The *total* market demand for goods or services consists of the sum of the individual demand relationships of all possible buyers. Some individuals will be willing and able to pay more for a particular good. Some individuals will be willing and able to buy more units at a certain price. The total market demand, then, may be found by summing all of the individual demand behaviors.

INVERSE DEMAND RELATIONSHIP

There are three reasons why price and quantity demanded have an *inverse* relationship (move in opposite directions). The first reason is the **income effect**. If price decreases, a consumer is willing to buy more at the lower price. At lower prices, the consumer has more purchasing power. This is called the income effect.

The second reason for the inverse relationship is called the **substitution effect**. If the price of item A, a substitute for item B, decreases, then people will buy more of A and less of B. Thus, the quantity demanded of A will increase when its price decreases.

The third reason for the inverse relationship is called the **law of diminishing marginal utility**. Economists assume that at any given price a person will continue to consume more and more of an item, but at some point that person starts receiving less and less additional satisfaction (utility) from each additional unit consumed. Therefore, beyond some point, the consumer will only purchase more of that item if the price of that item decreases.

In summary, the reasons given above for "inverse demand relationships" provide us with a somewhat more technical analysis for human behavior that we all instinctively understand—when the price of something goes down, we (as a group) buy more of it. But there is much more to our study of demand and supply than "price down, we buy more."

There are three basic methods of analysis that we will use in our study of demand and supply. We will use descriptive analysis, tabular analysis and graphical analysis. We have already used "descriptive analysis" (word-/concept-based analysis) in presenting the discussion above. We can now expand on these concepts using the tabular and graphical approaches.

Consider the tabulation of Prices and Quantities Demanded in the illustration below:

Price ($)	Quantity (d)
10	1
9	2
8	3
7	4
6	5

This table of prices and quantities is called a Demand Schedule.

DEMAND SCHEDULE AND THE GRAPH

This schedule is describing the change in quantity demanded as price decreases from $10 to $6. The entire set of prices and quantities is referred to as "Demand." The Demand for a product, then, describes the quantities of goods and services that consumers are willing and able to purchase as a function of prices at a given point in time.

Graphically, a Demand Line is always plotted with Price on the Y-axis and Quantity on the X-axis. The negative slope (downward trend) of a Demand

Line illustrates the "inverse relationship" described earlier — as prices increase, quantity demanded decreases and as price decreases, quantity demanded increases. The data from the Demand Schedule above is plotted on the Demand Graph. A change in quantity demanded is shown by a movement along the Demand Line. For example, notice that when the price decreases from $9 to $7, the quantity demanded will increase from 2 units to 4 units.

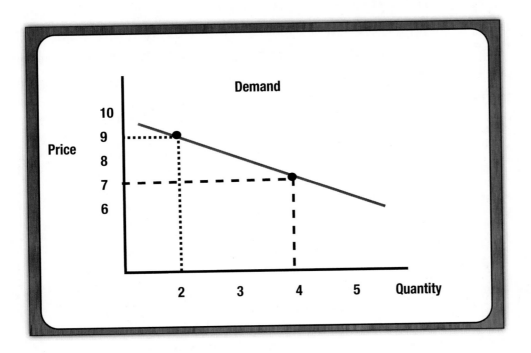

A change in price is, in fact, the only reason why there can be a direct "change in quantity demanded." If a factor other than price changes (such as income), then we will see a "change in demand" (notice the word "quantity" is not included in that last phrase).

In the next section, we will explore this idea of "change in demand." A Quick Preview: For several reasons, a consumer may view a product differently as time moves along. A consumer may either decide to buy more at a given price or buy less at that same price. In either instance, the quantity demanded at that price has changed. For example, in the illustration above, we observed a consumer buying 2 units of product when the price was $9. What might cause that same consumer to buy 4 units of the product even though the price stays exactly the same at $9? In the next section we will begin to answer that question.

CHANGES IN DEMAND

A Demand line may shift right, representing an increase in a demand behavior, or shift left, representing a decrease in that demand behavior. Circumstances affecting Demand can change for many reasons. For example, consider the change in demand for a seasonal item such as sunscreen lotion. A change in demand for the item is represented by adding a second demand schedule. If conditions favor sale of the item (summertime), then the second schedule (D2) lies to the right of the original schedule (D1). If the change in demand is constant, then the slope of the new D2 behavior will be the same as the slope of the original D1 behavior. Notice below that for every price, the increased Demand schedule D2 shows two more units demanded than the original (wintertime) demand schedule D1.

Price	Quantity Demanded 1 "D1"	Quantity Demanded 2 "D2"
$10	1	3
9	2	4
8	3	5
7	4	6
6	5	7

Because the quantities demanded increase at each price level, an "increase in demand" will always cause a right shift of the Demand line (see figure at right). If the quantities demanded decrease at each price level, the "decrease in demand" will always cause a left shift of the Demand line.

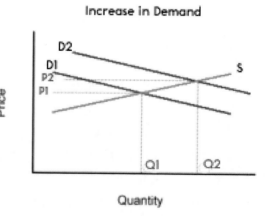

Increase in Demand

Tastes and Preferences

Number of Buyers

Determinants of Demand

Level of Income

Price of Related Goods

Consumer Expectations

DETERMINANTS OF DEMAND

When we describe the **Determinants of Demand**, we are saying that a change in any one of these fundamental factors will cause a consumer to buy more or less of a product at each price level. In effect, a change in any one of these fundamental factors will cause a Demand line to *shift*.

The **five** primary determinants of demand are:

Tastes and Preferences:

When consumers decide that one particular cell phone is much more desirable than another, the demand for this particular cell phone will increase (the Demand line will shift right). The demand for the other cell phone brands will, *other factors remaining the same*, diminish (shift left). Given a moment's thought, it is evident that advertising can have a great impact on consumers' Tastes and Preferences.

Number of Buyers:

If there are simply more people available to purchase a product at every price level, an increase in demand (shift right) will result. If fewer people are available to purchase at every price level, a decrease in demand (shift left) will result. This can occur when there is an overall population change, a geographic shift in population or a demographic change. For example, if more babies are being born in a certain part of the country, the demand for diapers (more new parents) will increase at every price level (right shift).

Level of Income:

If people have more income, they will purchase *more* items known as normal goods. Normal goods (sometimes called "superior goods") are items that consumers will instinctively increase their purchases of when they have an increase in income. An example of a normal good is a new automobile. An increase in the incomes of families across the country will typically result in an increase in the quantity of *new* cars being demanded (as opposed to "used cars").

An **inferior good** is one that consumers will buy *less* of when their incomes increase (other factors remaining the same). An example of an "inferior good" would, then, be the *used* car.

Price of Related Goods:

Two products that are viewed as replacements for each other are called **substitute** goods. Two goods that are purchased and consumed together are called **complementary** goods.

When two goods are *substitutes*, a change in the price of one will cause a change in the demand of the other in the <u>same</u> direction. When two goods are *complementary* goods, a change in the price of one will cause a change in the demand of the other in the *opposite* direction.

An example of a substitute situation is the relationship between Coke and Pepsi in the soft drink market. If the price of Pepsi *decreases* dramatically (think "half-price sale"), then the demand for Coke would *decrease* (shift to the left). An increase in the price of a substitute will cause an increase in the demand for the other item.

An example of two goods that are complementary would be computers and computer software. Each is directly related to the other and they are often purchased together. When the price of computers *decreases*, then more software will be purchased (an *increase* in software demand). If the price of computers increased dramatically for some reason, then less software would be purchased (a *decrease* in software demand).

Consumer Expectations:

If consumers expect the price of an item to *increase* in the future, they will tend to increase their *present* demand for the item. On the other hand, if consumers think that the price of the item will go down in the future, they will tend to decrease their present demand for that item. The demand for houses during the past 10 years has been an interesting example of changes in Consumer Expectations.

In our discussions up to this point, we have not yet seen any examples of exactly how the market price of an item is actually established. We must involve Supply in our discussion to create these examples. At this point, the examples of Demand display a *series of prices* and the *quantities demanded* that correspond to those prices. We have displayed Demand both in tabular form as well as graphically. Now it is time to bring Supply into the analysis.

SUPPLY

Conceptually, Supply and Demand are closely related in that both describe human behavior in relation to the price of a product. With Supply, however, we are describing the amount of a product that *business people* are willing and able to create at a moment in time (as opposed to the buying behavior of consumers). For "supply behavior," the relationship between price and quantity is direct, rather than inverse as it is with "demand behavior." For Supply, then, a higher price will result in a higher quantity produced (a "direct" relationship). A lower price will result in a lower quantity produced (again, a "direct" relationship). Graphically, we can say that the Supply curve will slope upward and to the right.

THE LAW OF SUPPLY

The Law of Supply is based on the "direct relationship" noted above. The Law of Supply summarizes the direct relationship between price and the **quantity supplied** by producers. If price increases, then the *quantity* supplied will also increase. The Law of Supply simply states that this direct relationship exists between price and quantity supplied at *every* level. When prices go up, greater quantities will be provided by producers at these higher price levels, all other factors remaining the same (remember our "ceteris paribus" from Lesson One).

The Supply curve for the total market is simply the summation of all suppliers' reactions to the various possible changes in price. Even though each *individual* producer tends to have a different reaction to a price change, the total quantity brought to the market by all producers at each new price is what creates the Supply curve (or Supply line).

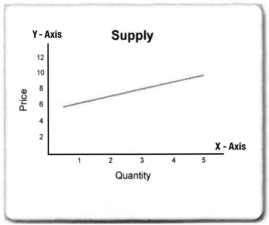

Since an increase in price leads to an increase in *quantity* supplied, the Supply line slopes upward and to the right. As with the Demand line, Price is on the Y-axis and Quantity is on the X-axis.

Price	Quantity Supplied
$10	5
9	4
8	3
7	2

A **Change in Quantity Supplied** is a movement along a given Supply line. This is caused by a change in price. An increase in price is the only variable that will increase the amount brought to the market by producers if all other variables remain the same.

A **Change in Supply** is a shift in the entire Supply line as more or fewer units of product are brought to the market by producers at a given price.

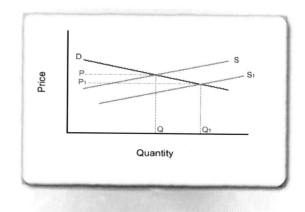

If there is an overall increase in suppliers' costs of production (i.e., wage costs go up), there will be fewer units of product brought to the market at each price level, resulting in a *left shift* in the Supply line.

If, however, there is an overall decrease in suppliers' costs of production (i.e., wage costs go down), there will be more units of product brought to the market at each price level, a right shift in the Supply line.

An illustration of an increase in the Supply is shown at the right with a change from S to S1.

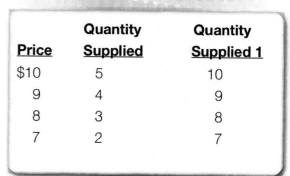

Price	Quantity Supplied	Quantity Supplied 1
$10	5	10
9	4	9
8	3	8
7	2	7

Determinants of Supply

- Resource Costs
- Number of Producers
- Production Substitute
- Future Prices
- Taxes or Subsidies
- Technology

DETERMINANTS OF SUPPLY

Just as with "change in demand," the phrase "change in supply" means that something other than price has changed. Remember that when price changes only quantity supplied will change as we move along the Supply line. But when there is a "change in supply," the entire Supply line will shift. We must re-plot the tabular data when the Supply line shifts—either left (a decrease in supply) or right (an increase in supply).

When we describe the **Determinants of Supply**, we are saying that a change in any one of these fundamental factors will cause producers to create more or less of a product at each price level. In effect, a change in any one of these fundamental factors will cause a Supply line to shift.

The **six** primary determinants of supply are:

Resource Costs:

Any increase in resource costs (that is, "factor of production" costs) will shift the Supply line to the left. Any decrease in those costs will shift the Supply line to the right. Examples: An *increase in the cost* of oil (or labor) will cause the Supply line to decrease (shift left). A *decrease in the cost* of labor (or capital equipment) will cause the Supply line to increase (shift right).

Number of Producers:

Any change in the number of businesses in a particular industry will also shift the Supply line. Example: Fewer suppliers of airline transportation services will cause the Supply line of "seats available" to decrease (shift left). More suppliers of ocean cruise line entertainment services will cause the Supply line of "cabins available" to increase (shift right).

Price of a Production Substitute:

An item that suppliers can produce in place of their current product is called a "production substitute." A change in the market price of a "production substitute" can cause an increase or decrease in the overall supply of the current product being produced. If many farmers are currently growing wheat but the market price of corn increases dramatically, then with the next planting those farmers may substitute corn for wheat production. This would result in a decrease in the supply of wheat (a left shift).

Conversely, if the market price of corn dramatically decreases, then with the next planting even more farmers will be producing wheat. This will result in an increase in the supply of wheat (a right shift).

Expectations about Future Prices:

Any increase in resource costs (that is, "factor of production" costs) will shift the Supply line to the left. Any decrease in those costs will shift the Supply line to the right. Examples: An *increase in the cost* of oil (or labor) will cause the Supply line to decrease (shift left). A *decrease in the cost* of labor (or capital equipment) will cause the Supply line to increase (shift right).

Taxes or Subsidies:

If increased taxes are imposed on producers in a particular industry, fewer units of that item will be supplied at each price level (a left shift). However, if government provides subsidies (money to increase production), then suppliers will provide more of that item at every price level (a right shift).

Technology:

If there is an increase in the technology used to produce an item, this will cause an increase in supply (a right shift). Increases in technology such as robotic manufacturing and other forms of automation can reduce production costs, which, in turn, will drive the increase in supply (the right shift).

MARKET EQUILIBRIUM

As consumers, we want the lowest price—as producers in the Circular Flow, we want the highest price. The market price or "**equilibrium**" price is where we try to get together. The equilibrium price is established where consumers as a group are willing and able to buy exactly that quantity that producers (as a group) are willing and able to produce. At the **equilibrium price**, every unit produced will be purchased—there will be no surplus left over and there will be no shortage of the product.

We need to keep in mind that markets provide that very valuable "allocation" function in our economy. Markets allocate resources and they do this primarily through the rationing effect of prices. A product's price reflects its relative scarcity. If a product becomes relatively more scarce (as would occur with an increase in demand or a decrease in supply), we would expect the market price to increase to reflect this increased scarcity. If the opposite occurs—a decrease in demand or an increase in supply—the product's equilibrium price will drop (the product is "less scarce").

ASSUMPTIONS:

Free Market Allocation of products and services is determined by the interaction of the Demand created by consumers and the Supply created by producers. Price determines the quantity demanded by the consumers and the quantity supplied by the producers. Recall that the Law of Demand states that there is an <u>inverse</u> relationship between price and quantity demanded while the Law of Supply states that there is a direct relationship between price and quantity supplied.

The Laws of Supply and Demand work together to create market **equilibrium**. The end result of this dynamic process is a market-clearing price, where the quantity demanded by consumers *becomes exactly equal* to the quantity supplied by producers. Ongoing adjustments in both buying behavior and production behavior allocate resources *toward* this market equilibrium. Note in the graph on market equilibrium that a market equilibrium exists when Quantity Demanded = Quantity Supplied at 2.75 units (think "pounds of T-bone steak per year") and a price of $7. The **Forces of Adjustment** *toward* market equilibrium are the natural instincts of suppliers toward making profit and the natural instincts of consumers toward satisfying their wants (gaining utility).

If the current price of a good is *below* **the equilibrium price**, then quantity demanded by consumers will be *more* than the quantity supplied by producers. This will result in a **shortage**.

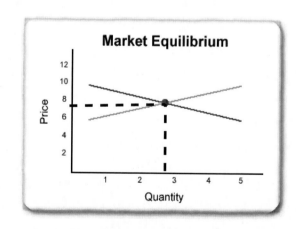

A Shortage will exist whenever the quantity demanded is more than the quantity supplied. In this situation, the producers will increase their asking price *and* their quantity supplied. Producers will continue with this approach until they realize that they are producing too much and have raised the price too high.

If the current price of a good is *above* the equilibrium price, then quantity demanded by consumers will be *less* than the quantity supplied by producers. This will result in a **Surplus**. A Surplus exists whenever the quantity demanded is less than the quantity supplied. In this situation, producers will decrease their asking price *and* their quantity supplied. Producers will continue with this approach until they realize that they are producing too little and have lowered the price too much.

If the current price of a good becomes *exactly equal* to the equilibrium price, then quantity demanded by consumers will be the *same* as the quantity supplied by producers. An equilibrium is established at that price where producers are willing to supply exactly the same amount of product as consumers are willing to purchase. In this situation (which usually does *not* last very long), producers will have no incentive to change either their asking price *or* their quantity supplied. Producers will stay with their present approach until they realize that there has been (or will be) a *shift* in Demand or Supply within their industry. These shifts are usually not far away in the "real world" and, in fact, often occur before an equilibrium is ever actually achieved—that is, *before* the asking price for a product rises or falls enough to become equal to the equilibrium price.

Shifts in Demand or Supply cause changes in Market Equilibrium and changes in the *location* of the *equilibrium price* and the *equilibrium quantity*. As expected, an increase in demand (shift right) with supply remaining constant will create an increase in the equilibrium price and an increase in the equilibrium quantity. Also, as expected, a decrease in supply (shift left) with demand remaining constant will yield an increase in the equilibrium price and a decrease in the equilibrium quantity. The resulting shortages *or* surpluses drive the markets toward these new equilibrium points. Once again, in the "real world," another shift in behavior often arrives before a market can really settle into its current equilibrium.

Market Disequilibrium exists when a current price is above or below an equilibrium price. Disequilibrium with a current price below an equilibrium price will yield a shortage. This type of disequilibrium causes producers to supply an amount of product that is less than the amount that consumers desire at that "low" price. Disequilibrium with a current price above an equilibrium price will yield a surplus. This type of disequilibrium causes producers to supply an amount of product that is more than the amount that consumers desire at that "high" price.

Complex shifts occur when *both* supply behavior and demand behavior shift at the same time. Both equilibrium price and equilibrium quantity will change, but the direction of these changes (increase or decrease) will be *indeterminate* until the magnitudes of the changes are considered. To illustrate such a "complex shift," one must draw two sketches of the shifts in the behavior lines. For example, the first sketch of a complex right shift would consider a *small* increase in demand along with a *moderate* increase in supply. The second sketch would consider a *large* increase in demand along with that *same* moderate increase in supply.

If both demand and supply decrease (shift left), the outcome on price is **indeterminate** (until the magnitudes of the demand shift is considered), but the equilibrium quantity definitely declines. If both demand and supply increase (shift right), the outcome on price is indeterminate, but equilibrium quantity definitely rises. If demand shifts right and supply shifts left, equilibrium price will definitely rise, but equilibrium quantity is indeterminate until the magnitudes of the shifts are considered.

For **complex shifts**, it is very important to sketch the magnitudes of the shifts as well as the direction of the shifts that are being considered.

At this point, it is also very important to recall and reflect on the idea that in a market system, prices function as a **rationing mechanism**. It is the market price that places a limit on the amount of a product that a consumer is willing and able to purchase. And it is the market price that places a limit on the amount of resources that a businessperson is willing and able to commit in the creation of that product.

A market-clearing price ensures that those willing and able to pay that clearing price will receive the product, but those unwilling (or unable) to pay that price will *not* receive the product. Depending on the product and the circumstances, this can seem a very harsh reality. It is for this reason that most societies have some blend of tradition-based *and* government-based approaches to complement the market-based approach.

We should also keep in mind that over the long run, only those suppliers who are willing to *accept* a market-clearing price from consumers will, in fact, be able sell their product. *Over the long run,* those suppliers who are seeking a higher price and are unwilling to accept a market-clearing price will usually not survive.

GOVERNMENT INTERVENTION

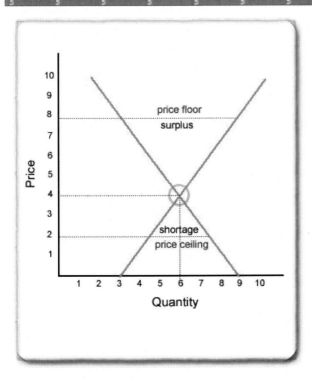

It was previously mentioned that most societies include some government based actions to complement a system that is essentially market based. Direct government intervention into the pricing of a product is one such action. This particular type of action can be very controversial. A direct government intervention into pricing will change both the quantity of product supplied and the quantity of the product demanded. Notice in the graph at left that equilibrium *without* government intervention is at Price of $4 and a Quantity of 6 units. But if a **price ceiling** at $2 is imposed, then the quantity supplied is 4.5 units and the quantity demanded is 7.5 units. This results in a shortage of 3 units. If a **price floor** is imposed at $8, then the resulting quantity demanded is 3 units and the quantity supplied is 9 units. This results in a surplus of 6 units.

Price Ceiling

A Price Ceiling is created when a government sets a legal *maximum* price on a product in order to keep the product price below the true equilibrium price. The term "price ceiling" is used because by law it places a "cap" on the price that can be charged for the product. The "price ceiling," however, will result in the quantity demanded by consumers being greater than the quantity supplied by producers. This means there will be a shortage of that product. An example of a "price ceiling" is when government sets a maximum rent that can be charged for an apartment. This results in more rentals being desired by consumers but fewer rentals being supplied by developers (a shortage of apartments).

Price Floor

A Price Floor is created when a government sets a legal *minimum* price on a product in order to keep the product price above the true equilibrium price. The term "price floor" is used because by law it creates a "support" for the price that can be charged for the product or service. The "price floor," however, will result in the quantity demanded by the buyers being less than the quantity supplied by the sellers. This means there will be a surplus of the item in the marketplace. An example of a "price floor" is minimum wage legislation. Firms are required by law to pay the minimum wage even though the equilibrium wage in that particular labor market may be somewhat lower. The minimum wage (price floor) increases the quantity of labor supplied by Households in the Circular Flow but reduces the quantity of labor demanded by Businesses. Yes, this tends to result in a surplus of labor also know as "unemployment." This is a topic we will spend more time on in the Lessons that follow.

For Lesson Three, you have now reviewed the Preview Questions and the Learning Objectives and you have completed the Video, PowerPoint and E-text components. To begin **applying** what you have learned, you should proceed immediately to the **Animations** & **Interactives** component.

Real-World Economics

Please access links through the online site Real-World Economics.

Key Terms

Demand: A schedule showing a series of prices and quantities that consumers would be willing and able to buy at a specific point in time.

Determinates of Demand: Changes in tastes, income, number of buyers and related goods that cause a fundamental change in the way consumers view a particular product or service.

Determinates of Supply: Changes in resource prices, technology, expectations, related goods, taxes and subsidies or the number of producers that cause a fundamental change in the way producers view a particular product or service.

Equilibrium: That point in an individual market where quantity demanded equals quantity supplied. It is always where the curves cross—the market is cleared with no surplus or shortage.

Law of Demand: This law assumes an inverse relationship between price and quantity. At a higher price, quantity demanded declines—at a lower price, the quantity increases.

Law of Supply: This law assumes a direct relationship between price and quantity. At a higher price, producers will produce more. At a lower price, the quantity will decline.

Market Shortage: The quantity demanded is greater than the quantity supplied.

Market Surplus: The quantity supplied is greater than the quantity demanded.

Market System: Where buyers and sellers meet. It provides for the free interaction of buyer and seller in the marketplace.

Price Ceiling: Government sets a price that is below the equilibrium price.

Price Floor: Government sets a price that is above the equilibrium price.

Price Function: In a market, price measures scarcity. If the product is more scarce, price goes up; if less scarce, it will go down. Price is an important mechanism for allocating scarce resources in a market.

Pure Competition: A large number of independently acting buyers and sellers in a marketplace where no one producer can unduly affect that market.

Quantity Demanded: On a demand schedule, this is the amount that corresponds to one price. A change in price will change the quantity demanded.

Quantity Supplied: On a supply schedule, this is one amount that corresponds to one price. A change in price will change the quantity supplied.

Applied Exercises

Exercise One:

Given the following Demand and Supply for cell phones, respond to the questions below.

Quantity Demanded	Price	Quantity Supplied
100	$300	500
200	$200	400
300	$100	300
400	50	200

A: What is the equilibrium price and quantity in this market?

B: What occurs at a price of $300?

C: What occurs at a price of $50?

D: What would happen if government sets a price ceiling at $50?

Exercise Two:

What effect would each of the following have on the **Demand** for cell phones?

A: The price of cell phones increases due to an increase in a component part.

B: There is an increase in income for most families.

C: Consumers anticipate the price of cell phones will be lower in the future.

D: There is a decrease in incomes caused by recession.

E: There is an increase in telephone connect charges required for cell phones.

Applied Exercises

Exercise Three:

What effect would each of the following have on the **Supply** for cell phones?

Quantity Demanded	Price	Quantity Supplied
100	$300	500
200	$200	400
300	$100	300
400	50	200

A: The government increases taxes on cell phone usage.

B: A decline in the number of cell phone firms in the industry.

C: The expectation that cell phones will be cheaper in the future.

D: Technology improves the processes for making cell phones.

E: The government provides a subsidy to cell phone production.

Exercise Four:

What effect will each of the changes in supply and demand have on **equilibrium price** and **quantity**?

A: Demand increases and Supply is constant.

B: Supply decreases and Demand is constant.

C: Demand decreases and Supply is constant.

D: Demand increases and Supply increases.

E: Supply decreases and Demand increases.

Applied Exercises: Answers

Exercise One:

A: What is the equilibrium price and quantity in this market?

Quantity = 300 @ Price = $100

B: What occurs at a price of $300?

Quantity Supplied = 500; Quantity Demanded = 100; Surplus = 400

C: What occurs at a price of $50?

Quantity Demanded = 400; Quantity Supplied = 200; Shortage 200

D: What would happen if government sets a price ceiling at $50?

Quantity Demanded = 400; Quantity Supplied = 200; Shortage of 200

Exercise Two:

A: The price of cell phones increases due to an increase in a component part?

No change to Demand, only a movement along a Demand line (change in quantity demanded).

B: There is an increase in income for most families.

Increase in Demand because a cell phone is a superior or normal good, more will be purchased at every price with an increase in income.

C: Consumers anticipate the price of cell phones will be lower in the future.

Decrease in Demand as consumers wait to make purchases.

D: There is a decrease in incomes caused by recession.

Decrease in Demand because a cell phone is a superior or normal good.

E: There is an increase in telephone connect charges required for cell phones.

Decrease in Demand because of this new tax.

Applied Exercises: Answers

Exercise Three:

A: The government increases taxes on cell phone usage.
Decrease in Supply.

B: A decline in the number of cell phone firms in the industry.
Decrease in Supply.

C: The expectation that cell phones will be cheaper in the future.
Decrease in Supply.

D: Technology improves the processes for making cell phones.
Decrease in Costs leads to increases in Supply.

E: The government provides a subsidy to cell phone production.
Increase in Supply.

Exercise Four:

A: Demand increases and Supply is constant.
Increase in equilibrium price and quantity.

B: Supply decreases and Demand is constant.
Decrease in equilibrium quantity and increase in price.

C: Demand decreases and Supply is constant.
Decrease in equilibrium price and quantity.

D: Demand increases and Supply increases.
Increase in equilibrium quantity and indeterminate change in price.

E: Supply decreases and Demand increases.
Increase in equilibrium price and indeterminate change in quantity.

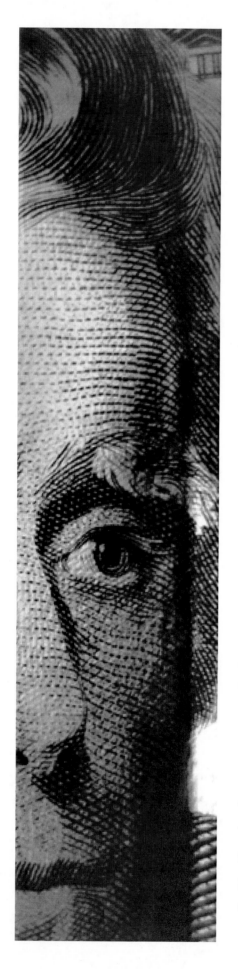

Lesson **Four**
The Public and Private Material World

Introduction

The one constant in our economic system has been change. This long-term evolution has taken place as we have reacted to various problems that have occurred in our system. A viable private and public sector—called a dual system—has been a direct result of these changes.

LEARNING OBJECTIVES

Please note the listed objectives. As you will see, the course materials are all objective driven. This provides you with a constant way to direct and monitor your progress throughout the course. Each objective is color-coded and corresponds to that particular section in the text.

OBJECTIVE ONE | 1

Provide an overview of the Public Sector in contrast to the Private Sector in the U.S. economy.

OBJECTIVE TWO | 2

Explain the concept of Externalities and the concept of Public Goods vs. Private Goods.

OBJECTIVE THREE | 3

Describe both the Functional Distribution of Income as well as the Personal Distribution of Income in the U.S. economy and the uses of that Income.

OBJECTIVE FOUR | 4

Identify the three Forms of Business Ownership and the advantages and disadvantages of each form.

OBJECTIVE FIVE | 5

Identify the major Economic Functions of Government along with the types of Government Spending and forms of Government Taxation.

INTERACTIVE EXERCISE

Use the Major Economic Models to demonstrate an understanding of the chain reactions resulting from human choices and how they move through an economy. Demonstrate an understanding of the Tradeoffs that result.

In Lesson Two, many of the major economic, political and social changes were described in some detail from an historical perspective. Some of America's most challenging economic problems, such as the monopoly and oligopoly power of the late 1800s, the labor unrest of the early 1900s, the Great Depression in the 1930s and the growing environmental problems in more recent years, gave rise to the conclusion that a pure market economy had difficulty solving certain problems. Historically, we have turned to government to help provide solutions to these problems.

Over the years, as government has assumed a larger role, it has become more accurate to describe our overall system as a mixed economy or dual system rather than a pure free-market system. Certainly there has been controversy about the growth and role of government, and many normative judgments have been made about this evolution.

Social Balance

One of the ways to begin analyzing the growth of government is with the concept of **social balance**, which is simply the allocation of resources between public and private sectors. By allocation, we mean spending by the private and public sectors. If we look at our current GDP (total spending in the economy), roughly one-third of the total is spent by government and two-thirds by the private sector. That is our current allocation of resources—the social balance. If we decide that we want more public goods, that balance will change and more taxes must be imposed or debt incurred to reflect that change. The public sector is dependent on the private sector for adequate tax revenue or the government must borrow funds.

Public and Private Sectors

The **Public Sector** of our economy consists of all branches of government, including city, county, state and federal levels. The largest expenditures are made by state and local government. During the past few years, we allocated about $1.7 trillion annually to state and local governments and $1.1 trillion annually to the federal government. See U.S. Department of Commerce, Bureau of Economic Analysis (www.bea.gov/national) for the latest information.

The **Private Sector** of an economy is the resource allocation (spending) by all consumers and businesses. The private sector is largely a market-oriented system of allocation based on consumer demand met by producer supply.

PUBLIC AND PRIVATE GOODS

Public Goods are typically unrestricted in availability (accessible to all) in contrast to Private Goods, which are produced by businesses and are restricted in availability. Private goods are offered only to individuals who pay for such a good or service. We conclude that private goods are subject to an exclusion principle while public goods are inclusive in principle. If you do not have the money for a private good, you are excluded from obtaining that good, but public goods are available without direct cost to the consumer.

Another distinguishing feature of public spending is that public costs do not increase with increasing use. Public goods do not usually have a marginal cost. An example is the cost of national defense. National defense is available to all (inclusive) and has no additional cost (marginal cost) by including more people.

PRIVATE SECTOR — INCOME

Private sector income is measured in two forms: personal distribution of income and functional distribution of income. Personal distribution of income is the allocation of total income per household, while the functional distribution of income is payments for production factors.

In the personal distribution of income, an individual can do one of two things with after-tax income—spend it or save it. Americans spend about 88 percent of their income for personal consumption and 12 percent for government taxes, and they save about 0 percent (in recent years) or may even have a negative savings in some months (meaning they borrow for some current expenditure). Americans have a lower savings rate than workers in other industrialized nations. See Figure 4.1.

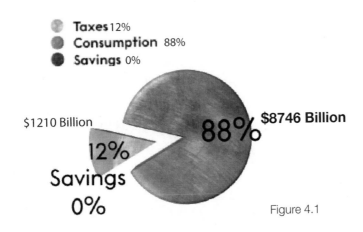

Taxes 12%
Consumption 88%
Savings 0%

$1210 Billion $8746 Billion

88%

12%
Savings
0%

Figure 4.1

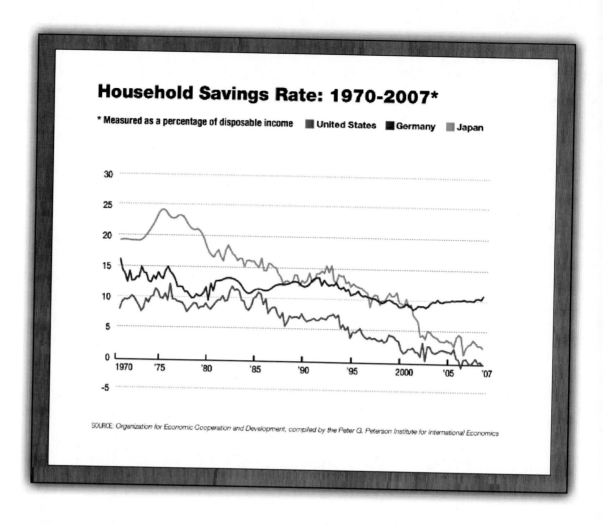

Household Savings Rate: 1970-2007*

* Measured as a percentage of disposable income ■ United States ■ Germany ■ Japan

SOURCE: *Organization for Economic Cooperation and Development, compiled by the Peter G. Peterson Institute for International Economics*

GLOBAL SAVINGS RATES

Note the household savings rate in Japan, Germany and the United States since 1970. Each nation has dramatically decreased its savings rate. Saving is necessary for capital investment but many industrialized nations have borrowed from developing nations, like China, for their investments. This debt is a claim by developing nations on borrowers' future income, employment and output.

Individuals spend 59 percent of their income for services (such as medical, education, child care, etc). Services comprise about 75 percent of our total national output. The next largest share of personal spending (29 percent) is for nondurable goods (goods lasting less than 3 years, such as food and clothing). The smallest expenditure, at 12 percent, is for durable goods (lasting more than 3 years), such as furniture and automobiles. See Figure 4.2.

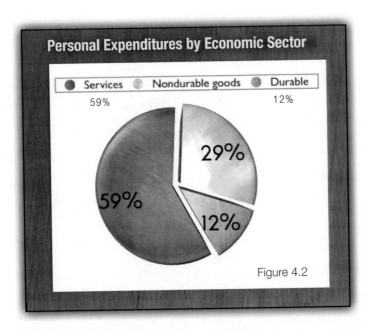

Personal Expenditures by Economic Sector

Services ● Nondurable goods ● Durable

59%   12%

29%

59%

12%

Figure 4.2

PRIVATE SECTOR—FUNCTIONAL DISTRIBUTION OF INCOME

The functional distribution of income is based on the factors of production and the income that comes to each. The factors of production are land, labor, capital and entrepreneurship. Each factor is paid according to its contribution to production. Laborers receive income for wages and salaries, entrepreneurs for profit, landowners for rent and capital providers for interest. Labor receives about 71 percent of national income, entrepreneurship about 23 percent, landowners about 5 percent, with the remaining 1 percent going to capital. See Figure 4.3.

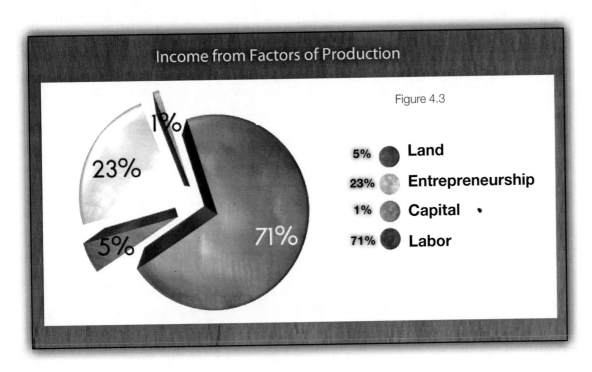

Income from Factors of Production

Figure 4.3

1%

23%

5%   71%

5% ● Land

23% ● Entrepreneurship

1% ● Capital ·

71% ● Labor

PERSONAL DISTRIBUTION OF HOUSEHOLD INCOME

The income of U.S. households is computed by the U.S. Census Bureau and is available in many different categories. The median (point where 50 percent made more and 50 percent made less) household income for 2007 was $50,233. The top 1.9 percent of households made more than $250,000, and the bottom 10 percent made less than $11,050. The lowest 20 percent of households made less than $19,178, and the top 20 percent made more than $90,000. Poverty, estimated at about $17,000 for a household, included about 12.7 percent of all households.

HOUSEHOLD INCOME GROWTH

Notice in the Real Median Household Income graph that the median household income increases between 1969 and 1996 have been modest. Median incomes during this period increased slightly, but there were also changes in the size and composition of the median household.

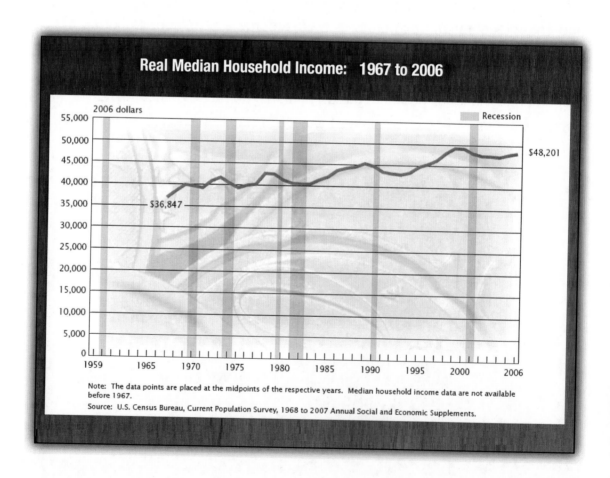

Real Median Household Income: 1967 to 2006

Note: The data points are placed at the midpoints of the respective years. Median household income data are not available before 1967.

Source: U.S. Census Bureau, Current Population Survey, 1968 to 2007 Annual Social and Economic Supplements.

PERSONAL DISTRIBUTION OF INCOME BY PERCENTILE GROUP

The personal distribution of household income describes the way income is divided into groups among households in this country. This is normally analyzed by dividing all U.S. households in 5 equal groupings of 20 percent each. If income were evenly distributed, each 20 percent segment would receive exactly 20 percent of income. Figure 4.4 shows that this is not the case. According to recent data, the top 20 percent received more than 50 percent of the total income and the bottom 20 percent received only 3.4 percent of the total income.

You will see further discussion of this important question in the PowerPoint presentation for this lesson.

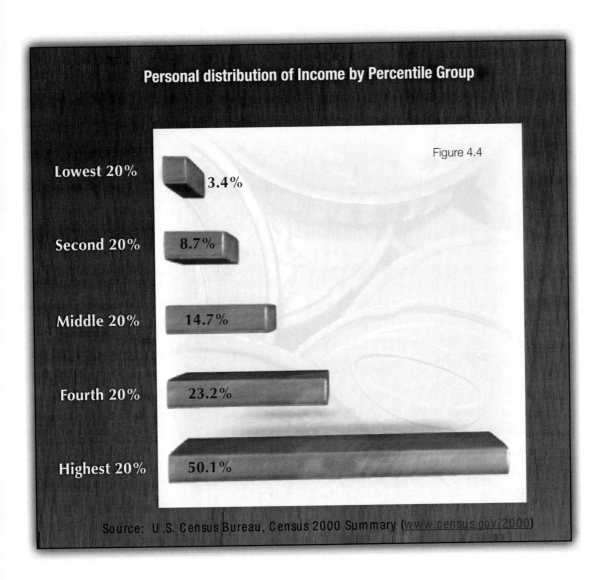

Personal distribution of Income by Percentile Group

Figure 4.4

Lowest 20%	3.4%
Second 20%	8.7%
Middle 20%	14.7%
Fourth 20%	23.2%
Highest 20%	50.1%

Source: U.S. Census Bureau, Census 2000 Summary (www.census.gov/2000)

What Determines Your Income?

Many factors determine an individual's income including education, age, skills, inheritance and location. However, the most important factors are education, experience and training. According to the U.S. Census Bureau, workers in 2006 with a high school education made $28,290 median income, while workers with a bachelor's or master's degree made $47,240 and $56,707, respectively. Professional degrees result in even higher incomes. Individuals with a professional degree, such as an MD (medical doctor), JD (lawyer), DDS (dentist) or DVM (animal doctor), made a median income of $121,340.

Comparison of U.S. Household Incomes 1990 to Present

The U.S. household median income is higher than in most nations if the comparison is made using parity pricing relationships (purchasing power parity or PPP). Parity comparison attempts to make purchases in each nation comparable by using an adjusted long-term exchange rate.

According to the Organization for Economic Cooperation and Development (OECD), only Switzerland's median income of $55,901 exceeds the U.S. median income of $50,233. And in Switzerland, if adjustments are made for comparable U.S. taxes and health insurance costs, the net median drops to $39,306. The United Kingdom's comparable median income is $34,000 and Singapore's is $30,000. Canada median income is $44,000, New Zealand's is $41,000 and Australia's is $38,000.

However, the median incomes of the majority of nations in the world are less than $10,000 per year. In fact, the majority of the world's population lives on less than $2 per day.

Forms of Business Ownership

Economists categorize output according to the three organizational forms of business. One may start a business enterprise in one of these three forms: sole proprietorship (alone), partnership (with one or more parties) or as a corporation (separate legal unit).

Corporations produce about 84 percent of the business output but only account for 20 percent of the total number of firms. Sole proprietors are 70 percent of the units but produce only 5 percent of the output. Partnerships account for 10 percent of business units and produce 10 percent of business output.

Figure 4.5	Sole Proprietorship	General Partnership	Corporation
Easy to Organize	X	X	
Permanence			X
Specialization		X	X
Limited Liability			X
Money Resources		X	X
Market Power			X
Tax Advantages		X	X

ADVANTAGES AND DISADVANTAGES OF OWNERSHIP FORMS

The ease of forming and operating a sole proprietorship or partnership is the main reason owners frequently choose this form of enterprise. These simple forms of ownership are easily understood and controlled by an owner. But, there is also a potential problem. The extent of personal liability is unlimited, meaning that the personal assets of the owners (sole or partners) may be taken if bankruptcy occurs. Therefore, sole proprietorships and partnerships are organized flexibly but have unlimited liability. Corporations have limited liability but lose control to stockholders. A corporation is considered to be an artificial legal entity and therefore assets of the corporation can be taken in bankruptcy but not the personal assets of the owners (stockholders).

THE ORGANIZATIONAL ENVIRONMENT: COMPETITION

Business organizations are engaged in varied competitive structures within the private economic sector. Some firms operate in highly competitive markets with many buyers and many sellers, such as the purely competitive model, while other firms operate in markets with little or no competition, such as the monopoly model. Pure competition is present when the market consists of a very large number of producers and consumers with easy entry, such as in agriculture. Monopoly is present when there is no competition and barriers exist to prevent competition. A monopoly is a one-firm industry. Competitive markets generally have greater efficiency in resource allocation and, as a result, have higher output and lower prices for consumers.

THE PUBLIC SECTOR

We have previously defined and described some elements of the public sector, but now we turn our attention to specific functions of government. Although most functions of government have come to be accepted, there is still an argument about the proper role for government and the overall social balance question: "How much of our economy should be private and how much public?"

THE ECONOMIC FUNCTIONS OF GOVERNMENT

PROVIDES A LEGAL FRAMEWORK:

The public sector provides a system of laws for businesses and individuals that is critical for both individual rights and commerce. A legal system must be fair and ensure compliance with laws through enforcement. Businesses must be able to expect stability and compliance with contracts, while individuals must be free to choose their role in the system.

CORRECTS FOR MISALLOCATION OF RESOURCES:

Government can reallocate resources when **negative** or **positive externalities** (also called spillover benefits or costs) affect the economic system. A negative externality is present when production or consumption inflicts costs on third parties not part of a market transaction. An example is pollution caused by automobiles. Individuals driving automobiles gain by having transportation and the automobile manufacturer gains by making the sale, but third parties that are not part of this transaction are given the cost of air pollution and traffic congestion.

Government attempts to correct or lessen negative externalities through regulation, taxes and fines. Taxes imposed on those who pollute increase costs and cause a decrease in supply. Regulation may also be imposed directly to decrease pollution. A combination of regulation and increased taxes has been used to decrease automobile pollution in the United States. This occurred when catalytic converters were *required* on cars, causing an increase in the costs to manufacture and use. There was a decrease in the supply schedule and a decrease in the equilibrium quantity with the increased cost. An increase in taxes causes a similar impact of decreasing supply, causing prices to rise and quantity produced to decrease.

A positive externality exists when third parties benefit from a transaction that they did not directly undertake. An example of a positive externality is education. When society spends funds on education, the student gains skills and the educational institution gains revenue. However, society at large is assumed to benefit through the productivity increase provided by a college-educated person. It is also a benefit to society. Such students with more education will be more likely to pay taxes and be less likely to be unemployed. Government subsidizes education and other public goods such as medical care, because they have a positive affect (externality) on society at large. Government subsidies cause a shift right (increase) in the supply for a good or service.

REDISTRIBUTES INCOME:

Government can also reallocate resources of an economy through taxation, by making social payments or by providing services. Federal income tax rates are higher (progressive) on higher-income individuals. By taking more funds through personal income taxes and providing welfare funds (transfer payments), resources are reallocated. Transfer payments are funds given for welfare, Medicare (elderly medical care) and Social Security (retirement payments). Transfer payments are paid without goods or services given in return to government. Government also provides services directly to some low-income individuals for health benefits (Medicaid). These taxes and transfers change the overall personal distribution of income.

MAINTAINS A STABLE ECONOMY:

Government (mainly the federal branch) can promote a stable economy by increasing spending and/or decreasing taxes in recessions and decreasing spending and/or increasing taxes during inflationary times. The government actions of taxation and spending are part of a fiscal policy that can be used to exert a counter-cyclical effect on our overall economy. This, as well as the use of monetary policy, will be discussed in much more detail in later lessons.

ENCOURAGES AND ENSURES COMPETITION:

Government helps ensure the existence of competition. Monopoly power can significantly reduce the efficient use of resources within society. Since the passage of the Sherman Antitrust Act of 1890 and other, more recent regulation, an important function of government has been facilitating competition within the market. Recently, the U.S. Justice Department has been given broad regulatory authority to monitor competition in private markets.

THE SOCIAL BALANCE DEBATE

Over the past century, there has been a continuous trend of increased spending by government as a percent of national income. In 1900, the branches of government spent about 10 percent of total national income as compared to about 30 percent today. There are many reasons why government spending has increased, including war and defense, population growth (more people need services), urban areas requiring more government services, and the concept of equal opportunity. Government is involved in allocating resources to provide expected services and to assist low-income families with opportunities. These services were not expected in 1900. The arguments about the proper role of government will, undoubtedly, continue. However, if we look at the broad issue, most economists would agree that our dual system has worked reasonably well over many years.

TAXATION

As we have seen, government has the ability to impose taxes, which provides the major means to pay for public goods. Although no one likes to pay taxes, they are a fact of life. As Supreme Court Justice Oliver Wendell Holmes said, "Taxes are the price that we pay for living in a civilized society." Everything has a cost—public goods are no different.

AN EFFECTIVE TAX

Several basic economic questions need to addressed in order for a tax system to be effective:

- Is it fair and equitable to all taxpayers?

- Is it collectable? If enough taxpayers see it as unfair, it may be difficult to collect.

- Does it provide sufficient funds for effective government?

- Does it avoid over-reliance on any one tax?

- Is it regressive in its effect?

CATEGORIES OF TAXATION

ABILITY TO PAY

One long-term taxation principle suggests that those who have a greater ability to pay should pay at a higher tax rate than those who do not. Such taxes are called progressive; individuals with higher incomes are taxed at a higher rate. This approach to taxation has long been applied to personal income taxes. A higher marginal rate is applied to increasing incomes and, as of this writing, varies from 10 percent to 35 percent on the additional taxable income.

Figure 4.6

Federal Personal Income Taxes (2006) on Taxable Income

Marginal Tax Rate	Single	Married
10%	$0 - $7,550	$0 - $15,100
15%	$7,551 - $30,650	$15,101 - $61,300
25%	$30,651 - $74,200	$61,301 - $123,700
28%	$74,201 - $154,800	$123,701 - $188,450
33%	$154,801 - $336,550	$188,451 - $336,550
35%	$336,551 +	$336,551 +

The marginal tax rate is applied to taxable income at varied levels of listed income. Taxable income refers to income that is left over after standard deductions and exemptions, as qualified by the tax code, are applied. Therefore, using the table in Figure 4.6, we can find the tax for a married couple making a taxable income of $16,000. This couple would pay 10 percent on $15,100 = $1,510 and 15 percent on $900 = $135 for a total tax of $1,645.

Benefits Received

The **benefits received** principle is very simple. This principle argues that only those who receive the benefits of the tax should have to pay the tax. The best example of this would be a toll road. Those who drive on toll roads pay the toll fee. They receive the direct benefit from paying the toll. If people do not use the road, then they do not pay the tax.

Even though the benefits received tax might seem to be a very fair type of tax in some cases, it is difficult to apply universally. For example, if government is providing education as a public good, which is done throughout this country, how could government structure an ongoing tax system based on a benefits received principle that would be fair to all people, including future generations? We assume all of society benefits from the increased education of its citizens because of the resulting increased goods and services produced. However, a tax only on those students who receive an education would be burdensome and result in decreasing educational levels, thus not promoting the overall public good. Given these types of difficulties, most of our tax structure relates more to the "ability-to-pay" concept than to the "benefits received" concept.

Classification of Taxes

Progressive taxation is present when marginal (additional) tax rates increase with additional taxable income (i.e., a rising marginal rate is found in the federal income tax). Personal income taxes in the United States are progressive as individuals with higher income are taxed at a higher rate.

Proportional (flat) taxation is simply a flat rate that is applied to all individuals, regardless of income or wealth. Property taxes are imposed as a flat tax on assessed value (generally market value). A specific rate is applied to the value of the property to determine the amount of the tax. All property is taxed at the same rate. For example, assume a 1 percent tax applied to the market value of a home valued at $100,000; the tax would be $1,000 ($100,000 $\times$ .01). Local school districts are often funded through a flat tax on property.

Regressive taxation is present when marginal (additional) tax rates actually decrease with additional taxable income; a decreasing marginal rate is found with a general sales tax or payroll (Social Security) tax. Sales taxes are regressive because low-income individuals spend more of their income on taxable items. For example, assume a family makes $20,000 per year and spends $4,000 for food that is taxed at 10 percent, paying $400 in taxes in contrast to another family making $100,000 per year and spending $6,000 on food with a tax of $600. The lower-income family is taxed at $400 on $20,000 or 2 percent, while the higher-income family is taxed at $600 on $100,000 or 0.6 percent.

Social Security taxes are also regressive because the tax rate only applies to a maximum amount of $102,000 (2008) with no taxes after one reaches this maximum. Individuals making $102,000 per year would be taxed the same amount as individuals making $1,000,000 or even higher annual incomes. Thus, the tax _rate_ will _decline_ as income _increases_ above $102,000. From these examples, you can understand the controversy of regressive taxation.

CALCULATING TAX RATES

The economic calculation of marginal vs. average tax rates is found by comparing tax amounts with income. A marginal tax rate is the change in taxes divided by the change in income, while an average tax rate is the amount of taxes divided by the total income.

Notice in Figure 4.7 that the average tax is the amount of the tax divided by the amount of the income. At $10,000, the tax is 1,000, therefore 1/10 = .10.

The marginal tax is the tax on additional income. When income increased from $10,000 to $20,000 and the tax increased from $1,000 to $4,000, the marginal tax rate is the change in tax ($4,000 − $1,000) over the change in income ($20,000 − $10,000); therefore, the result is $3,000 divided by $10,000 or .30.

Marginal tax rate is the change in taxes divided by the change in income. Marginal taxes describe the tax rate when taxable income increases or decreases.

When taxes are progressive, marginal tax rates increase as taxable income increases. When taxes are regressive, marginal tax rates decrease as taxable income increases.

Figure 4.7

Illustration of Progressive Tax Rates

Income	Tax	Average Tax	Marginal Tax
$10,000	$1,000	10%	10%
$20,000	$4,000	20%	30%
$30,000	$9,000	30%	50%

INTENT AND EFFECT

The intent of a tax is simply the purpose lawmakers had in mind when a tax law is passed. Most taxes are intended as progressive or proportional. A tax law is usually not intended to be regressive, which would impose a greater burden on low-income workers. However, economists find some taxes are progressive, some are flat and others are regressive to some income groups.

The intent and impact of a tax may be different when we look at its real-world application. The sales tax is intended to be proportional but, as stated earlier, higher-income groups may not have to use all their income for consumption. They may save or invest the remaining portion. Lower-income groups do not have the same discretionary choices and are therefore taxed at a higher rate.

TAX INCIDENCE

The incidence of a tax describes who actually pays the tax. Some taxes may be shifted away from the intended party to someone else. Corporate taxes are directed toward the firm, but if such taxes are shifted to the price, then the consumer pays some tax. In this case, the corporation has effectively shifted the tenant, depending on the price sensitivity of demand and supply for rental units.

TAX LOOPHOLES

A tax loophole is a tax reduction built into our federal tax code for individuals or corporations. "Loopholes" are intended to promote a specific action. For example, the tax code allows homeowners to deduct interest and taxes on their homes to encourage home ownership. Charitable contributions can also be deducted to lessen tax liability to encourage donations to worthy causes. Loopholes allow tax avoidance, which is legally reducing one's tax liability.

Tax evasion, however, is when taxes are owed but not paid. Tax laws are purposefully written to make tax liability visibly apparent and compliance enforceable by law officials. The Internal Revenue Service (IRS) is particularly diligent in enforcing payment of tax liabilities.

FEDERAL GOVERNANCE: INCOME AND EXPENDITURES
FEDERAL FINANCE

As you look at Figures 4.8 and 4.9, observe the broad categories that compose federal finance for both income and expenditure. Consider a few summary points:

The federal government gets funds from personal income taxes (45 percent); payroll taxes, including Social Security (37 percent); and corporate income taxes (13 percent). Other sources of funds include excise taxes and tariffs. See Figure 4.8 below.

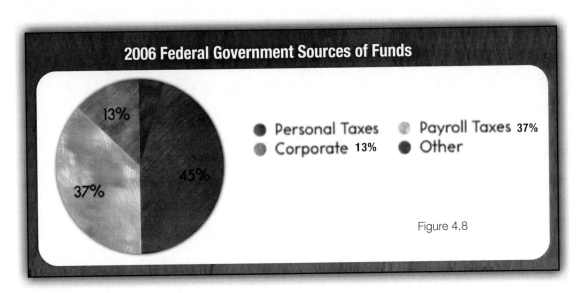

2006 Federal Government Sources of Funds

- Personal Taxes
- Corporate 13%
- Payroll Taxes 37%
- Other

13%
45%
37%

Figure 4.8

The federal government uses funds for income security and pensions (35 percent); health (21 percent); national defense (20 percent); and interest on national debt (7 percent). See Figure 4.9.

Fiscal federalism is when the federal government shares revenue with state, local and other governmental units for poverty, health and highway programs.

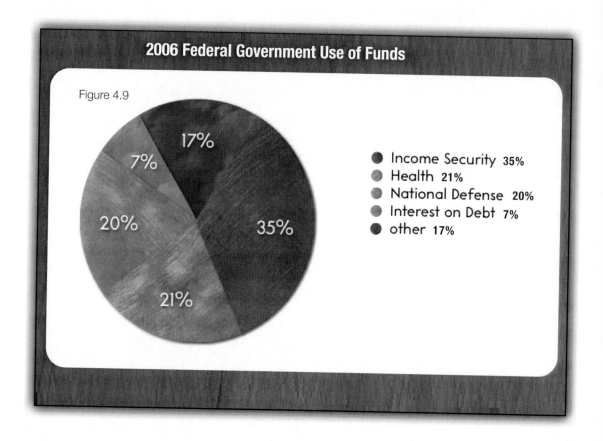

2006 Federal Government Use of Funds

Figure 4.9

17%
7%
20%
35%
21%

- Income Security 35%
- Health 21%
- National Defense 20%
- Interest on Debt 7%
- other 17%

Government has two ways to spend money—transfers and purchases. A transfer payment, as discussed earlier, is government spending for which nothing is directly received in return. Examples include welfare payments or subsidies paid to farmers. However, government also purchases goods and services just as a consumer or a company would. Transfer payments are currently about half of the total federal government's spending and growing rapidly as a percent of total spending.

TAX AND LOCAL FINANCE:

Texas gets 59 percent of operating funds from tax collections (mostly sales taxes), 25 percent from federal aid (revenue sharing by federal government), and 6 percent from interest income. Texas uses funds for education (44 percent), human services (18 percent) and transportation (11 percent), with the remainder going toward operating expenses. A relatively new source of funds for states is a lottery, which is a game of chance run by the state to raise revenue.

Texas receives much of its tax funds from sales taxes, which are regressive. Most states in the United States receive significant funding from revenue sharing from the federal government and from state income taxes. Texas is one of the few remaining states that does not have an income tax.

SUMMARY

Both the private and public sectors are essential to the American economic system. Each sector provides a critical economic function for the other. The efficiency of the private sector promotes growth, while the public sector seeks to promote stability, equity and competition.

Real-World Economics
THE ROLE OF GOVERNMENT?

Since the early 1980s, Democrats and Republicans have debated ideas about the proper role for government. During the recent presidential campaigns, the issue has grown more evident.

What is the proper role for government? How do tax cuts really affect our economy? Are lower taxes always better for economic growth? How have these changes affected our society?

Consider these two opposing views, and consider how this issue has come to be a part of our pop culture after watching the Daily Show link. What do you think?

Please access links through online E-text.

Key Terms

Ability to Pay: A principle of taxation that suggests that those who have more should pay more tax.

Benefits Received: A category of taxation where only those who pay the tax receive the benefits of the tax. A good example is a toll road.

Corporation: A form of business ownership characterized by a legal entity owning the enterprise.

Dual System: A mixed economy with a viable role for public and private sectors in the allocation of resources.

Durable Goods: Goods with an expected useful life of more than three years.

Effect of a Tax: The true, real-world impact of a tax.

Functional Distribution of Income: Dividing total income into resource or factor categories (i.e., wages, rents, profits, etc.).

Government Purchase: Public sector purchases of goods and services.

Incidence of a Tax: The individual or entity that a tax is directed toward. If that entity can get someone else to pay the tax, we conclude that the incidence has been shifted.

Intent of a Tax: What lawmakers intend a tax to be when it is passed into law. All taxes are intended to be progressive or proportional.

Negative Externality: When private production shifts part of the cost to a third party. With pollution, there is a misallocation of resources because the costs of private production are shifted to society in general.

Nondurable Goods: Goods with an expected useful life of less than three years.

Partnership: Similar to a sole proprietorship but with multiple owners.

Personal Distribution of Income: Total income divided by total households or spending units.

Private Sector: All consumers and private firms organized with a profit motive.

Progressive Tax: A type of tax where the rate of taxation (marginally) increases as does taxable income.

Key Terms

Proportional or Flat Tax: A type of tax that does not change as taxable income increases.

Public Sector: All segments of government—federal, state and local.

Regressive Tax: When a tax has a greater impact on lower-income groups than on upper-income groups.

Social Balance: The conscious decision made by a society in the way that resources are allocated between public and private sectors.

Sole Proprietor: A form of business ownership characterized by a single owner.

Tax Loopholes: Items built into the federal tax code that allows a reduction in personal and corporate tax liability for certain activities, such as home ownership, charity, etc.

Transfer Payments: Spending on the part of government for which nothing is received in return.

Applied Exercises

Exercise One:

Calculate the average and marginal tax rates for the following table. Is this tax progressive? How do you know? What generalizations can you offer concerning the relationship between marginal and average tax rates?

Income	Tax	Average Tax Rate	Marginal Tax Rate
$ 0	0	_____	
			_____
100	10	_____	
			_____
200	30	_____	
			_____
300	60	_____	
			_____
400	100	_____	
			_____
500	150	_____	

Exercise Two:

Given the following Federal Tax Table, find the taxes for an individual in contrast to a couple making a taxable income of $100,000. What is the average tax rate for each?

Marginal Tax Rate	Single	Married
10%	$0 - $7,550	$0 - $15,100
15%	$7,551 - $30,650	$15,101 - $61,300
25%	$30,551 - $74,200	$61,301 - $123,700
28%	$74,201 - $154,800	$123,701 - $188,450
33%	$154,801 - $336,550	$188,451 - $336,550
35%	$336,551 +	$336,550 +

Applied Exercises

Exercise Three:

Given the table of current dollar and real dollar GDP values from the Bureau of Economic Analysis, find the following:

A: How much has GDP grown adjusted for inflation between 2000Q1 and 2009Q1?

B: When was a recession present?

C: How much inflation has occurred between 2000q1 and 2009q1?

Year/Quarter	Current $ GDP	Real $ GDP
2000Q1	$9,629	$9,696
2000Q2	9,823	9,848
2000Q3	9,862	9,837
2000Q4	9,954	9,906
2001Q1	10,022	9,876
2001Q2	10,129	9,906
2008Q1	14,151	11,946
2008Q2	14,295	11,727
2008Q3	14,413	11,712
2008Q4	14,200	11,522
2009Q1	14,090	11,354

Applied Exercises: Answers

Exercise One:

Income	Tax	Average Tax Rate	Marginal Tax Rate
$ 0	0		
			.1
100	10	.1	
			.2
200	30	.15	
			.3
300	60	.2	
			.4
400	100	.25	
			.5
500	150	.3	

Yes, it is progressive. Marginal rates rise faster than the average rates.

Exercise Two:

A: Single individual making $100,000: $755 on first $7,550, 15 percent on $7,551 to $30,650, 25 percent on 30,651 to $74,200, 28 percent on $74,201 to $100,000. ($755 + $3,435 + $10,887 + $7,224) = $22,301. The average tax rate is $22,301/$100,000 = an average tax rate of 22 percent.

For a couple making $100,000: $1,510 on first $15,100 and 15 percent on the next $46,200 and 25 percent on the final $61,300. ($1,510 + $6,930 + $9,675) = $18,115 or an average tax rate of 18 percent.

Applied Exercises: Answers

Exercise Three:

A: How much has GDP grown adjusted for inflation between 2000Q1 and 2009Q1?

2001Q1 = $9,697 and 2009Q1 = $11,354, therefore the difference is the real growth ($11,354 − $9,697) = $1,658 or $1,653/$9,697 = 17 percent.

B: When was a recession present?

A decrease in real GDP occurred in 2000Q3 and 2001Q1 and again in 2008Q2, Q3 and Q4, officially creating a recession with 3 quarterly declines in real GDP.

C: How much inflation has occurred between 2000q1 and 2009q1?

Assuming constant dollars from 2000q1, then 2009Q1 14,090/11,354 = 1.24 or approximately 24 percent total inflation of the nominal GDP over the real GDP.

Lesson Five
National Income Accounting

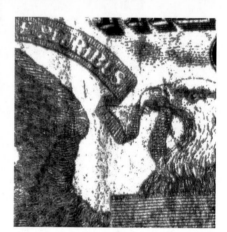

Introduction

National Income Accounting broadly refers to all the methods used to measure and evaluate economic activity. This diagnostic information about the health of our economy helps us formulate appropriate policy—usually fiscal or monetary policy. Through this, the government exerts a counter-cyclical approach where government stimulates the economy during recession and attempts to slow the economy during inflation.

LEARNING OBJECTIVES

Please note the listed objectives. As you will see, the course materials are all objective driven. This provides you with a constant way to direct and monitor your progress throughout the course. Each objective is color-coded and corresponds to that particular section in the text.

OBJECTIVE ONE [1]

Define GDP, describe the "value added" concept of GDP and contrast GDP with GNP.

OBJECTIVE TWO [2]

Calculate GDP using the Expenditure Approach and explain the significance of each component in the calculation.

OBJECTIVE THREE [3]

Calculate GDP using the Income Approach and explain the significance of each component in the calculation.

OBJECTIVE FOUR [4]

Create a Price Index, use it to adjust for Inflation, and explain the importance of that adjustment using the appropriate terms.

OBJECTIVE FIVE [5]

Describe the limitations of GDP as a measure of "well-being" and the importance of the Social Accounts.

INTERACTIVE EXERCISE

Use the Major Economic Models to demonstrate an understanding of the chain reactions resulting from human choices and how they move through an economy. Demonstrate an understanding of the Tradeoffs that result.

Specifically, we use National Income Accounting to:

- Measure and describe economic activity.

- Compare data with past performance.

- Compare our economy with other nations.

- Provide information to evaluate economic policy.

GROSS DOMESTIC PRODUCT

Gross domestic product (GDP) is the largest aggregate measure of economic activity. GDP is the monetary value of all final goods and services produced in the nation within a year. GDP reflects the cost or price of an item to the final user and can be measured at the sale to the end user and not at any one point before the sale.

GDP is measured as the cost to the final user or the total value added at each stage for participants in production. The sum of income for each stage results in the cost to the end user of the product.

To illustrate "value added," assume a consumer purchases an oak rocking chair from a furniture store for $495. This cost to the final user is equal to the value added to an economy from this new production at each stage.

Value Added: Stage	Buy	Sale	Value Added
1) Farmer grew lumber	$0.	$100	100–0 = 100
2) Craftsman makes chair & sells it to wholesaler	100	$250	250–100 =150
3) Wholesaler sells to retailer	250	$350	350–250 = 100
4) Retailer	350	$495	495–350 = 145

Figure 5.1

In Figure 5.1, the farmer cut the lumber and added value by selling it for $100 to the craftsman. The craftsman built the chair from the lumber, which cost him $100, and sold the chair for $250. The craftsman added a value of $150 to the economy. The wholesaler paid $250 and sold the chair for $350, adding

$100 of value. Finally, the retailer bought the chair for $350 and sold it for $495, adding $145 in value.

The sum of the value added at all stages of production is the cost to the final user. The craftsman added a value of $150 to the economy. The wholesaler paid $250 and sold the chair for $350, adding $100 of value. Finally, the retailer bought the chair for $350 and sold it for $495, adding $145 in value. The sum of the value added at all stages of production is the cost to the final user.

Notice in the example above that only by summing the value added at each stage do we obtain the national output cost to the final user ($495). If we added the value paid at each stage, we would be double counting because we would be including values already counted. Counting the value at each stage yields the value of intermediate goods rather than the value for its final use.

As an example of a final use vs. intermediate use, consider the purchase of fuel, seed and fertilizer by a wheat farmer. These purchases are intermediate costs that will be included in the final price of the wheat but will not be included as a final product until the product is sold to the final user.

THE RULES FOR GDP

Although new production is measured at value added or cost to the final user, many transactions are NOT counted in GDP. GDP includes all new goods and services produced in a year but does not include used products that are resold. The sale of used items does not represent new production. GDP also does not include non-production transactions, such as financial transactions or public or private gifts. Stocks sold are exchanges of ownership and do not constitute a change in production. However, any commissions on the sale of used goods, as well as commissions on financial transactions, are counted in the GDP as cost of services.

GNP AND GDP

GDP and gross national product (GNP) are two different measures of the aggregate activity of an economy. While GDP is a measure of total output for a nation, GNP is a measure of what is produced by Americans throughout the world. Since many Americans work outside of the United States, the GNP accounts for the aggregate of all goods and services produced by Americans regardless of location.

TWO SIDES TO GDP—EXPENDITURE

The expenditure approach to GDP is a calculation that accumulates output for each of the four major sectors of an economy. The four major sectors are: consumers, investors, government and foreign. The formula for the expenditures approach is:

$$GDP = C + I + G + Xn$$

Figure 5.2

C is Personal Consumption Expenditure

I is Gross Private Domestic Investment

G is Government spending at all levels

Xn is Net Exports (Exports – Imports)

Personal consumption expenditure (PCE) is the spending by households on all final goods and services but does not include purchases of new homes because such purchases are counted as investment goods.

Gross private domestic investment (GPDI) is the amount of all business investments added to an economy and includes both replacing what equipment was depreciated (used) and new investment in capital goods and inventories as well as new homes.

Government spending at all levels (G) includes government consumption, government investment and transfer payments, such as Social Security.

Net exports are the amount of products and services that foreigners buy from our economy (exports) less what we bought from their economy (imports).

Investment is the amount of funds spent by businesses for new plants and equipment as well as increases in inventory accumulated during the year. Investment represents the amount of capital stock that was produced for businesses. This does not include stock market certificates that represent ownership and are bought and sold on stock exchanges nor does it include bonds that are debt contracts.

GPDI includes new additions to the capital goods in our nation and the replacement of capital goods that have been worn out or made obsolete. Thus, in a growth economy, the amount of total new investment is more than what was used or destroyed. The amount destroyed is called consumption of fixed capital (CFC).

The total investment or GPDI is for both replacement of destroyed capital (CFC) and new additions called net private domestic investment (NPDI). This is expressed in the equation:

$$GPDI = NPDI + CFC$$

Gross private domestic investment is net private domestic investment plus consumption of fixed capital. Total investment is the replacement of depreciated capital plus new additions or deletions to capital.

In a growth economy, NPDI is positive, but in a constrictive economy, NPDI is negative. Thus, CFC must be replaced in order for investment to be greater than the previous year. Economies that are in a recession or decline will not have sufficient new investment to replace depreciated capital because investors are unwilling to put financial capital into a declining economy. New investment is put into an economy when profit expectations are high, not when there is a lack of confidence in the economy.

Figure 5.3

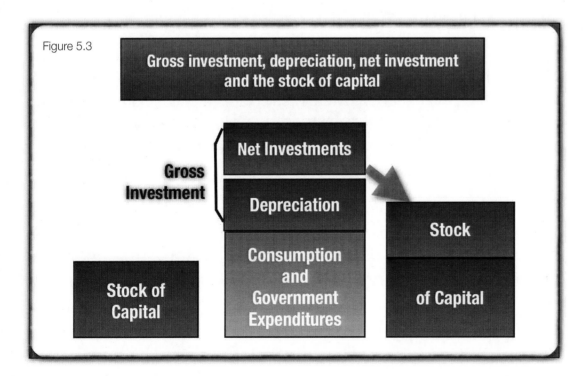

Gross investment, depreciation, net investment and the stock of capital

Expenditures Approach to GDP		Income Approach to GNI	
Personal Consumption Expenditure	$3,500	Compensation of Workers	$3,650
Gross Private Domestic Investment	500	Rents	100
Government Purchasers	1,000	Interest	300
Net Exports	0	Profit	550
	$5,000	**National Income**	
		Indirect Business Taxes	200
		Consumption of Fixed Capital	300
		Net Foreign Income earned in US	**−100**
Figure 5.4		**GNI = GDP**	$5,000

THE INCOME APPROACH

The **Income Approach** to gross national income (GNI) follows the flow of income to each sector of the economy and concludes with the GDP. The gross national income is equal to the gross domestic product as the sum of the income flow is equal to the cost of the goods and services at final use.

GNI is the sum of all incomes of the production process, including payment for the factors of production as well as taxes and depreciation. Thus, GDP is equal to GNI, with each calculation arriving at the same value with one using products produced (GDP) and the other incomes generated (GNI).

The U.S. Department of Commerce, Bureau of Economic Analysis (BEA) maintains the database for national income accounting for the U.S. government. These accounts are carefully calculated and compared with other economic data to assure reliability and validity. The following accounts are available to represent the first quarter of 2007 for the U.S. economy (Figure 5.5).

The data in Figure 5.5 is an accurate description of the American GDP and its expenditure components in 2007. The value of each sector represents its importance relative to the total for the nation. GDP for the United States is $13.6 trillion, and this is greater than for any other nation. China and Japan are the second and third largest economies in the world, each with a GDP about half of that for the United States.

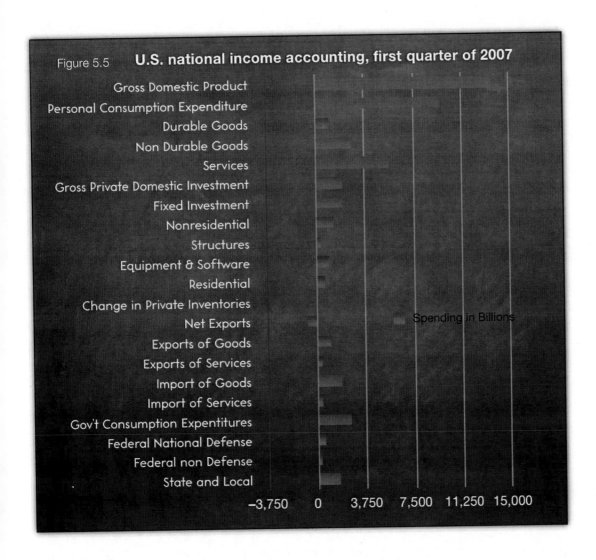

Figure 5.5 **U.S. national income accounting, first quarter of 2007**

Gross Domestic Product
Personal Consumption Expenditure
Durable Goods
Non Durable Goods
Services
Gross Private Domestic Investment
Fixed Investment
Nonresidential
Structures
Equipment & Software
Residential
Change in Private Inventories
Net Exports
Exports of Goods
Exports of Services
Import of Goods
Import of Services
Gov't Consumption Expentitures
Federal National Defense
Federal non Defense
State and Local

Spending in Billions

-3,750   0   3,750   7,500   11,250   15,000

The allocations among GDP are widely varied. Consumers' purchases account for about 70 percent of the total GDP, while government expenditures account for a much smaller amount—about 20 percent—and investment expenditures account for only 16 percent. The role of investment is essential for capital formation and growth. However, the foreign sector, in its present state, presents a unique problem, yielding a <u>decrease</u> in total output because our exports are less than our imports. The history and implications of the balance of trade (exports less imports) will be discussed in a later lesson.

The personal consumption expenditure (PCE) is the total expenditures of consumers and is the largest component of the economy. Increases or decreases in PCE affect employment, income and output significantly. Businesses expand production when consumers increase spending and contract production when consumers decrease spending.

GPDI is the most important sector determining the future direction of economic activity. When investment is strong, momentum is built for future expansion in income, employment and output. Economists examine changes in GDPI to predict future economic growth or recession.

The net export (Xn) is exports minus imports. This sector is growing in importance for the American economy. Currently the United States imports about $800 billion more in goods and services than it exports, thereby resulting in a decrease in GDP. This

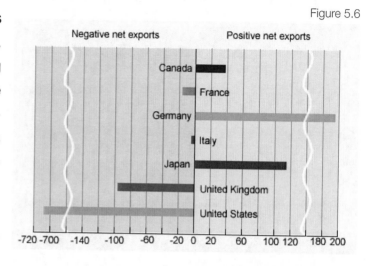

Figure 5.6

imbalance does pose a problem in the longer term unless changes are made. See the chart above, showing nations with deficits (imports > exports) and nations with a surplus (exports > imports).

INFLATION

Inflation of economic values is an increase in the general price level of an economy. Just as individuals experience inflation in the cost of products, the economy in general tends to experience a rise in prices over time. Inflated values must be adjusted to real values to make comparisons. Real values in national income accounting are those that have been adjusted to remove the impact of inflation so meaningful comparisons of the value of goods can be made. The price index, as compiled by the BEA, is the measure of inflation used by the government to compute real values.

PRICE INDEX

Price indices are calculated by comparing output prices for a given year to prices for the same output at a specific year, called the base year. In order to take out the effect of inflation, an adjustment must be made for price changes. For example, assume a basket of food goods costs $200 in the base year, 2000, and in 2001 the same goods cost $202; the price has increased by $2 from a base of $200 to $202, yielding an increase of 2/200 or 1percent. The price index in 2001 is 101, as shown in Figure 5.7.

Figure 5.7

$$\frac{\text{Price of Goods in Specific Year}}{\text{Price of Same goods in Base Year}} \times 100 = \text{Price Index in Given Year}$$

$$\times 100 = 101$$

$$\frac{\$202}{\$200}$$

Thus the price index has increased by 1% or and index value from 100 in 2000 to 101 in 2001.

An application of the calculation of a price index is given below for a base year of 2000 through 2002.

A further application of this concept can be illustrated showing adjustments to output, such as gross domestic product accounts. The price index for a group of specific goods in 2002 compared to the same goods in the base year 2000 can be calculated. This value is found by first examining the output of the specific goods (prices times quantity produced during 2000) to find the total cost at the base year. Then the total cost of the specific goods in 2002 is computed (prices times goods produced).

Figure 5.8

Year	Output Units	Price of Apples	Price Index	Nominal GDP	Real GDP
2000	10	$1	100	$10	$10
2001	20	2	200	40	20
2002	25	2	200	50	25

In Figure 5.8, the price index base year is 2000 and the price of apples is $1 each. However, in 2001, the price of apples has increased to $2, which means that the base year 2000 price index has doubled from the base of 100 to a value of 200. Therefore, prices have doubled (200/100 = 2). The nominal GDP is the value of output produced in a specific year at the price level of that year. The nominal GDP in 2001 is 20 units at a new price of $2 with a GDP of $40. However, adjusted for inflation, this value must be reduced if a comparison with constant or real value is to be determined.

Real values take out the impact of inflation. Prices between 2000 and 2001 have doubled, so the GDP value of 40 must be divided by the price index of 200 to find an adjusted or constant dollar value of 20. The nominal GDP comparison between the two years was an increase from $10 to $40, but this did not adjust for the doubling of prices so the adjusted or real GDP was $40/200 × 100 or a real value of $20. Output has doubled and, therefore, the increase in prices taken out and real GDP has increased from $10 to $20 in real terms. These same adjustments are made to the aggregate output of the nation, as shown in Figure 5.8.

Year	Nominal GDP	CPI	Real GDP
2004	$11.712	190.2	$6.157
2005	12.456	197.4	6.310
2006	13.247	202.6	6.538

Amounts in trillions of dollars.

Figure 5.9

PRICE ADJUSTMENTS TO GDP

The 2005 GDP was $12.456 trillion in nominal terms and it was $13.247 in 2006. Does this mean that the economy grew by $13.247–$12.456 or $791 billion? In nominal terms, the answer to this question is yes, but the value adjusted for inflation requires further adjustment for price changes (inflation).

CONSUMER PRICE INDEX

The price index used above is the consumer price index (CPI) as computed by the Department of Commerce for a basket of goods and services purchased by an average family in an urban setting. For more information on the CPI, visit www.bls.gov/cpi/.

Notice that on this website, a calculator is available to adjust any past value to a current price. If you input $100 in the base year 1980, you will find that these funds in 1980 would be worth about $250 today. Prices have increased on average by a factor of 2.5, so that a dollar in 1980 is worth $2.50 today.

An increase of $791 in GDP must be adjusted for inflation to make constant comparisons. The $791 increase must be divided by the price index, so the real value in 2005 is 6.310 and in 2006 6.538. Therefore, the amount of the real increase (after adjusting for inflation) is $228 rather than the nominal increase of $791.

Figure 5.10

Nominal GDP	/	Price Index	X	100	=	Real GDP
12.456	/	197.4	x	100	=	6.31

Year	Nominal GDP	Price Index	Real GDP
2005	12.456	197.4	6.310

The information on adjusting for inflation can be summarized by restating some of the information above. Real GDP is the value of GDP in constant dollars without inflation. Such a GDP value is termed constant dollars, real dollars or adjusted GDP. Over time, the general price level changes due to changes in prices. Inflation is a rise in the general price level. Adjustments for these changes can be made to remove the impact of inflation. This "real value" is calculated by dividing the nominal (unadjusted or current dollar value) value by the price index for that year times 100.

The income of an individual can also be adjusted for purchasing power through this same process. Consider that you were making $40,000 in income in 2005 and you are making $44,000 in income in 2006. How much has your income increased in real terms? Assume the price index of the CPI has increased from 197.4 to 202.6 or a change of 2.6 percent (202.6−197.4=5.2, then 5.2/197.4 × 100=2.6). To adjust your income of $44,000 to base year values in 2005, you would compare values of $40,000/197.4=$20,263 and $44,000/202.6= $21,718. Therefore, in real 1980–1982 price index terms, your real income increased by $1,455.

Notice that your income increased in nominal terms by $4,000 or 10 percent and inflation increased by 2.6 percent. You would hope your income increased by a similar percentage as inflation. Because individual income has social implications, other means of analyzing income changes over time have been developed.

THE SOCIAL ACCOUNTS

The social accounts are another way of measuring national income. In this approach, the major economic accounts are described with values beginning with the largest GDP and considering social influences in lesser sums until the resulting personal savings is listed. The social accounts measures the well-being of a nation's economy based on all allocations of resources by society.

Figure 5.11

List of Social Accounts in Billions (2002)

Gross Domestic Product (GDP)	**$10,446**
Consumption of Fixed Capital	−1,393
Net Domestic Product (NDP)	9,053
Net Foreign Factor Income Earned in U.S.	−10
Indirect Business Taxes	−695
National Income (NI)	8,348
Minus Income Earned But Not Received	
Social Security Contributions	−748
Corporate Income Taxes	−213
Undistributed Corporate Profits	−141
Plus: Income Received But Not Earned	
Transfer Payments	+1,683
Personal Income (PI)	8,929
Minus Personal Taxes	−1,113
Disposable Income (DI)	7,816

The social accounts in Figure 5.11 provide a means for examining each of the components of gross domestic product that affects society. The following discussion explains the basis for the social accounts analysis of individual income.

THE SOCIAL VALUES OF GDP

The GDP less CFC is net domestic product (NDP). These figures measure the output less depreciation on a nation's capital goods. This measure is needed to estimate how much a nation must spend to continue current GDP. If capital consumed (CFC) is not replaced, then GDP will fall. A growing gap between GDP and NDP indicates increasing obsolescence of capital goods while a narrowing of the gap indicates that the condition of capital is improving.

The CFC is important because it indicates whether the economy is increasing or decreasing its capital base. A growing economy will have more invested in new capital, NPDI, than is depreciated through consumption of fixed capital. The gross private domestic investment (GPDI) is the total amount of investment put into an economy, but the consumption of fixed capital (CFC) is the total used or depreciated. Therefore, NPDI is the amount of additions or deletions to investment.

The next group of calculations derives personal income or the income people receive. The national income figure is reduced by income that individuals and businesses earn but are not allowed to keep as an income flow because it is retained in the business as undistributed profits or the funds are taxed away through Social Security insurance and corporate profit taxes.

Other components of the social accounts indicate how GDP is being used. Net domestic product less indirect business tax (sales taxes) yields national income (NI). NI is the total income earned by sectors, including landowners (rent), capitalists (interest), labor (wages and salaries) and entrepreneurs (profits).

The national income figure is increased by the amount that people receive but did not earn in the year through production. This income flow is called transfer payments and consists of veterans' payments, welfare and Social Security payments. National income less income earned but not received plus transfer payments equals the amount of funds available to individuals as personal income.

From the personal income figure, disposable income is found by subtracting required payments of personal taxes. The disposable income figure represents the funds that individuals have available for uses after taxes have been paid. Finally, from the disposable income number, personal consumption expenditure (the C in the expenditures model used to calculate GDP) is subtracted to arrive at savings by all individuals within our economy. The amount of funds left for savings is critical within an economy because it represents the funds available for investment back into the economy for capital goods.

SHORTCOMINGS OF GDP

There are many shortcomings of gross domestic product when it is used to measure economic well-being. Many people think of the GDP number as being solely representative of how well people live but this is not completely accurate. The quantity of goods and services is, at best, only a partial representation. Numerous studies have tried to modify this number to better measure a quality of life index but no common consensus has been reached on a substitute measure.

One problem is that GDP does not consider byproducts. One of the byproducts of GDP is the amount of pollution produced by an economy to obtain goods and services. This is the negative externality or negative spillover from the GDP production process.

The amount of leisure time for individuals is also an important measure of social welfare but is not considered in GDP calculations. Americans work more hours per week than people in any other culture. Although Americans today may work fewer hours than their great-grandparents, the GDP does not adjust for this difference.

Another factor not considered in GDP is the quality of products produced. GDP measures only an aggregate of price times quantity produced but not the resulting utility to consumers. Today's cars are better made than those manufactured 30 years ago, yet there is no consideration given to the quality of products.

Another shortcoming involves productivity that we cannot measure. Maintaining a household, cooking, cleaning, making home repairs and caring for children are all productive activities but are not really measurable. Certainly, one could make a case that such activity is valuable for a society, but it is difficult to measure in terms of a benchmark of economic activity.

Further, many unreported economic activities are not calculated, such as individuals working for cash unreported to the Internal Revenue Service. This so-called underground economy is not measured but includes economic activities that are often illegal but unreported.

All these social considerations are important to our economy, involve value judgments and are very difficult to quantify or measure. These qualitative judgments—the quality of life vs. quantity of life—have long been an issue in economic discussions. That debate among students and policymakers continues. The quantity (goods consumed) of life is not a measure of happiness, which seems to be well recognized in other parts of the world.

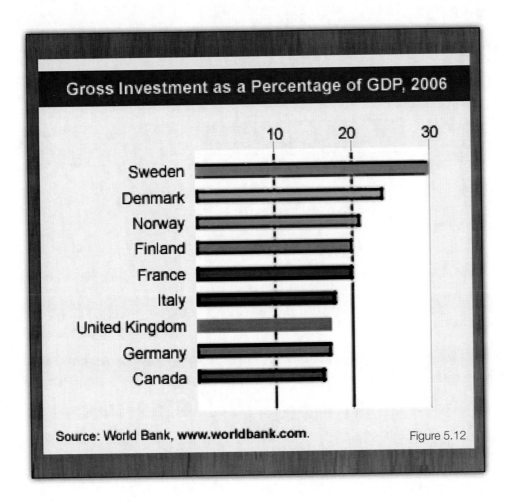

Gross Investment as a Percentage of GDP, 2006

Source: World Bank, www.worldbank.com.

Figure 5.12

Real-World Economics

In our system of national income accounting, GDP is largely a price times quantity figure—it makes no qualitative judgments about our lives and how they may be improving.

Please access links through online E-text.

Key Terms

Adjusted GDP: GDP date adjusted for price changes by using the price index.

Base Year: The arbitrary beginning year or benchmark for any statistical index.

Consumer Price Index: A measure of price changes in our economy during a given period by tracing the prices of a predetermined number of consumer items.

Consumption of Fixed Capital: Replacing worn-out capital—depreciation.

Expenditure GDP: The total of all categories in the economy, including consumers, businesses, government and net exports.

Gross Domestic Product: The total, final sales price of all goods and services produced in our economy in one year. GDP measures only domestic production (inside U.S territory).

Gross National Product: A measure of production for all American firms throughout the world.

Gross Private Domestic Investment (GPDI): Total, business investment spending for depreciation and new capital in a given year.

Indirect Business Tax: A correction that is made to expenditure GDP to account for sales taxes that are collected at the point of final sale, which is a more accurate measure for the final price.

Personal consumption: The total spending of all consumers in the U.S. economy, which makes up about two-thirds of all consumption in a given year.

National Income Accounting: Measurers of economic activity and monetary flows that track changes in spending and impact on the business cycle.

Net Domestic Product: Overall GDP corrected for depreciation or the consumption of fixed capital.

Net Exports: A comparison of monetary flows as goods are imported and exported and the economic impact.

Key Terms

Net Private Domestic Investment (NPDI): Spending on new capital equipment in a given year.

Personal Income: Personal income minus personal income tax leaves the consumer with disposable income.

Price Index: A percentage comparison from a fixed point of reference (base year) that adjusts for price changes.

Social Accounts: The accounting of income as generated from expenditure GDP.

Unadjusted GDP: A price times quantity figure with no adjustment made for price changes—inflation or deflation.

Underground Economy: Unreported economic activity and income, usually with the intent to evade taxes on that income.

Applied Exercises

Exercise One:

Given the following national income accounts, compute the values requested below.

Government Purchases	$70
Indirect Business Taxes	20
Personal Consumption Expenditure	300
Consumption of Fixed Capital	25
Exports	20
Gross Private Domestic Investment	50
Imports	25
Net Foreign Factor Income Earned in US	15

A: What is GDP?

B: Calculate NDP.

C: What is National Income?

Exercise Two:

Given the following national income accounts, compute the values requested below.

A: The purchase of Exxon Mobil common stock.

B: The purchase of a new car.

C: The purchase of a used textbook.

D: The sale of a factory to a new company.

E: An increase in the hours worked throughout the United States.

F: A gift to a son by his family.

G: Rent paid for a business building.

H: Social Security payment to a retired worker.

Applied Exercises: Answers

Exercise One:

A: $C + I + G + Xn$

$300 + 50 + 70 + 20 - 25 = 415$

B: $NDP = GDP - CFC$

$415 - 25 = 390$

C: National Income = NDP − Net Foreign Factor Income Earned in United States − Indirect Business Taxes

$390 - 15 - 20 = 355$

Exercise Two:

Excluded: A, C, D, E, F; Included: B, G

Lesson **Six**
Instability - Business Cycles

Introduction

A major macroeconomic problem for modern nations is the tendency toward periodic instability—the (seemingly) constant threat of economic conditions turning toward either inflation or recession. In this lesson, we will define and discuss instability—the business cycle—relative to the causes, expected effects and possible remedies. In later lessons, we will explore the counter-cyclical mechanisms of government fiscal and monetary policy, which are the policy weapons available to deal with recession and inflation.

LEARNING OBJECTIVES

Please note the listed objectives. As you will see, the course materials are all objective driven. This provides you with a constant way to direct and monitor your progress throughout the course. Each objective is color-coded and corresponds to that particular section in the text.

OBJECTIVE ONE | 1

Explain the nature of the Business Cycle and the problem of economic instability.

OBJECTIVE TWO | 2

Describe the causes of Inflation using the Aggregate Supply/Aggregate Demand model and explain the effects of Inflation on the economy.

OBJECTIVE THREE | 3

Describe the causes of Recession using the Aggregate Supply/Aggregate Demand model and explain the Effects of Recession on the economy.

OBJECTIVE FOUR | 4

Explain the various Types of Unemployment and how they are measured.

OBJECTIVE FIVE | 5

Describe the social impact of Economic Instability (Inflation and Unemployment).

INTERACTIVE EXERCISE

Use the Major Economic Models to demonstrate an understanding of the chain reactions resulting from human choices and how they move through an economy. Demonstrate an understanding of the Tradeoffs that result.

BUSINESS CYCLES

Business cycles are the ups and downs (usually short-term) of real GDP or fluctuations in economic activity. Attempts to maintain constant or increasing business activity are not always successful. Macroeconomic instability describes the irregular, unexpected changes in business activity. The economic result of these fluctuations will vary depending on the phase of the cycle. We may experience periods of recession and unemployment (or even depression), which may be followed by inflation and an overheated economy. Figure 6.1 presents a hypothetical business cycle. A larger version is available in the Interactive Exercises.

Business cycle phases can be divided into the peak, which is the maximum point of economic activity, and the trough, which is the lowest point of business activity. A recovery is a period of renewed economic activity between the trough and the peak. A recession is a period of decreasing economic activity between the peak and trough.

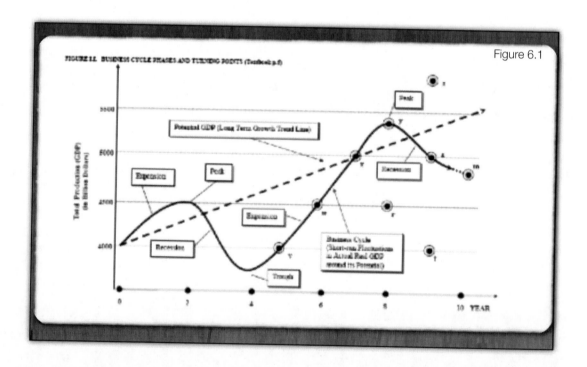

Figure 6.1

CYCLICAL VARIATIONS

A downward slope in economic activity results in decreases in output, income and employment and may lead to a longer-term recession. The Bureau of Economic Research (NBER) is the accepted authority on when a recession begins and ends. This prominent group of economists is considered to be nonpolitical. The NBER officially declares a recession in the United States after two consecutive quarterly declines in real national income; however, the NBER may judge a recession to exist with any combination of other business activity changes.

The major causes of cycles include war, monetary policy changes, speculation, political events and even technological changes. War is devastating to individuals and to the economy because it reduces available resources and diverts existing resources to the war effort. Too much available money relative to the supply of goods and services causes inflation, which initiates a new business cycle. Speculation in the stock market may drive prices to an unsustainable high, and political actions or reactions may overly stimulate or depress business activity. Technology improvements can increase economic activity, provided that production costs are reduced and the economy can absorb those workers who become unemployed as a result of technological improvements. All these events may trigger a business cycle.

INFLATION

Inflation is one of the most difficult problems of business cycles. Inflation is a rise in the general price level. Inflation can reduce real income, employment and output because of its affect on business investment and the general economy.

CAUSES OF INFLATION

Inflation is often a result of changes in the business cycle but economists can isolate different types of inflation. There are many theories of what causes inflation in an economy.

DEMAND-PULL

The demand-pull theory argues that inflation is caused by too much money in an economy with too few goods. If the growth of money is faster than the growth of goods and services, pressure is placed on producers to sell more than they can efficiently produce. Increasing output often causes unit costs to increase and, thereby, prices to rise. When demand in our economy is greater than our ability to meet that demand, the usual result is inflation.

The demand-pull theory is illustrated by Keynesian analysis comparing prices (inflation) on the Y-axis and real national output on the X-axis, as shown in Figure 6.2. Keynes assumed that an economy with high unemployment (Stage 1) would have a flat aggregate supply (AS) line, with an intersecting decreasing sloped aggregate demand (AD) line. As the aggregate demand line shifts right (increases from AD1 to AD2), there would be no inflation. In Stage 2, as AD shifts right (increases from AD3 to AD4) along an upward sloping AS line, both output and prices increase (P1 to P2). However, as the aggregate demand line approaches the capacity on the aggregate supply vertical line (Stage 3), inflation occurs (price increases from AD5 to AD6), with no increase in output. At full employment, increases in aggregate demand will only cause inflation with no increase in real national output.

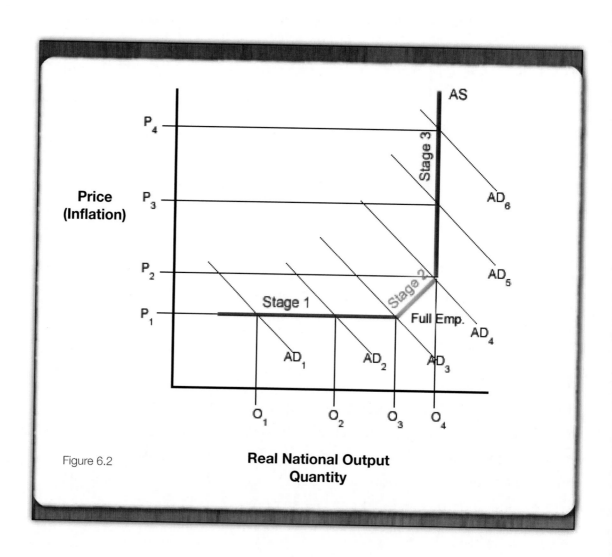

Figure 6.2

**Real National Output
Quantity**

Cost-Push Inflation

Cost-push is another theory of what causes inflation. In this model, inflation is determined by owners of resources increasing their prices, which causes cost increases for all producers and eventually consumers. This action effectively "pushes up" prices throughout an economy.

Three Types of Cost-Push Inflation:
Increasing Resource Prices

Perhaps the leading cause of cost-push inflation is the scarcity of basic resources. In our world today, increases in oil prices represent the best example of how a basic commodity can cause inflation throughout producer and consumer allocations.

Wage-Price Spiral

Although we have not seen very much of this type of inflation in recent years, it has to do with labor unions' demands for higher wages when demand-pull inflation is occurring. When (or if) these demands are met, it increases the cost of production, resulting in more inflation, which, in turn, may again increase union demands.

Monopoly Power

If there is very little competition in a given market, producers may raise prices simply to increase profits. This is difficult to do in a competitive market or in a recession, but we are seeing increasing levels of market power exhibited in many parts of our economy.

There are other theories of inflation that argue inflation is likely if the economy is nearing capacity and therefore resources are in high demand. We may also see labor moving from one job to another that pays more. Thus, resources are attracted through higher compensation but higher output is not attained—only higher prices.

Inflation—Overall Effects

Inflation is normally associated with the expansionary side of the business cycle. The definition is simple. Inflation occurs when there is a general and sustained increase in prices. The major measures of inflation are the **Consumer Price Index (CPI)** and the **Producer Price Index (PPI)**.

Both indices relate to the idea of a "general and sustained price increase." The CPI notes inflation for a family of four in a city, while the PPI notes inflation at the wholesale level of business. These measures are statistically complex but result in a very useful tool for analysis. Each index weighs (gives measured component value to) a wide diversity of purchases by consumers or businesses to provide an aggregate cost value for a given month. This value is then compared to the same value in the following month to determine the change in prices for the aggregate of the purchases.

- According to the U.S. Bureau of Labor Statistics (BLS), "Prices for the goods and services used to calculate the CPI are collected in 87 urban areas throughout the country and from about 23,000 retail and service establishments. Data on <u>rents</u> are collected from about 50,000 landlords or tenants.

- The weight for an item is derived from reported expenditures on that item as estimated by the Consumer Expenditure Survey." Source: <u>www.bls.gov/cpi/</u>

The CPI is computed with and without food and energy because of the volatile nature of food and energy. Notice the high inflation of food/energy followed by deflation (decrease in prices) in 2007 and 2008.

U.S. inflation rates are generally lower than most industrialized nations; however, the inflation rate has varied from its current 2 percent to 13 percent in 1979. Other national rates vary widely, from a low rate in most of Western Europe to a high rate in an African nation of more than 4000 percent.

INFLATION ARITHMETIC

The impact of inflation on prices over time can be calculated by the rule of 70. The rule of 70 is a measure of how long it will take for prices to double at a given annual inflation rate. The compounded inflation rate is divided into the number 70 to find the number of years for prices to double. For example: if a nation's prices are inflating at 10 percent per year, it will take seven years for the prices to double (70/10 = 7 years). However, if inflation is 2 percent, it will take 35 years for prices to double (70/2 = 35 years).

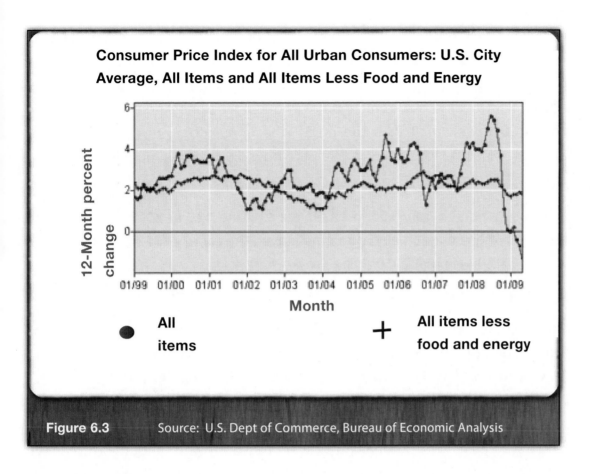

Consumer Price Index for All Urban Consumers: U.S. City Average, All Items and All Items Less Food and Energy

All items •   All items less + food and energy

Figure 6.3   Source: U.S. Dept of Commerce, Bureau of Economic Analysis

INFLATION BASICS

Although numerous theories attempt to explain inflation, we have previously discussed the two major causes of inflation. Demand-pull inflation, which is "too much money chasing too few goods," means that there is excessive demand (see Stage 3 in Figure 6.2). Money is available but supply is usually limited in the short run so prices are bid up. The other major theory of inflation is the cost-push model. With cost-push, the costs of production are increasing, which "pushes" up overall prices.

REDISTRIBUTION OF INCOME AND WEALTH

When the rate of inflation exceeds wage or profit increases, wages and profits are reduced in real terms. This process rewards those workers or firms with market power and penalizes those without. With market power, one can increase prices to keep up with increasing costs or even gain through inflation by increasing prices more than the general price level increases. In contrast, people living on a fixed income will decrease their purchasing power by the amount of inflation.

For example, if you receive a monthly $1,000 pension for life and after one year inflation is 10 percent, then your monthly income in real terms is only $900. Nominal vs. real income is the issue of inflation's effect on purchasing power. Real income is current income divided by the price index at a base year times 100. For example, assume in 2010 that your income was $20,000 and in 2011 your income increased to $22,000; how did your real purchasing power change?

If prices increased from 100 in base year 2010 to 110 in 2011 (a 10 percent increase), then your actual real income stayed the same — $22,000 divided by 1.10 = $20,000 in real 2010 dollars.

BORROWERS MAY GAIN AT THE EXPENSE OF LENDERS

Unanticipated inflation reduces the value of the money that is paid back to the lender. Assume you borrowed $100,000 at a fixed rate of 7 percent for 30 years to purchase a house. If the inflation rate increases to 7 percent or more, you are repaying with funds less valued than the interest rate because the lender did not anticipate such inflation. Through unanticipated inflation, lenders actually lose purchasing power. You borrowed something (money) that was worth more at the time than the money that you later returned to the lender.

The effect of inflation (if anticipated) will result in savers earning higher interest rates to accommodate for inflation. If banks (savers) anticipate an inflation rate of 5 percent and require a return of 5 percent, then interest rates are set at 10 percent. If unanticipated inflation rises from 5 percent to 10 percent and interest rates are set at 10 percent, banks (savers) will lose their expected return of 5 percent.

REAL INTEREST RATES

Real interest rates are the actual return a saver receives for loaning money. The real interest rate is the nominal interest rate minus the inflation rate.

Real Interest Rate = Nominal Interest Rate minus Inflation Rate

If interest rates for a given loan are 12 percent but there is 4 percent inflation, the real rate of interest is (12-4) 8 percent.

INFLATION DISCOURAGES SAVING

If you are being paid a 5 percent return on your savings and inflation is running at 7 percent, it is not logical to save money for a purchase. The value of your money is declining in real terms while in your account. In addition, the item that you may be saving to purchase is increasing in price as inflation takes place. It may be a more sound decision to borrow the money now to buy the item that is increasing in price rather than save to purchase it in the future.

INFLATION ENCOURAGES SPECULATION

As mentioned, if the value of your saved money is declining, it is logical to put your money into an investment that is keeping pace with inflation. Inflation interrupts the normal borrowing-saving relationship and results in speculative investments with market power to increase prices without increasing output. During 2007–2008, as seen in the CPI graph of oil, oil markets were representative of this speculative process (Figure 6.3).

The impact of inflation creates a great deal of uncertainty and risk. To accommodate for possible inflation increases, savers/lenders may require a premium interest rate to hedge against a possible loss from unanticipated inflation.

CREEPING (ANTICIPATED) INFLATION

A slower rate of inflation (creeping) will not have as negative of an effect as those just mentioned. Most businesses would argue that a small amount of inflation (2 percent or 3 percent) might actually be beneficial for the economy. Creeping inflation may encourage some economic growth and profits as investors anticipate stable returns.

NONCYCLICAL CHANGES

Noncyclical fluctuations are economic fluctuations other than business cycles. Seasonal variation and secular trends are two examples of such fluctuations.

Seasonal fluctuations form a regular (predictable) pattern of economic activity during a year. Retail activity, for example, follows a seasonal pattern, higher in November and December and lower in January, while farm output is higher in the summer and lower in the winter.

A secular trend is a long-term average of economic activity. Examples are the ownership of cell phones and iPods over a time period. Secular trends illustrate long-term movements. A secular trend is illustrated on the cycles graph (Figure 6.1) by the dashed line.

AGGREGATE SUPPLY IMPLICATIONS FOR GROWTH

The secular trend (or Long-Term Trend Line) represents the path of a long-run movement in the economy. Secular trends are driven by the relatively slow rightward shifts of the AS curve. These rightward shifts in AS are also responsible for long-run growth discussed in Lesson 2 (PPF). When AS shifts left with a given AD, prices raise (inflation) and national output declines, but when AS shifts right, prices decline and real national output increases.

The rightward shifts in AS are also responsible for long-run growth of output in our ongoing studies of the Circular Flow diagram that we began in Lesson 1. Although there are technical differences in the graphs, an insight into the factors that cause rightward shifts in the Aggregate (Macro) Supply curve can be gained by reviewing the factors that caused rightward shifts in the Market (Micro) Supply Curves in Lesson 3. The "macro" models of the economy are all strongly linked together (with the AS/AD driving changes in the others.) Supply and demand shifts at the micro level ultimately drive the changes in the "macro" AS/AD. Keep these points in mind along with our ongoing theme of "Making Good Choices for Healthy Growth" as the course continues to unfold.

EFFECT OF RECESSION — UNEMPLOYMENT

Recession is generally defined by the NBER as occurring when two consecutive declines in quarterly GDP occur. This is somewhat inexact but we know that unemployment is one of the major characteristics of a slowing business cycle. Unemployment in economics is normally defined as workers who are willing and able to work for pay but are unable to find work (Lesson Two). The **unemployment rate** is the number of unemployed (those unable to find work) *divided* by the total labor force. The total labor force includes those willing and able to work whether employed or unemployed. Some adjustments to this definition are made by the BLS.

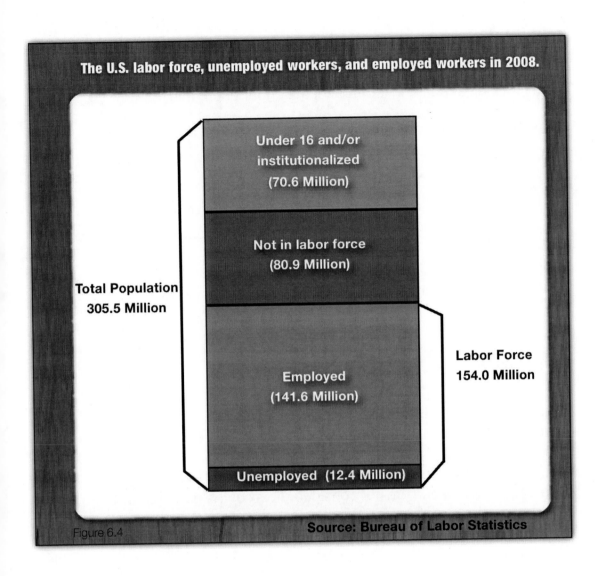

The U.S. labor force, unemployed workers, and employed workers in 2008.

Total Population 305.5 Million

Under 16 and/or institutionalized (70.6 Million)

Not in labor force (80.9 Million)

Employed (141.6 Million)

Labor Force 154.0 Million

Unemployed (12.4 Million)

Source: Bureau of Labor Statistics

Figure 6.4

THE THREE TYPES OF UNEMPLOYMENT

Cyclical unemployment is present when there is insufficient demand for labor in an economy due to a decline in the business cycle. The lack of demand for workers results in increased unemployment.

Frictional unemployment occurs when workers are moving between jobs. There is a period of adjustment as a worker is temporarily unemployed while looking for a job or moving to a new job. Frictionally unemployed can be unemployed by choice. This is quite different from those who cannot find work due to a recession.

Structural unemployment is the most difficult type of unemployment for society to correct. Structural unemployment occurs when workers do not have the required skills for existing jobs. If workers' skills do not keep up with job demands or, more broadly, workers lack basic reading, writing and computational skills, an expanding job market may not benefit this group.

CALCULATING UNEMPLOYMENT

The unemployment rate is calculated by the BLS monthly figures based on a sample survey of 60,000 households. A person in this survey is classified as employed if the person did any work for pay or profit during the survey week. Part-time and temporary workers are considered employed even if they work for only one hour.

To be considered unemployed, an individual must be:

1) Able to work

2) Willing to work

3) Seeking a job during the previous month

4) Not retired, under 16 years of age, or institutionalized

Individuals who are under 16, retired or institutionalized in prison or hospitals, as well as homemakers, are not considered part of the labor force so they cannot be unemployed.

Unemployment rates are often criticized because these values do not consider the above groups, who may wish to work but are unable to find jobs, nor do they consider people who do not actively seek work.

People who have not made active efforts within a month before the survey are considered **discouraged workers** and not unemployed. Also, self-employed workers and retired workers without work who wish to work are not considered unemployed. Underemployment may also occur as workers are forced to take available jobs below their skill levels, but these workers are not defined as unemployed.

COSTS OF UNEMPLOYMENT

An economy experiences many negative individual and social consequences from unemployment. There are lost goods and services but also personal and social costs as well as government costs associated with unemployment.

The social and individual costs include the inability of people to pay bills, mental stress resulting in illness, and even increases in crime and suicide. The individual and social costs, combined with the loss of goods and services, increases in governmental costs for unemployment, welfare and health services, and the loss of tax revenues, illustrate the high cost of unemployment. These economic costs are unlikely to be recovered once lost.

THE "EXPECTED RATE OF UNEMPLOYMENT"

The **natural rate of unemployment** is the unemployment rate at full employment. The natural rate of unemployment is the combined frictional and structural unemployment rate <u>excluding</u> cyclical unemployment. The current goal of the natural unemployment rate is 4 percent. At this rate, production output is assumed to be at a maximum. The natural unemployment rate varies with social conditions over time. This rate has decreased from 6 percent in 1980 as more employment opportunities exist within the workforce.

High unemployment rates (rates above the natural rate) cause a gap between what is produced and what is possible at full employment. The **GDP gap** is the difference between potential output at full employment and current output.

UNEMPLOYMENT AND LOST GDP

Economists often use **Okun's Law** to estimate the loss of GDP associated with an increase in unemployment. Okun's Law estimates that for every 1 percent increase in unemployment above the natural rate, a GDP gap of 2 percent occurs. Thus, if an economy has 5 percent unemployment when 4 percent is the estimated natural rate, a 1 percent gap yields a 2 percent loss of GDP.

5%–4% = 1% gap times 2 = 2% loss of GDP

The average annual unemployment rate of the United States is less than in most industrialized nations of the world. A comparison of unemployment rates throughout the world can be found at the International Monetary Funds Internet website or at the CIA World Book website.

Policy Trade-Offs of Inflation and Unemployment

There are inevitable trade-offs that are always at play in our economy. If we have inflation, it normally means that we have a rapidly growing, overheating economy but we have more jobs (at least with demand-pull inflation). If we have recession, it normally means that the economy is slowing with fewer jobs, but at least we don't have to worry about inflation.

In the 1970s, and more recently, we have (unfortunately) experienced the "worst of both worlds." With the oil price shocks of 1972–1973 and 2007–2008, we seem to see history repeating itself. The new word in the mid-70s was stagflation and we currently fear repeating this cycle.

Stagflation

This term was coined by combining two different words to describe a perplexing economic problem. If our economy is "stagnant" or not growing but is experiencing, at the same time, a significant degree of inflation, the result is "stagflation."

Some economic theories suggest that we cannot have high unemployment and high inflation at the same time. If we look at the demand-pull model, this would appear to be true. However, most of our price shocks, then and now, have resulted from cost-push factors that center on the price of oil.

In the mid-1970s, a barrel of oil increased from $1.75 at the wellhead to $8. While this seems incredibly cheap today, it still represented a quadrupling of oil prices. From 2007–2009, we have seen oil prices vary by a similar multiple—from approximately $35 per barrel to more than $140 and then back to under $100.

With this kind of price change for such a critical commodity, varying inflation is the inevitable result—regardless of other economic variables.

Summary

Business cycles are a common problem for capitalism. Both inflation and unemployment present hazards for an economy but are inevitable occurrences over time. There are significant costs associated with both inflation and unemployment that ultimately affect the national economy.

History of the NBER

Founded in 1920, the National Bureau of Economic Research (NBER) is a private, nonprofit, nonpartisan research organization dedicated to promoting a greater understanding of how the economy works. The NBER is committed to undertaking and disseminating unbiased economic research among public policymakers, business professionals and the academic community.

Over the years, the NBER's research agenda has encompassed a wide variety of issues that confront our society. The NBER's early research focused on the aggregate economy, examining in detail the business cycle and long-term economic growth. Simon Kuznets' pioneering work on national income accounting, Wesley Mitchell's influential study of the business cycle, and Milton Friedman's research on the demand for money and the determinants of consumer spending were among the early studies done at the NBER.

The NBER Today

The NBER is the nation's leading nonprofit economic research organization. Sixteen of the 31 American Nobel Prize winners in economics and six of the past chairmen of the President's Council of Economic Advisers have been researchers at the NBER. The more than 1,000 professors of economics and business now teaching at universities around the country who are NBER researchers are the leading scholars in their fields. These NBER associates concentrate on four types of empirical research: developing new statistical measurements, estimating quantitative models of economic behavior, assessing the effects of public policies on the U.S. economy and projecting the effects of alternative policy proposals.

The NBER source: http://www.nber.org/info.html

Real-World Economics

RECESSION AND DEPRESSION—
WHAT'S THE DIFFERENCE?

It usually comes as a surprise to students but the word "depression" is not really an economic term. It came to be used as such during the early days of the Great Depression in the 1930s. One of President Hoover's economic advisors said that they could put a more positive "spin" on the crisis if they could get the press to use the word depression instead of the word that they were using.

Today, we know that the word depression is very scary and one that politicians avoid. How could that word sound less frightening? Well, the word that was being used to describe our imploding economy was "panic." Maybe depression does sound better.

President Harry Truman, when asked by a reporter what the difference is between the two, replied: "It's a recession when your neighbor is out of work . . . it's a depression if you lose your own job."

All that is to say, there is no precise definition for a depression.

Please access links through online E-text.

Anticipated or Creeping Inflation: A small amount of inflation—less than 3 percent.

Business Cycle: Unexpected changes in overall GDP. Fluctuations in spending.

Consumer Price Index: Measuring inflation by tracking the costs of a market basket of consumer goods (i.e., 80,000 items) month to month.

Cost-Push Inflation: Inflation caused by increasing costs of production, which may come from resource price increases, labor demands or simple monopoly power.

Cyclical Unemployment: Those unable to find a job because of the decline in economic activity.

Demand-Pull Inflation: A theory that attempts to explain inflation by saying that when demand is excessive, relative to supply, prices are "pulled" up by the level of spending that is occurring.

Discouraged Worker: Someone who is no longer looking for work and is not counted in the unemployment statistic.

Frictional Unemployment: Those who are unemployed by choice and may be in school or training to improve skills.

GDP Gap: The difference between potential GDP (100 percent) and actual GDP for a given year.

Inflation: A general and sustained price level increase. Measured by the CPI.

Natural Rate of Unemployment: The combined frictional and structural rate of unemployment.

Okun's Law: A method of estimating changes in GDP based on changes in unemployment.

Producer Price Index: A calculation similar to the consumer price index that traces increases in production cost.

Recession: When GDP declines for two successive quarters.

Rule of 70: A measure to determine how long it will take inflation to double prices.

Key Terms

Seasonal Variation: An expected change in overall spending during certain times of the year such as pre-Christmas or back to school.

Secular Trend: A fundamental change in our economy that is occurring over a much longer period of time. Example: Over the past 30 years, there has been a secular trend in the United States toward a service economy rather than manufacturing.

Stagflation: When there is rapid inflation and a high rate of unemployment occurring at the same time. The word was coined by combining stagnant and inflation.

Structural Unemployment: Those whose skills do not keep up with changing job requirements or do not possess very basic skills.

Unanticipated or Galloping Inflation: A relatively high degree of inflation (over 5 percent) when the negative effects of inflation begin to occur.

Underemployed: A worker who settles for a job that is below his skill and normal pay level.

Wage-Price Spiral: Inflation caused by labor demand for higher wages.

Applied Exercises

Exercise One:

Given the data below, find real GDP in each year. On the basis of this information, can we conclude that there was real growth or recession in 2009 and 2010?

Year	Nominal GDP	Price Index
2008	$500	100
2009	$550	105
2010	$575	110

Exercise Two:

Answer the following as True or False.

_____1. The production of durable goods is more stable than the production of nondurables over the business cycle.

_____2. People who work part time, but desire to work full time, are considered to be officially unemployed.

_____3. The natural rate of unemployment in the United States is about 5 percent.

_____4. Unanticipated inflation benefits some groups in the economy.

_____5. During the past 10 years, the U.S. economy has experienced three recessions.

Exercise Three:

If we assume that the natural rate of inflation for Nation X is 5 percent but the current economy has 11 percent inflation, according to Okun's Law, what is the loss in GDP?

Applied Exercises: Answers

Exercise One:

Year	Nominal GDP	Price Index	Real GDP
2008	$500	100	500/100 x 100 = $500
2009	550	105	550/105 x 100 = $523.8
2010	575	110	575/110 x 100 = $522.7

Real growth occurred between 2008 and 2009 as real GDP increased by $23.8 but declined between 2009 and 2010 by $1.1.

Exercise Two:

Numbers 1, 2, 5 are False.

Exercise Three:

If we assume that the natural rate of inflation for Nation X is 5 percent but the current economy has 11 percent inflation, according to Okun's Law, what are the costs to GDP?

The opportunity cost or lost goods and services according to Okun's Law would be 11 percent − 5 percent = 6 percent times 2 for a loss of GDP of 12 percent per year.

Lesson **Seven**
Classical Economics and Modern Theory

Introduction

Economics began as a field of study in 1776 with the publication of "An Inquiry into the Wealth of Nations" by Adam Smith. Smith became known as the "father of economics" with this publication. He was a Scotsman who held a professorship in Moral Philosophy at Glasgow University. Smith traveled the globe as a tutor for a merchant's family and, while touring, began to investigate reasons for differences in nations' material goods.

LEARNING OBJECTIVES

Please note the listed objectives. As you will see, the course materials are all objective driven. This provides you with a constant way to direct and monitor your progress throughout the course. Each objective is color-coded and corresponds to that particular section in the text.

OBJECTIVE ONE　1

Describe the history and evolution of the Classical Theory in economics.

OBJECTIVE TWO　2

Explain the Basic Concepts of the Classical Theory using the "Bathtub" model.

OBJECTIVE THREE　3

Explain the role of Flexible Prices, Wages and Interest rates in the Classical Theory.

OBJECTIVE FOUR　4

Explain the fundamental role of Full Employment in the Classical Theory using the Aggregate Supply and Demand Model.

OBJECTIVE FIVE　5

Describe recent challenges to the Classical Theory.

INTERACTIVE EXERCISE

Use the Major Economic Models to demonstrate an understanding of the chain reactions resulting from human choices and how they move through an economy. Demonstrate an understanding of the Tradeoffs that result.

CLASSICAL THEORY

Smith's explanations of national economic living standards became known as the Classical Theory. His principles emphasized the invisible hand and laissez-faire economics (see Lesson 1). The invisible hand principle argues that competition moves an economy to efficiency and a higher standard of living as if guided by an invisible hand. Laissez-faire economics is the idea that an economy with less government restriction serves people best by allowing unrestricted, free allocation of resources. According to this theory, "the government that governs least is thought to be the government that governs best."

Smith's principles of economics were modified in 1803 by Jean-Baptiste Say, a French businessman, who wrote a book titled "A Treatise on Political Economy." He contributed an additional principle to the Classical Theory, stating "It is not the abundance of money but the abundance of other products in general that facilitates sales." ("A Treatise on Political Economy," 4th ed, p.138)

Modern interpretations of Say's work simplified his writing to mean that supply creates its own demand. If production is created, then there will be sufficient flow of funds from this creation to purchase everything that is produced (Circular Flow). When people have more money, they will spend it on other goods and the amount of income generated will equal the amount of spending. Say concluded, "If one has money, it is irrational to hoard it." Thus, recession was unlikely since people receive money to produce and the funds they receive will be spent to buy other goods. Although temporary adjustments were possible, Classical Theorists believed that there were several relationships built into an economy that would guarantee price stability and full employment.

The combination of Smith's theory and Say's theory resulted in a broader Classical Theory based on the assumption that a free-market economy will operate at full employment. The principles of Classical Theory evolved even further with the writings of James Mill, David Ricardo, John Stuart Mill and others into the "Law of Markets," which represented the Classical Theory from the mid-1800s to the 1930s.

This evolving theory held the basic belief that a market economy was inherently stable—always adjusting, after a relatively short time, to a full-employment, efficient and stable position. Classical Theorists did believe that events such as war, disease, natural disasters, etc. could cause an extended disruption, but—barring these major problems—stability and full employment would be the norm.

The Law of Markets Theory argues that recession (low business activity) is not due to a lack of demand by consumers but rather a lack of supply. Accordingly, business activity can be increased by stimulating supply. Hence, a lack of supply for goods creates a lack of business activity, resulting in a lack of income and therefore a decrease in consumer consumption. This insufficient supply will be adjusted by decreases in prices and wages to restore consumption and finally cause renewed levels of sustainable supply.

There are several important assumptions made with Classical Economics. In order to simplify the economic system, early Classical Theory assumes there is neither government influence nor international trade within the economy. Further, it is assumed that businesses do not hold savings. With these simplifications, Classical Theory can analyze the basic elements of economic activity. These restrictions would be a significant limitation today but were less so from 1800 to 1930, when these sectors were a smaller part of the total economy.

THE BATHTUB MODEL

A bathtub analogy can be used to visualize the important cause-and-effect relationships within a Classical Economy. If we imagine a bathtub full of water, our analogy would describe the water as total spending in our economy. It follows, then, that anything that allows water to flow out of the tub through the tub drain would mean that spending was decreasing with predictable effects. Savings is analogous to water draining from the tub and is referred to as a leakage or withdrawal. If we save more, it means that we are spending less. Thus, too much saving may slow our economy in the short run, all other things remaining the same.

Further, we know that a tub also has a faucet that will allow water to run into it—hence, more spending. Anything, such as investment, that allows more spending will expand our economy. Investment is seen as an injection of water into the tub. In this tub, the drain is connected to the faucet by the credit market. Hence, saved dollars may become the source of borrowed dollars for investment. If we have a $1 million economy and we are saving $100,000, there is a potential problem—our economy may slow down. However, if business investors borrow the $100,000 of savings and spend that money, then the saved dollars that were taken out of the economy are put back in through investment borrowing. Supply can still create its own demand if all of the $1 million is used for spending by either consumers or business investors.

The Classical Theory can be viewed as a closed-system bathtub with input of resources, the working of resources and the withdrawal of resources that are then reinjected into the tub (Figure 7.1). The resources going into a tub represent injections to the flow of income, employment and, ultimately, output from the economy. Injections to a Classical Economy include consumption and investment. This theory assumes that a change in employment will change income and output in the same direction by the same amount. The water in the tub represents the working economy with full employment, which generates output and income. The leakage (withdrawal) represents income saved that is borrowed by businesses and reinjected into the economy. Leakages are held back as savings but reinjected as investment.

According to **Classical Theory**, an economy is almost always at full employment. The level of water in the tub (employment, income and output) is at the

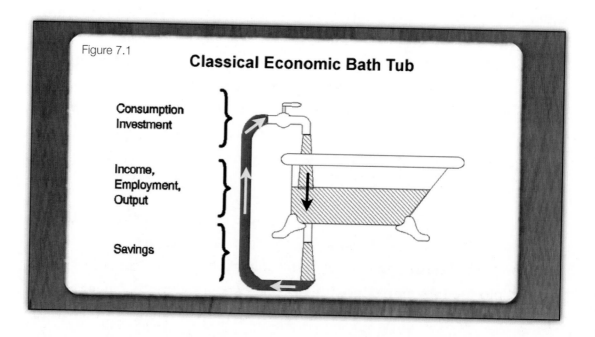

Figure 7.1

Classical Economic Bath Tub

Consumption
Investment

Income,
Employment,
Output

Savings

maximum because national quantity supplied (aggregate supply) is assumed to create an equivalent national quantity demanded (aggregate demand). The level of water in the tub remains constant because the amount of injections of investment is equal to the leakage of savings. Consumption remains constant and savings (S) is equaled by investment (I).

FLEXIBLE INTEREST RATES

Savings is linked to investment through a flexible interest rate. Although savings is a leakage from consumer spending, it is borrowed by businesses and spent as investment for capital goods. Savings is equaled by investment. If businesses want more funds, the interest rate will increase and people will save more money, but if businesses want fewer funds, the interest rate will decline, resulting in smaller savings. All income, however, will be spent either by individuals for consumption or businesses for investment as adjusted by a flexible interest rate in the Classical Theory.

FLEXIBLE WAGES AND PRICES

A final challenge to constant consumption is that people may decrease their spending for a short time. If this occurs, according to Classical Theory, inventories will increase on business shelves and this will induce owners to reduce prices and decrease wages that, in turn, will cause consumers to restore spending and clear the shelves of excess inventory. This price-wage flexibility restores the economy to full employment in the long run.

Classical Theory assumes that the economy is capable of adjusting itself to full employment without government. Competition and laissez-faire forces will drive the economy to continuous adjustments of allocation to full production. The mechanisms of a flexible interest rate will eliminate excess savings, and flexible prices and wages will maintain constant consumption.

AGGREGATE SUPPLY AND AGGREGATE DEMAND

The Classical Theory can be applied as a national model by using the same principles of economics related in Lesson 3 to individual products with supply and demand. Although there are technical differences between the microeconomic supply and demand in Lesson 3 and the macro version here in Lesson 7, many of the basic concepts are the same. Aggregate demand (AD) is the national quantity of goods and services purchased at various national prices.

Aggregate demand in Classical Theory includes purchases by consumers and investors. Notice in Figure 7.2 that there is an inverse relationship between national quantity demanded and national prices. More goods and services will be purchased at lower prices and fewer goods and services will be purchased at higher national prices.

Aggregate supply (AS) is the national quantity of goods and services brought to the market by producers at various prices. A direct relationship exists between the nation's supply of all national goods and services and the national price of all goods. Producers will bring more goods and services to the market at higher prices.

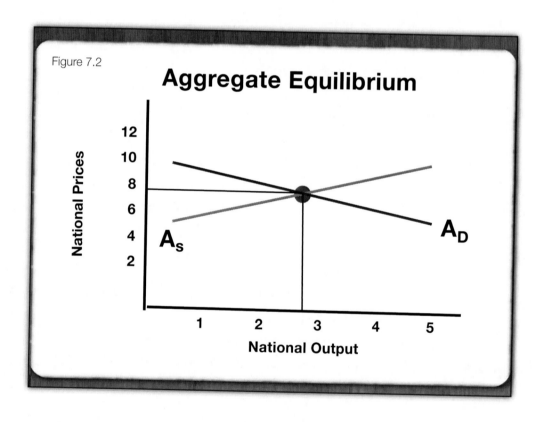

Figure 7.2

Aggregate Equilibrium

Figure 7.2 illustrates the traditional view of AD and AS relationships. The intercept of AS/AD determines the national price (P) and the national output (Q). On a national basis, price relates to the level of prices and is representative of inflation or deflation. Price changes are represented as prices increase or decrease from intersections of AD along the AS line. A resulting upward movement in national prices represents inflation and, contra-wise, a downward movement represents deflation. Figure 7.2 illustrates that equilibrium exists between AS and AD at a national price of 8 and a national output of 2.8.

In the Classical Theory application of AS/AD, the aggregate demand consists only of consumption and investment. Consumption (C), as noted in Lesson 5, is personal consumption expenditure, and Investment (I) is gross private domestic investment. Together, C and I form the amount of aggregate demand at various national prices. AS is the quantity of products/services brought to the market and can be defined as net domestic product (NDP), as discussed in Lesson 5. Net domestic product is gross domestic product less consumption of fixed capital (depreciation) or the value of product/services actually brought to the market.

Aggregate Demand

The aggregate demand line is downward sloping, meaning that at higher national prices, a lower quantity of national output would be demanded. The slope of the AD is negative because:

- If prices are higher, people will have less purchasing power and thereby purchase less quantity.

- If prices are higher, real interest rates (the nominal interest rate minus inflation) must also be higher, therefore, increasing the cost of goods sold and resulting in a price increase and lower aggregate quantity demanded.

- Finally, when prices are higher in a nation, fewer products will be purchased for export by international markets, therefore, aggregate quantity demanded will be lower.

Aggregate Supply

Aggregate supply is the total national output of goods at various prices, but since Classical Theory assumes full employment, the aggregate supply line is always vertical (red line in Figure 7.3A), adjusted to full employment with only variations in national prices (inflation).

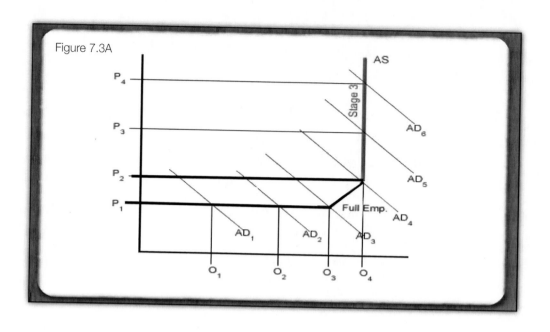

Figure 7.3A

In this limited Classical Model using only national consumption and national investment, aggregate demand is assumed constant and at full employment. An increase in the quantity of AS is not possible with a given AS curve. If aggregate demand increases, only an increase in prices (inflation) is possible because employment is already full. This is represented by a movement of AD up the AS line, as shown from AD5 to AD6 (Figure 7.3B).

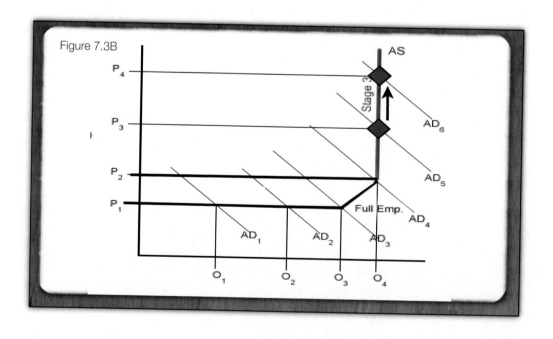

Figure 7.3B

Aggregate supply (AS, red line) will find equilibrium with aggregate demand (AD) along the vertical stage of aggregate supply. If there was any intervention by government (in a modified Classical Model) to increase aggregate demand at this point, it would only result in a movement up the aggregate supply line with an increase in prices (inflation).

Classical Theory was questioned in the early 1930s with the onset of the Great Depression in the United States. In 1929, the U.S. stock market fell, which in turn caused decreases in business investment spending that led to rising unemployment. As less income was earned, consumption fell, reducing economic activity even further. Government had less revenue from taxes and believed in a balanced budget (spending = taxes collected), therefore government spending was reduced, further magnifying the fall in the economy. In addition, within the foreign sector, exports were reduced as foreign consumers had less income to spend. Every sector of the economy was affected, with declines in spending by consumers, businesses (fewer investments), government and the foreign sector. GDP = C + I + G + Xn became an interactive exercise for a falling economy.

EFFECT OF RECESSION — UNEMPLOYMENT

Classical Theory was unable to satisfactorily explain the reductions in economic activity in the 1930s. It was assumed that activity would be restored through the mechanisms of adjustment with flexible interest rates, flexible wages and flexible prices, and AS = AD. However, the mechanisms did not restore the economy and economists began to consider the flaws in the Classical Theory.

Say's Law that supply would create sufficient demand for full employment and automatic clearing of product markets proved to be untrue as inventories rose with increased unemployment. The aggregate supply was significantly greater than aggregate demand, prompting businesses to make more cuts in employment and output as inventories further increased.

The adjustment mechanisms of flexible interest rates and flexible wages and prices did not restore economic activity. Within the bathtub theory, the savings were greater than the investment and thereby the quantity of AD was less than the quantity of AS. Businesses did not make new investments, so savings was not returned to the economy through lower interest rates.

Savings was greater than investment and AD continued to fall. AD = C + I and both C (consumption) and I (investment) fell significantly. Reductions in interest rates did not induce businesses to borrow more money when they already had too much capacity. The flexibility of interest rates did not cause investment to equal savings.

Further bathtub theory negatives were experienced as consumption fell and could not be restored through reduction in wages and prices. Although wages and prices did fall, consumption fell more and resulted in AS being greater than AD. The flexibility of wages and prices did not return the economy to full employment.

The basic elements of the Classical Theory were called into question as economic activity fell throughout the early 1930s. New theories of economics began to emerge to supplement the long-held views of the Classical Theory.

The events of the Great Depression in the 1930s led to the development of the Keynesian Theory, which will be discussed in Lesson 8. Classical Theory was out of vogue from the late 1930s until the late 1960s, when the Keynesian Theory itself was challenged and "new" (or enhanced) Classical Theories were developed. We will discuss the revitalization of the Classical Theory with the developments of Monetarism in the 1950s and Supply Side Economics in the 1980s before concluding this Lesson.

MODERN PRINCIPLES FROM CLASSICAL THEORY

Classical Theory principles offer an analytical framework of how capitalism works and emphasize the efficiency of market-based economies—economists continue to value the efficiency of competitive private markets. But by the 1970s, severe recession was again present in spite of (some say because of) the primary Keynesian approach that had been adopted. In response, some economists proposed enhancements to the Classical Theory (which included Supply Side Economics) as proposed solutions.

Criticisms of the Keynesian Theory actually began in the late 1940s and grew through the 1960s and into the 1970s. The new Classical Theory began to challenge Keynesian Theory soon after World War II. The early new school of Classical Theory, Monetarism, was launched by Milton Friedman in the late 1940s and expanded into the 1950s. Milton Friedman won the Nobel Prize in Economics in 1976 when his new Classical view became widely accepted. This theory was based on the influence of money in the economy. This monetary theory argued that moderate money growth was essential to balanced growth for an economy in the long run. The growth rate in the money supply was fundamental to sustained growth in goods and services. According to Monetarism, the money supply should only grow at the rate of real growth in GDP, thus promoting balanced, noninflationary growth in the economy. The Monetarist Theory also encouraged limited government and, therefore, used a modified application of the Classical principles.

In the late 1970s, the new Classical Theory was formed with a combination of Monetarism and Supply Side Economics. The new Classical Theory emphasized the promotion of producer interests to increase AS. During President Reagan's administration, Supply Side principles were a guiding force for coordinated efforts between fiscal and monetary policy. See Figure 7.4.

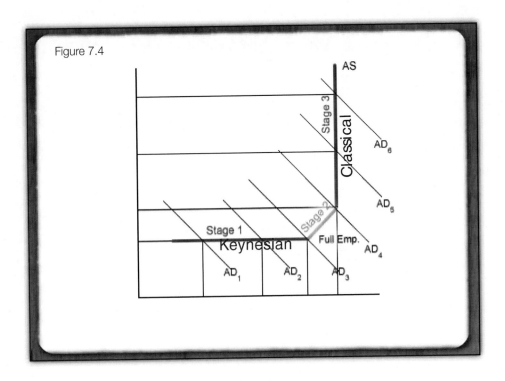

Figure 7.4

SHIFTS IN AGGREGATE SUPPLY AND AGGREGATE DEMAND: NEW CLASSICAL THEORY

The AS/AD relationships were re-examined through the new Supply Side perspective in the 1980s during President Reagan's administration. The essential elements of the new Classical Theory were applied to a more modern economy. The assumptions of competition, limited government and increasing AS were still fundamental principles. The question then was centered on how to increase AS (shift right aggregate supply). To address this question, economists turned to Growth Theory, which is an analysis of how to increase AS (goods and services). As we discuss the elements of growth from the Supply Side, keep in mind that adequate demand is also necessary to purchase the increases in aggregate supply.

Notice in the AS shift right graph (Figure 7.5), as AS increases to AS_2 in Stage 3, prices decline but output increases from O_4 to O_5. An increase in output with a given input of resources is the concept of growth in goods and services. An increase in AS not only increases output but also lowers prices.

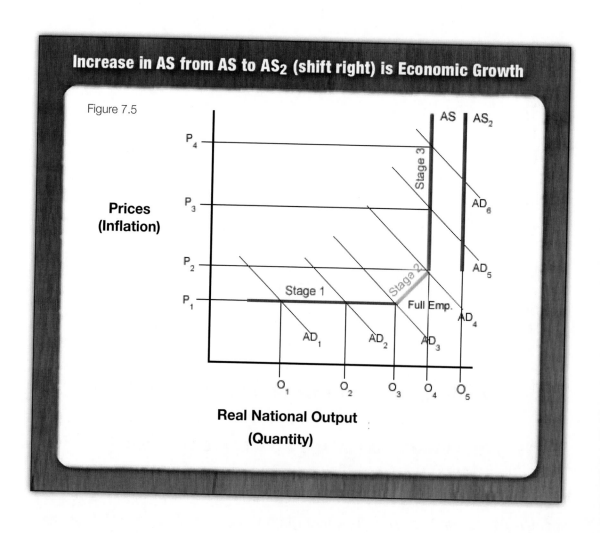

Increase in AS from AS to AS₂ (shift right) is Economic Growth

Figure 7.5

Notice in the AS shift left graph (Figure 7.6), as AS decreases to AS_1 in Stage 3, prices increase from P_3 toward P_4 and output decreases from O_4 to O_3. When there is a decrease in AS, there will be a compound negative response with a decrease in output and an increase in prices.

How can an economy increase AS from its existing position? Growth economics is a field of economics established to analyze the means for increasing output. This methodology was given attention throughout the 20th century, but this attention increased significantly in the 1980s.

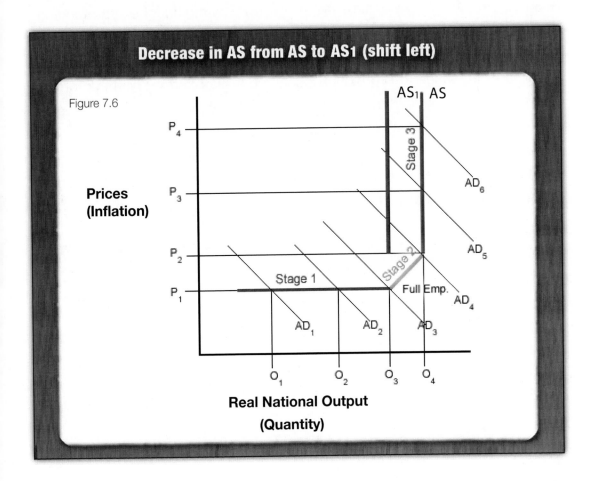

Decrease in AS from AS to AS1 (shift left)

Figure 7.6

GROWTH ECONOMICS

Economic growth for a nation is measured by increases in real Gross Domestic Product (GDP) and increases in real GDP per capita. The latter figure compares the growth of goods and services with the growth in population. If GDP real growth is not greater than population growth, then consumption per person is actually declining.

Most firms and consumers are sensitive to national economic growth. Consider how different an environment is when consumers are without work. During a recession, individuals lose their purchasing power and firms lose revenue and profits. Contrast this situation with a high-growth economy, where incomes are growing and consumption is increasing. Most firms and households experience cyclical variation, receiving more income with national economic growth and less with recession.

WHAT ARE THE CAUSES OF ECONOMIC GROWTH?

The theory of growth was discussed in Lesson 6 by relating the importance of increasing aggregate supply (AS right shift) to increases in real national output at every price level. Two factors shifting the AS line right were decreases in taxes and decreases in production costs (such as energy prices). Improvements in technology will be discussed more in Lessons 8 and 9. Lesson 12 will discuss the important influence of a steady, moderate growth in the money supply, encouraging an outward shift of the Production Possibility Frontier (PPF) that is driven by a right shifting AS. Generally, then, with this overview, what are the major factors that determine macroeconomic growth?

THE PRIMARY SUPPLY SIDE FACTORS OF MACROECONOMIC GROWTH

- The amount of resources available

- Technology

- Education and training of workers

- The number of workers

- Opportunity cost of resource inputs

- Amount and quality of capital used

- Availability of savings for investment

By considering the factors above, economists conclude that an increase in economic growth is basically from either using more resources or better (more efficient) use of the same amount of resources. Better use of resources is also referred to as increasing productivity. Productivity is generally measured as an increase in output per worker hour. Productivity is closely monitored by the U.S. Department of Commerce and is relatively easy to measure at the aggregate level.

Most economic growth is due to productivity increases caused by better use of capital or technology or improvements in education and training. However, economic growth by increased productivity can be difficult without attendant increases in the number of workers and the amounts of natural resources.

AMERICAN GROWTH

Economic growth in the United States is actually an ongoing economic study that continues to evolve, with new theories explaining growth. In the 1950s, the growth model of Solow-Swan emphasized the importance of capital and investment. In the 1980s–1990s, the Lucas-Barro model emphasized the importance of technology through improvements in human capital (knowledge, education and skills).

The United States has experienced much growth over the last 200 years, resulting in a significant increase in the standard of living. American real GDP growth has averaged about 3.5 percent per year and 3.2 percent per year in real GDP per *capita* over the last 50 years. With this growth rate, GDP will double in real terms every 25 years.

Although this growth has been cyclical, over most decades there has been an overall growth in real GDP. In the last few decades, however, the rate of growth has slowed. During a period beginning in late 2007, growth was actually a *negative* number.

Micro Lessons in the second semester of this course contain more discussion on the American and global growth experience.

GROWTH POLICY IMPLICATIONS FOR GOVERNMENT

As we have seen, Classical Theory assumes that the economy is almost always in the full employment vertical stage of the AS line and that AD shifts up and down along this line. Therefore, if the economy is already at full employment, any increase in AD will only cause increasing inflation.

The new classical view of the economy developed in the 1980s assumed that a shift left in AS (decrease in AS) could be caused by high rates of taxation and excessive government regulation. By decreasing tax rates and government regulation of business, Supply Side Economics assumed that the AS line would actually shift right and result in lower prices and higher levels of national output given a specific AD line. With these assumptions of the new Supply Side Theory extended to the AS/AD model, significant decreases in tax rates and government regulation were then implemented.

Economists have argued about the results of these changes, but tax rates were reduced under the assumption that people would work harder, produce more and thereby earn more income, which, in turn, would produce more tax revenues. Tax revenues did increase, but government spending increased even faster, resulting in larger and larger government deficits. The economy, however, did grow significantly during the 1980s and unemployment did decrease.

SUMMARY: SHIFTING AS CURVE WITH CONSTANT AD

The basics of Classical Theory added much to the knowledge of how an economy worked from 1776 to 1930, when the Great Depression began and economists began to question some of the relationships. In the 1950s, a modified Classical Theory began to unfold with Monetarism. Beginning in the 1980s, a second new Classical Theory emerged that also used some of the basics of the earlier theory. The emphasis in the 1980s on Supply Side Economics was to promote increases in AS to increase output and decrease prices. The new Classical Theorists thought that government could govern best by reducing regulations and tax rates and holding to a moderate growth in the money supply.

The new Classical Theory of Monetarism and Supply Side Economics will be further discussed in Fiscal Policy, Lesson 9, and in Monetary Policy in Lesson 12. Modern employment theory encompasses elements of Classical, new Classical and Keynesian theories.

Key Terms

An Inquiry into the Wealth of Nations: First book of economics by the "father of economics" Adam Smith, published in 1776.

Aggregate Demand: The price level to output level demanded by a nation as a schedule or graph. In Classical economics, AD consists of Consumption + Investment.

Aggregate Supply: The price level to output level supplied by producers as a schedule or graph. In Classical economics, AS is assumed to be maximum output at full employment.

Assumptions of Classical Theory: Classical Theory assumes full employment, Savings = Investment due to a flexible interest rate, AD = AS because supply creates demand.

Bathtub Theory: Vision of an economy relative to a bathtub with injections of water represented by Consumption and Investment in Classical Theory and withdrawals of savings recirculated as investment due to a flexible interest rate in Classical Theory.

Classical Theory: Theory begun by Adam Smith in 1776 that assumes that the economy of a nation is always at equilibrium with full employment because of self-adjusting mechanisms.

Invisible Hand and Laissez-Faire Economics: Concepts of successful capitalism according to Adam Smith. Invisible hand relates to the idea of competition, and laissez-faire economics assumes government should be limited to encourage private sector success.

Say's Law: Classical Theory component arguing that supply creates demand; therefore, an economy will operate at full employment because supply generates sufficient funds to purchase production.

Applied Exercises

Exercise One:

Using Classical Theory, explain how an economy would adjust to full employment if aggregate demand is $500 and aggregate supply is $550.

Using Classical Theory, describe how an economy would adjust to full employment if aggregate demand is $550 and aggregate supply is $500.

Exercise Two:

Assume there is a nominal interest rate of 10 percent in an economy with inflation of 4 percent. What is the rate that economists use when discussing interest rates and what is the rate given this information?

Exercise Three:

Given the Classical Theory Bathtub below, how is the inflow of water equal to the outflow allowing for continuous full employment?

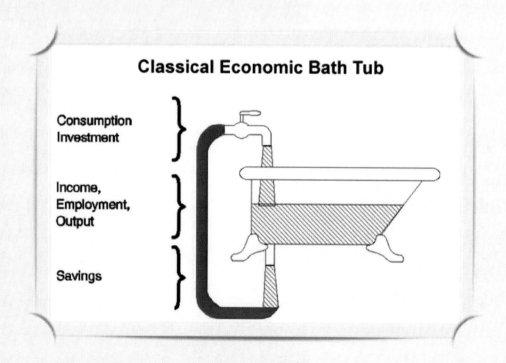

Classical Economic Bath Tub

Consumption
Investment

Income,
Employment,
Output

Savings

Applied Exercises: Answers

Exercise One:

If AS > AD, then Classical Theory assumes that more money is generated within the economy through increased production, which means people have higher incomes and will spend more money. Therefore, the economy will expand to full-employment maximum output.

If AD > AS, then Classical Theory assumes that consumers want more products and producers will respond by increasing output to full employment and maximum output.

Exercise Two:

Nominal interest = 10 percent − inflation of 4 percent = real interest of 6 percent.

Exercise Three:

In Classical Theory, the leakages of Savings are equal to the injection of Investment. Whenever there is more savings than investment, it will cause a decrease in the flexible interest rate, encouraging businesses to borrow and invest more. With an increase in savings (decreased consumption spending), there would also be more inventory for merchants to deal with, causing them to reduce wages and prices to encourage buyers to purchase more.

Lesson **Eight**
The Aggregates and the Multiplier

Introduction

We now turn our discussion to Keynesian Economics, which became the primary challenge to Classical Theory in the 1930s. Decreased economic activity during the 1930s caused people to question the basic tenets of Classical Theory. Classical Theory assumed that business activity would always remain at full employment with only minor short-term adjustments. As the Depression continued in the 1930s, economists began to question the theory of self-correction they had so long espoused.

LEARNING OBJECTIVES

Please note the listed objectives. As you will see, the course materials are all objective driven. This provides you with a constant way to direct and monitor your progress throughout the course. Each objective is color-coded and corresponds to that particular section in the text.

OBJECTIVE ONE 1

Describe the rise of the Keynesian Theory in the history of macroeconomics.

OBJECTIVE TWO 2

Explain the basic concepts of the Keynesian Theory in relation to Classical Theory.

OBJECTIVE THREE 3

Use the Aggregate Supply/Demand model and the "Bathtub" model to explain the dynamics of recession and inflation using the Keynesian Theory.

OBJECTIVE FOUR 4

Explain the application of the Multiplier Process in the Keynesian Theory.

OBJECTIVE FIVE 5

Provide an example of the dynamics of the Keynesian Theory using the Circular Flow Model.

INTERACTIVE EXERCISE

Use the Major Economic Models to demonstrate an understanding of the chain reactions resulting from human choices and how they move through an economy. Demonstrate an understanding of the Tradeoffs that result.

THE RISE OF THE KEYNESIAN THEORY

Numerous theories were formulated to provide an alternative to the Classical Theory. Some critics advocated the Soviet Union's planned economy or Italy's command economy, believing that these controlled systems would not experience depression. Other economists advocated a more modified form of capitalism.

One of the most analytical challenges to the Classical Theory was proposed by John Maynard Keynes. His influential work, "The Economic Consequences of the Peace" (1919), described the economic principles at work after World War I. He published several more books and became known for his explanations of economic events. Keynes became best known for expressing his economic theory in "The General Theory of Employment, Interest and Money," published in 1936.

With the continuation of the Great Depression in the 1930s, Keynesian explanations of economic activity were widely studied. Although considered an attack on previous fundamentals of economics, his theory was less extreme than Hitler's Fascist approach in Germany and the Communist/Socialist alternative being used in the Soviet Union. Keynes believed that a depressed economy would not automatically adjust to full employment—a key element of the Classical Theory. He proposed that government must actively intervene to promote restoration to full employment.

The Keynesian Theory accurately predicted continued depression in the 1930s and offered an explanation consistent with the economic activity. While Classical Theory emphasized the role of supply through Say's Law, the new Keynesian alternative was different. Keynes suggested that demand would create its own supply. As the Depression continued through the 1930s, more attention was given to the Keynesian Theory.

As we moved beyond the 1930s and 1940s, the impact and influence of Keynesian ideas continued to grow. By the 1960s, there was a feeling among many economists that we finally had an ability to manage our economy with these new tools and end the extreme instability problem.

An Explanation of the Keynesian Theory

Keynesian ideas centered on most of the same questions that the Classical Theorists had pondered but had come to very different conclusions. In this new economic theory, the term aggregate demand took on great importance and was seen as the key element to explain the business cycle. As the aggregate demand dynamics in the circular flow came to be understood more fully, these interactions were recognized as being important structural elements. These flows could move too slowly, as in recession, or too rapidly, as in inflation.

Keynesian Savings/Profit Motives

Keynesian economics recognized the many cause-and-effect interactions in our macroeconomy. This model emphasized the importance of aggregate demand—the cause—and the many effects that grew from changes in overall demand. Aggregate demand was seen as the locomotive that could power our economy—the engine that could pull the train of economic activity but seemed to periodically speed up or slow down. According to Keynes, savings, consumption and investment determine business cycles. Savings and investment were seldom equal because:

- Savings is sometimes accumulated by consumers for deferred transactions (income set aside to make household purchases in the future).

- Savings is sometimes accumulated for speculation (income set aside to fund unique profit opportunities that present themselves in the future).

- Savings is also set aside for precautionary reasons (income set aside because of fear of individual financial distress in the future).

These motives are similar to "demand for money" motives (more short-term in nature) that are discussed in Unit 4. Also, these motives for saving do not respond equally to a flexible interest rate.

Keynes then emphasized that Investment by business managers (in contrast to Savings by consumers) is determined by profit expectations. Keynes concluded that since Investment and Savings result from different motives, they are seldom equal.

KEYNESIAN WAGE/PRICE FLEXIBILITY

Keynes also believed that product prices and wages paid to labor were not totally flexible. During a recession, wages and prices may adjust downward to some degree, but the fall in aggregate consumption spending would overwhelm these adjustments. This meant that businesses' inventories would actually increase and not decrease, as predicted by the flexible prices approach used in the Classical Theory.

Keynes saw that wages and prices were not totally flexible because monopoly power on the Business side of the Circular Flow can set prices with little regard for competition. He also saw monopoly power on the Labor side of the market (unions) and the fact that Labor is not always easily replaceable in a modern production process. In addition, Keynes saw that minimum wage legislation could limit the downward adjustability of wages. Wages and prices were considered to be "sticky downward" (resistant to downward movement) and, therefore, not totally flexible in a recession as the Classical Theory had assumed.

A NEW MODEL: INVESTMENT SPENDING IN THE KEYNESIAN BUSINESS CYCLE

Like Classical Theorists, Keynes argued that Savings and Investment are important in determining economic activity—but he differed from the Classical Theorists when he argued that Savings and Investment are seldom equal. Businesses strongly impact economic activity according to their Investment decisions. **Planned Investment** by business is what businesses intend to invest to maintain inventory at current levels. Economic activity will decrease when Savings are greater than Planned Investment (what businesses intend to invest without increases or decreases in inventory).

> **Planned Investment > Savings = growth impact**
>
> **Planned Investment < Savings = recessionary impact**

<u>**Income**</u> = Consumption + Savings, so when savings increase, then consumption must fall. When consumption falls, inventories (unsold goods) will

increase. When their inventories increase, businesses will begin to reduce their investment spending on equipment and facilities—and they will begin to reduce their employment and their output. In this Keynesian approach, then, Savings and Investment are not made equal by a flexible interest rate and this difference can affect economic activity in a very major way.

In the Keynesian approach, there is also an impact from Unplanned Investment. Unplanned Investment results when there are unexpected reductions or increases in inventory due to unexpected increases or decreases in sales. When sales unexpectedly increase, more investment must be injected to replace inventory lost because sales increased and depleted inventory. When sales unexpectedly decrease, less investment will be injected because inventories are too large and new inventory investment will be reduced. See Figure 8.1.

Unplanned Investment + Planned Investment = Total Investment

Investment > Savings = growth impact

Investment < Savings = recessionary Impact ·

Figure 8.1   **Unplanned Investment**

Disposable Income = GDP	Consumption	Savings	Investment	Aggregate Demand	Unplanned Inventory
$2000	$2040	-40	40	2080	-80
2200	2200	0	40	2240	-40
2400	2360	40	40	2400	0
2600	2520	80	40	2560	40
2800	2680	120	40	2720	80
3000	2840	160	40	2880	120

If **Total Investment** (Planned + Unplanned) is *less* than Savings, then economic activity will decrease. Overall, with Savings seldom being exactly equaled by

Investment, the resulting impact on aggregate demand is a major influence on economic activity. If more is invested than saved, then aggregate demand will increase (assuming constant or increasing consumption). If, however, savings increases (decreasing consumption) and the increases in savings are not reinvested, economic activity will decrease.

Business Cycles According to Keynes

Keynesian Theory considers that fluctuations in economic activity are due to changes in effective demand (changes in aggregate demand). Aggregate demand consists of spending for consumption, investment, government and net exports. Recall from Lesson 7 that aggregate demand in Classical Theory consisted only of Consumption plus Investment. Also recall from Classical Theory that consumption was assumed to be stable and investment was equal to savings. Keynesian economics expands aggregate demand to include the government sector and international markets as active components.

Keynesian aggregate demand on the AS/AD curve (Figure 8.2) is the total demand, including consumers, government, business investment and the foreign sector, and their expenditures at various prices within Stage 1. The intersection of aggregate demand (AD) with aggregate supply (AS) determines national price levels and real national output.

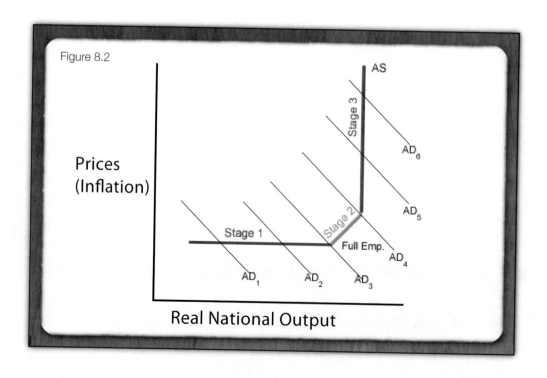

Figure 8.2

When AD shifts right (AD$_1$ to AD$_2$), inventories will decrease due to increased consumption and, therefore, businesses will increase employment and output to replace inventories (increase in unplanned investment). This replacement of inventories will increase national income as well as employment and output (Real GDP). With more income, more consumption will occur and the utilization of productive capacity will increase. These dynamics will occur without inflation in the horizontal area of Stage 1. If AD decreases (AD shifts left from AD$_3$ to AD$_2$), business inventories will increase, resulting in businesses cutting back employment and output, with resulting decreases in national income and consumption.

Keynesian Theory assumptions are well illustrated in the AS/AD graph in Figure 8.2. Stage 1 assumes that the economy is at a relatively low level of employment. Thus, AD can be increased without inflation. Because there is unused capacity, if government stimulates an increase in AD, then income, employment and output can increase nearer to the full-employment area (Stage 2) without increasing prices.

THE KEYNESIAN BUSINESS CYCLES—A REVISED BATHTUB

Keynesian Theory can also be visualized in a revised bathtub illustration. The Keynesian Bathtub illustrates expenditure injections (Figure 8.3). Expenditure injections (increases in AD) are due to increases in government and export spending in addition to consumption spending and business investment. These are shown as increased water flows into the tub.

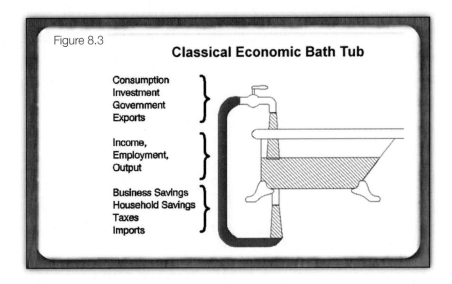

Figure 8.3

Classical Economic Bath Tub

Consumption
Investment
Government
Exports

Income,
Employment,
Output

Business Savings
Household Savings
Taxes
Imports

Increasing the flow of any of these four expenditures will increase the employment, output and income (water level in the tub). Decreases in any of these four expenditures will decrease the level of water in the tub, assuming constant leakages. Fluctuations in the leakages (withdrawals) may occur at the same time as inflow fluctuations and, therefore, will also affect income, employment and output (water level in the tub).

The Keynesian withdrawals or leakages from the tub consist of taxes, business savings, personal savings and national imports. If injections and leakages remain equal, then the level of water in the tub will remain constant, and the level of economic activity will neither increase nor decrease.

When injections increase with constant leakages, the level of water (income, employment and output) will increase, limited only by the capacity of the economy (size of the tub). Likewise, if leakages increase with constant injections, the resulting level of water (income, employment and output) will decrease.

The relationships of consumption, investment and savings also illustrate the interactive change. If savings decrease (implying an increase in consumption), then the water level increases (all other factors remaining the same, certis paribus). If savings increase (decrease in consumption), then the water level decreases.

The relationship of AD (spending for consumption, business investment, government projects and exports) to AS (employment, output and income) determines economic activity. When the quantity of AD is greater than the quantity of AS, business investment will increase to make up for the shortage in inventories. When the quantity of AD is less than the quantity of AS, business investment will decrease to adjust for the surplus that is building up in inventories.

GOVERNMENT POLICY IN KEYNESIAN THEORY

The recommended government actions of Keynesian Theory are very different from those of Classical Theory. With a recession, Classical Theorists recommend that government decrease spending and raise taxes if necessary to balance the government budget. According to Keynes, this action will make the recession even worse because it will reduce AD. When President Herbert

Hoover raised taxes in 1932, Keynes correctly predicted that economic activity would fall even further. Keynes argued for increasing government spending in a recession (or possibly cutting taxes) to increase AD (shift right).

Keynesian concepts were tried by President Franklin Roosevelt during the Depression in the 1930s with only limited results. New spending by government was adopted in a series of programs to increase AD and stimulate employment, output and income. Some economists believe Roosevelt should have spent even more, but they believe that the "limited results" at least saved the economy from a total collapse. Other economists believe that the "limited results" actually prevented the economy from completing its natural adjustment. The Classical Theorists remained convinced that increasing government spending was not necessary and would only result in a deficit between tax revenues and government spending and make matters worse in the long run. The U.S. economy (and the entire global economy) stumbled through the 1930s and only the massive military spending for Word War II in the 1940s finally ended the Great Depression.

Keynesian Theory advocates the use of government deficits to manage a recessionary economy. Fiscal policy is the action of the government when it adjusts spending and taxation to influence the economy. The term counter-cyclical fiscal policy is applied when the government uses its spending and taxing powers to attempt a smoothing of natural business cycles. Keynes encouraged government spending increases during a recession and reducing government spending (and even increasing taxes) during a demand-side inflation.

Classical Theorists reacted negatively to Keynesian initiatives in a recession by saying that deficit spending by government would only make funds unavailable to the private sector and these funds borrowed by the government would be spent for wasteful programs. This criticism is termed the crowding-out effect. Funds borrowed by the government, because there is a limited amount of savings available, will cause interest rates to rise and this will place additional limitations on the amount of funds available to the private sector.

Keynes responded to this criticism by stating that government deficits are appropriate when unemployment is consistently high because there is no motivation for business to expand and use the funds that have been saved. If government increases aggregate demand that, in turn causes employment, output and income to increase, then investment by businesses would be encouraged or **crowded in**. The implementation of counter-cyclical measures is still criticized by classical and neoclassical (new classical) economists today who developed the Public Choice Theory.

Public Choice Theory

This theory argues that the expansion of government spending results in bureaucracy and payments to special interest groups and has very little positive economic impact in the long run. Keynesian policy is very controversial to advocates of Public Choice Theory because it promotes government spending that seems to result in an ongoing series of budget deficits.

THE KEYNESIAN MULTIPLIER CONCEPT

Keynesian Theory includes the idea that changes in any of the components of AD (C, I, G or Net Exports) could actually have a magnified effect. Government spending can have a significantly larger impact on aggregate demand than just the initial increase in government spending. When government spending is increased, these funds will become income to Households (Circular Flow). In turn, this income will be spent on consumption, leading to increases in income in the next round for another Household's or individual's spending (Figure 8.4).

Figure 8.4	CHANGE IN INCOME	CHANGE IN CONSUMPTION (MPC = .8)	SAVINGS (MPS = .2)
Increase in Government spending of	$10.00		
First Round	$10.00	$8.00	$2.00
Second Round	$8.00	$6.40	$1.60
Third Round	$6.40	$5.12	$1.38
Fourth Round	$5.12	$4.10	$1.02
All Other Rounds	$20.48	$16.38	$4.00
TOTAL	$50.00	$40.00	$10.00

This multiplier process will continue until a new level of economic activity is achieved. By the numbers, the multiplier process will end when the net amount of increased savings (leakage) from the multiplier process ($10 in Figure 8.4) is equal to the initial increase in government spending (injection).

The extent of the multiplier process is influenced by the consumption pattern of the individuals involved. Several calculations are used in Keynesian analysis to describe this consumption behavior and its impact on the multiplier process.

The average propensity to consume (APC) is the average tendency (propensity) to spend income at a given income level. The APC is the amount of consumption spending divided by the amount of income at a specific point. To illustrate this concept with a simple example, assume an individual consumes (spends) $8,000 of his $10,000 income—the APC is $8,000/$10,000 = 0.8.

The average propensity to save (APS) is the average tendency to save income at a given income level. APS is the amount of savings divided by the amount of income at a specific point. If one saves $2,000 of $10,000, then the APS is 0.2.

At any income level, individuals either spend or save their income so the APC + APS must equal 1.0.

Figure 8.5

Average Propensity and Marginal Propensity

Disposable Income	Personal Consumption	Savings	APC	APS	MPC	MPS
$2000	$2,040	-40	1.02	-.02		
2,200	2,200	0	1.00	0	.8	.2
2,400	2,360	40	.99	.01	.8	.2
2,600	2,520	80	.97	.03	.8	.2
2,800	2,680	120	.96	.04	.8	.2
3,000	2,840	160	.95	.05	.8	.2

Another calculation of importance is the amount of spending or savings from additional income. An increase in income is called marginal income. The tendency to spend or save marginal income is called **marginal propensity to consume (MPC)** or **marginal propensity to save (MPS)**, respectively.

To illustrate these concepts with a simple example, assume income increases from $10,000 to $20,000 (an increase of $10,000) and $9,000 of the new income is consumed. The MPC would then equal 0.9 (9,000/10,000 = 0.9). MPS in this example would be 0.1 ($1,000/$10,000 = 0.1). The total use of the additional $10,000 must equal 1.00 (or 100 percent) or MPC + MPS = 0.9 + 0.1 = 1.0. Illustrated in Figure 8.5.

THE MULTIPLIER

The Multiplier applied to increases in spending is dependent on the marginal propensity to consume. According to this concept, when there is a change in any one of the aggregate demand components (C, I, G or Net Exports), a multiple impact on employment, income and output will occur because of the interactions after the initial increase in AD.

The Multiplier in its simplest form is defined as 1 divided by 1-MPC, which is simply 1 divided by the MPS. If the MPC is 0.8, the MPS must be 0.2 (1−0.8 = 0.2). The Multiplier is then 1 divided by 0.2 or 5. If an aggregate demand component, such as investment or government spending, is increased by $10, then the total possible amount of change in spending (as well as income and output) would be $10 times 5 = a maximum increase of $50 for the nation.

The multiplier approach for Consumption, Investment and Government uses the Simple Multiplier illustrated above. The multiplier for tax changes and for

Figure 8.6

Disposable Income = GDP	Consumption	Savings	Investment	Aggregate Demand	Unplanned Inventory	Propensity of Employment
$2000	$2040	-40	40	2080	-80	Increase
2200	2200	0	40	2240	-40	Increase
2400	2360	40	40	2400	0	Equilibrium
2600	2520	80	40	2560	40	Decrease
2800	2680	120	40	2720	80	Decrease
3000	2840	160	40	2880	120	Decrease

the foreign sector, however, is a bit different and may be covered as a separate topic by your instructor.

Figure 8.6 applies the Keynesian Theory to a macroeconomy and a change from one level of GDP to another level of GDP through the multiplier process. We will assume that MPC and MPS for this economy will remain constant and, therefore, that the same percentage of additional income will be saved or spent at all levels of GDP. We are also assuming that the production of each level of GDP generates an equivalent amount of Disposable Income (GDP = DI) in the economy (Circular Flow).

In Figure 8.6, assume that the economy is at a DI (or GDP) of $2,400 and that Personal Consumption is at $2,360, with Savings = $40 and Business Investment stable at $40. At this point, Savings = Investment and AD = AS, therefore the economy is in equilibrium. Disposable Income is assumed to be generated from the production of the GDP, which is the AS for our purposes here. AD is Personal Consumption + the given level of Business Investment at $40. At this time, then, DI = GDP = AS = AD at a level of $2,400.

If an additional $40 of Investment is injected with MPS = .2, then the multiplier applies with a value of 5 (1/.2), which increases Disposable Income by $40 times 5 or $200. From $2,400, the DI (or GDP) rises by $200 to $2,600, where a new equilibrium is established. Notice at the $2,600 level that Savings of $80 would now be equaled by Investment of $80 (initial $40 plus the new $40).

THE BALANCED BUDGET MULTIPLIER

The spending and taxation policies of government have a multiplied impact on the economy, as described in the section above. However, the amount of the magnification does depend on the specific type of government action created. The Balanced Budget Multiplier quantifies the magnification applied when government increases spending and increases taxes by the same amount. Recall from previous discussions that if government increases spending but does not increase taxes, then it will have to borrow the money for the new spending (deficit spending).

Changes in G will have greater impact on the economy than changes in T because government spending goes directly into the economy, while taxation changes impact disposable income (take-home pay). Only a portion of the increase in DI will actually become spending based on the marginal propensity to consume (MPC). When G is increased or decreased, the multiplier is applied directly because government spending is an injection to the economy, as noted in the Bathtub Theory. However, when T increases, there are leakages—income and, therefore, consumption decreases, so the MPC must be applied.

For example: An increase in government spending (G) of $100 billion is undertaken to promote a publicly approved activity, such as education, ecology or public health. Let's assume this action is paid for by increasing taxes (T) by the same amount, $100 billion. The amount of impact on the economy (according to the simple multiplier) would be determined by the MPC and MPS relationships. If MPC is .8, then MPS is .2 (1−.8) and, therefore, the Simple Multiplier would be 1/.2 or 5.

The predicted result, then, of the $100 action initiated above would be an increase in economic activity from the increase in G and a decrease in economic activity from the increase in taxes. The impact of the change in G on the economy would be found by multiplying the change in G ($100) times the Multiplier (5) for a total maximum change of $500. The impact of the change in T on the economy is found by multiplying the change in taxation ($100) times the Multiplier (5) for a $500 total decrease in income and then times the MPC of .8 for a total of a $400 decrease in consumption spending by households. Notice that the impact of a change in taxes must be filtered through its impact on consumption spending, which is determined by MPC.

Government spending increases are directly magnified by the Multiplier because government spending (G) goes directly into the economy. However, the effect of an increase in taxation must be determined through its indirect impact on consumption spending (C). Bottom line (as they say in Accounting), is that the net impact of increasing T and increasing G is the amount of the initial change in G. In our example, an increase of $100 billion in G will (with the multiplier) expand the economy by $500 billion, but an increase in T will decrease the economy by $400 billion, so the net impact is $100 or the amount of the initial increase in G. If G and T are changed in different directions or by different amounts, the net impact would need to be derived through the same multiplier process.

The relationship between government policy and economic activity can be somewhat complex, but an understanding of the economic impact of government is *essential* for an informed electorate to make good choices when voting on public issues and electing representatives. Since 1980, government has enacted many changes in government spending (G) and taxation (T) with very different intentions. As discussed previously, taxes were reduced in the 1980s and economic activity did increase. In the early 1990s, government increased personal income taxes for upper-income individuals (those making more than $250,000), increased gasoline taxes ($.05 per gallon) and increased several federal excise taxes. However, economic activity increased from 1992–1999 and resulted in a budget surplus (T was greater than G). In 2001–2008, taxes were reduced again for most, but they were especially reduced for upper-income groups, reversing the tax increases implemented in the 1990s for upper income groups.

Partially as a result of tax reductions, but also as a result of major military and social spending, the economy incurred major deficits (G>T) in the early years of the 21st century. As the first decade of the 21st century came to a close, these deficits doubled and tripled in size as the government sought to bail the economy out of its worst recession since the 1930s.

OTHER NON-INCOME DETERMINANTS OF ECONOMIC ACTIVITY

The changes in economic activity according to Keynes involved many variables and their interactions. However, he considered income the most important determinant of consumption, savings and investment. We know today that there are several non-income and psychological determinants of Household and Business spending. Non-income determinants include the following:

- The level of personal debt that exists in our economy

- The value of assets held by individuals

- The current tax code as it provides incentives to spend or save

- Expectations of job loss or income gain

- Interest rates as they affect consumption

- Cultural attitudes toward savings or spending

Each of the above elements seems to have had an impact on the American economy in recent years and they will probably continue to do so in the future. It can be difficult to attribute specific changes in economic activity to any one variable or to forecast the future impact that a change in any one variable might have when many variables are changing at one time.

MODERN EMPLOYMENT THEORY

Traditional Aggregate Demand Theory (Keynesian Theory) describes the movement of AD along the flat portion of the AS line. More modern theories, however, also focus on long-term growth in the economy (as opposed to just the short-term fluctuations of AD) and these are concerned with the aggregate supply curve in Figure 8.2. A longer-term shift to the right in the AS would represent real growth in the economy as you saw in Lessons 6 and 7. Long-term shifts in the AS to the right tend to be relatively slow when compared to AD shifts.

A shift to the left in the AS (or backward shift) would represent a decrease in production at any given price level. Alternatively, the leftward shift in AS would represent a higher price level for the same level of production that was previously available. This situation is referred to as "cost-push inflation" or "stagflation" if it is an ongoing trend. Sustained increases in the price of oil (or other forms of energy) or sustained price increases in any of the four basic resources can result in this type of leftward shift.

SUMMARY

We have explored both Classical Theory and Keynesian Theory as well as modified versions of each of these Schools of Thought. We will be adding to these explorations in upcoming Lessons that extend our coverage of Fiscal Policy, Growth Policy and Monetary Policy. To begin **applying** what you have learned, you should proceed immediately to the **Animations & Interactives** component.

Key Terms

Aggregate Demand (AD): consists of Consumption and Investment in Classical Theory but also includes government and export expenditures in Keynesian Theory compared to prices at each level.

Average Propensity to Consume (APC): The average amount of income spent of total income = consumption/income.

Average Propensity to Save (APS): The average amount of income saved of total income = savings/income.

Aggregate Supply (AS): The amount of output provided by all suppliers at varied price levels.

Balanced Budget Multiplier: The amount of magnification caused by an increase in government spending (G) and taxation (T) when applied at the same time. G has a greater impact because it does not have to be processed through personal spending. G impact = G times the multiplier while T impact = T times multiplier times MPC.

Counter-cyclical Government Policy: Discretionary or nondiscretionary fiscal policy that helps stimulate the economy during recession and dampen demand in an inflationary period.

Government policy of changing taxes and/or government spending to alter recession or inflation in national income, employment and output from its current course by increasing spending and/or decreasing taxes in recession or decreasing spending and/or increasing taxes in inflation.

Crowding-out Effect: Actions to increase government spending may crowd out private sector spending by diverting existing savings and increasing interest rates.

Crowding-in Effect: Keynesian term relating to increasing government spending to stimulate the economy that will increase income and result in more available savings for the private sector.

Fiscal Policy: Government policy for taxation and spending to encourage growth and price stability.

Key Terms

Keynesian Theory: Macroeconomic theory assuming capitalism is characterized by business cycles due to changes in savings, consumption and investment but cycles can be moderated by government taxation and spending policy.

Keynesian Bathtub: Injections to the tub include government, consumption, investment and exports and leakages include taxes, imports and savings by both households and businesses.

Keynesian Multiplier: When AD factors of C, I, G and Net Exports are changed, a magnification of the change will take place because each new expenditure will change another's income and result in greater total change. The Multiplier formula is: 1/MPS or 1/1-MPC.

Planned Investment: Expected investment by a firm to maintain operations at current levels.

Public Choice Theory: Conservative economic theory arguing that increases in government spending result in more inefficiency and waste but little or no benefit for society.

Stages of AS:

- **Stage 1** is illustrated with a flat horizontal line showing no price increases when output increases.

- **Stage 2** is illustrated with an upward sloping line showing price and quantity increases.

- **Stage 3** is illustrated with a vertical line showing no increase in output but increases in prices.

Unplanned Investment: Changes in inventory needed to adjust inventories due to unexpected changes in sales.

Applied Exercises

Exercise One:

REAL GDP	CONSUMPTION	PLANNED INVESTMENT	AGGREGATE DEMAND	UNPLANNED INVESTMENT	REAL GDP WILL (UP/DOWN)
$30,000	$28,000	$1,000			
$28,000	$26,500	$1,000			
$26,000	$25,000	$1,000			
$24,000	$23,500	$1,000			

A. This economy will be in equilibrium at a GDP of _____.

B. If real GDP is producing at $28,000, the economy will tend to (expand or contract)?

C. Why would the economy tend to expand or contract?

D. The MPS for this economy is _____.

E. The multiplier for this economy is _____.

F. Describe what economists mean by the multiplier concept.

Applied Exercises

Exercise Two:

A. Assume that $100 billion is spent by government for environmental improvements. If the MPC is .8, what is the multiplier? What would the maximum impact on the economy be and would this increase or decrease output?

B. Continuing the example above, what would the impact be if taxes are raised to pay for the $100 billion expenditure? How would this impact output and in which direction?

C. Finally, what would the impact be on the output if A and B are both implemented at the same time?

Applied Exercises: Answers

Exercise One:

REAL GDP	CONSUMPTION	PLANNED INVESTMENT	AGGREGATE DEMAND	UNPLANNED INVESTMENT	REAL GDP WILL (UP/DOWN)
$30,000	$28,000	$1,000	$29,000	-$1,000	Down
$28,000	$26,500	$1,000	$27,500	-$500	Down
$26,000	$25,000	$1,000	$26,000	$0	Nether
$24,000	$23,500	$1,000	$24,500	$500	Up

A. This economy will be in equilibrium at a GDP of $26,000.

B. If real GDP is producing at $28,000, the economy will tend to contract.

C. Why would the economy tend to expand or contract? AD < AS (GDP)

D. The MPS for this economy is 500/2000 = .25.

E. The multiplier for this economy is .1/.25 = 4.

F. The multiplier concept states that changes in aggregate demand (comprised of consumption, investment, and government spending) will cause a magnified (greater) change in income, employment and output (GDP).

Applied Exercises: Answers

Exercise Two:

A. Assume that $100 billion is spent by government for environmental improvements. If the MPC is .8, what is the multiplier? What would the maximum impact on the economy be and would this increase or decrease output?

The multiplier is 1/mps or 1/.2 = 5. A change in government spending of $100 will cause a total change of $100 billion x 5 = $500 billion increase in income, employment and output.

B. Continuing the example above, what would the impact be if taxes are raised to pay for the $100 billion expenditure? How would this impact output and in which direction?

An increase in taxes of $500 billion will be subject to the multiplier but also the average propensity to spend therefore $500 increase in taxes will cause $100 billion x 5 x .8 = $400 billion decrease in income, employment, and output.

C. Finally, what would the impact be on the output if A and B are both implemented at the same time?

If government spending is increased and taxes are increased at the same time, government spending will relate to an increase in income, employment and output of $500 billion but increases in taxation will cause of decrease in income, employment and output of $400 billion with a net impact of an increase in income, employment, and output of $100 billion.

> "The temptation to form premature theories upon insufficient data is the bane of our profession."
>
> Sherlock Holmes

Lesson **Nine**
Fiscal Policy and Public Debt

Introduction

While the world's greatest detective was undoubtedly referring to a frequent failing on the part of criminologists, the temptation to make premature declarations on sketchy information plagues the economics profession as well. With economic decision making, there are even more clues and variables to contemplate.

LEARNING OBJECTIVES

Please note the listed objectives. As you will see, the course materials are all objective driven. This provides you with a constant way to direct and monitor your progress throughout the course. Each objective is color-coded and corresponds to that particular section in the text.

OBJECTIVE ONE | 1

Describe Fiscal Policy and the objectives of Fiscal Policy.

OBJECTIVE TWO | 2

Explain the Mechanics of Fiscal Policy and how it works.

OBJECTIVE THREE | 3

Describe the Budget Implications of surpluses and deficits.

OBJECTIVE FOUR | 4

Describe Discretionary and Nondiscretionary Tools.

OBJECTIVE FIVE | 5

Describe Public Debt and the true burdens and myths associated with it.

INTERACTIVE EXERCISE

Use the Major Economic Models to demonstrate an understanding of the chain reactions resulting from human choices and how they move through an economy. Demonstrate an understanding of the Tradeoffs that result.

All theories—ultimately—come from our belief about our world and our behavior as we interact with that world. As we have seen in our discussion in this unit, Classical Theory was the first real attempt to theorize about our economic behavior from the macro standpoint. Based on observation and data, Classical Theorists reached certain conclusions about the predictability of our economic behavior and the effects that would follow. Later theorists would conclude that the Classical Theorists were asking the correct questions but did not provide the correct answers.

By the late 1930s, Keynesian Economics became the set of ideas that would challenge the older theory (Classical). While this new school of thought was still looking at the old questions, the answers were different and seemed to be more supported by data and empirical evidence. These emerging ideas promised a new way of looking at economics and, even more importantly, suggested that there were "counter-cyclical tools" that could help us manage the periodic instability that had long plagued our system.

In this lesson, we will be focusing on Keynesian Theory and how these ideas attempted to provide insight into the most perplexing area of macroeconomics—how do we maintain a stable, growing economy without slipping toward inflation or recession? As a part of this model, it will also be necessary to gain some understanding of the way our federal budgets are managed and the role of public debt.

Normative Economics

As we have seen a number of times, the normative elements in economics are numerous. As we look at the impact of budget deficits, surpluses and the many political decisions that govern both discretionary (by our actions) and nondiscretionary (by adjustments with) policy, we must recognize that the decisions to use these models come from the beliefs of policymakers and have much to do with their perception of the world and their beliefs about the role of government. As we have also seen in earlier discussions, all economic theories require assumptions.

Fiscal Policy

Although fiscal policy is relatively complex, the definition is fairly simple: It is the action taken by government (usually federal) to change tax rates and/or spending levels for the purpose of stabilizing our economy. While the definition is simple, the discussion between our elected policy makers that usually predicates governmental action is quite a different story. Keep in mind that fiscal policy is largely a political answer to an economic problem and involves many different normative judgments.

The presentation of the principles in this lesson will be consistent with the assumptions of Keynesian Theory. As Keynes viewed the world, he came to several conclusions:

- A market economy is inherently unstable.

- There are no built-in economic devices in a market economy that will guarantee stability.

- Government has the ability, and the responsibility, to attempt to steer our economy toward price stability, growth and full employment.

Objectives of Fiscal Policy—Employment Act of 1946

The objectives of fiscal policy were identified by federal legislation that was passed in 1946. This legislation really did not do that much—it contained no regulations or appropriations. However, it did say that the federal government should make every effort to:

- Help maintain a stable economy relative to recession or inflation

- Encourage economic growth

- Promote full employment

These three simple objectives don't sound very difficult individually, but accomplishing all three at the same time is a major challenge. Although this legislation was passed in 1946, it would not be until the early 1960s that an active attempt would be made to carry out these objectives through fiscal policy. Legislation introduced by President Kennedy proposed an across-the-board tax cut to stimulate a sluggish economy. This policy action was based on an application of Keynesian Theory.

Discretionary Fiscal Policy

The overall intent of fiscal policy is very direct—the government is attempting to influence aggregate demand. If you think back to our model, we know that aggregate demand is what drives our economy in the short run. If the economy is moving too slowly, AD has to increase for us to move from recession. If it is moving too rapidly, it must be slowed to reduce the possibility of inflation. According to the Keynesian model, managing AD, during recession or inflation, can (in the short run) achieve our objectives of stability, growth and full employment.

As we look back to our bathtub model in Figure 9.1, we know that raising or lowering taxes has a predictable effect on AD as does a change in government spending. However, we must also consider the effect on the federal budget with any of these actions and, more importantly, understand the implications of the effects of these decisions for the longer run.

SUMMARY:
DISCRETIONARY FISCAL POLICY WITH LESS THAN FULL EMPLOYMENT

If taxes are raised—AD declines and the overall economy slows

If taxes are lowered—AD increases and the economy grows

If government spending is raised—AD increases and the economy expands

If government spending is lowered—AD declines and the economy slows

If we apply the Keynesian model and our economy is in recession, we must use fiscal policy to stimulate aggregate demand, which means that we would lower taxes and/or increase government spending. When the desired result is accomplished—an increase in AD to create an expanding economy—it would also normally result in a budget deficit.

If we are suffering from inflation, the opposite policy would be appropriate—raise taxes and/or lower spending. This would reduce aggregate demand and slow the economy. With higher tax revenues and less spending, we might then incur a budget surplus.

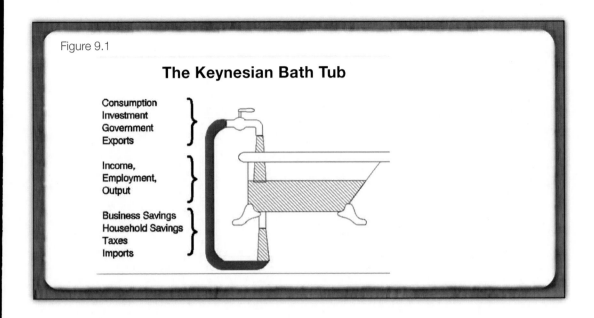

Figure 9.1

The Keynesian Bath Tub

Consumption
Investment
Government
Exports

Income,
Employment,
Output

Business Savings
Household Savings
Taxes
Imports

BUDGETARY IMPACT

As we look more closely at the finer points of fiscal policy, it is important to understand that some of these elements are counterintuitive—they may not seem logical. Could it be beneficial in some situations if the federal government did not maintain a balanced budget? Keynes would say yes, if incurring a short-term deficit or surplus would help promote our longer-term objectives of stability, growth and employment. In a Keynesian approach, the federal government is the only entity in our system that can assume this responsibility. State governments do not have the ability nor do corporations or consumers.

When the economy is stable and at full employment, a balanced budget would seem to be appropriate because it would not create an expansion or contraction. During a period of instability, however, the federal government can attempt to provide the impetus for a change in aggregate demand. If the economy is slowing, then fiscal policy would call for policy action to encourage an increase in AD, which would mean a cut in taxes and/or an increase in federal spending.

The result of this action is potentially a budget deficit because of less federal tax revenue (because of the tax cut) or the increase in spending. The net effect is an increase in AD as less money flows out of the tub because of lower taxes and more flows into the tub through greater federal spending. In effect, there is more water in the tub as a result of the budget deficit.

When inflation in the economy is accelerating, the opposite action would be appropriate and the goal will be to try to slow the right shifting AD. This would mean a cut in government spending and/or an increase in taxes. This action would translate into a budget surplus (or a smaller deficit)—more money flowing into the tub and less flowing out. The political consequences could be considerable, however, when elected officials tell taxpayers that raising their taxes will have a positive economic benefit.

What does President Kennedy's quote about a rising tide really mean? His message was that if the economy is growing and improving, then everyone benefits. All boats respond to a rising tide. One of the main problems, however, with fiscal policy (as envisioned by Keynes) was public perception and opinion. Many questions have to be answered and many normative judgments must be made. Does government have the right to take these actions and the right to spend more money than tax revenues allow? How could spending more money than you have available be a good thing? What will the money be spent for? Whose taxes will be raised or lowered?

In responding to some of these questions, Keynes would argue that deficits year after year would *not* be appropriate any more than constant surpluses. However, if an economy was in a severe decline, government policy should provide a "jump-start." If this did help to get the economy moving again and increase employment, then the longer-term benefit outweighs the short-term deficit. He argued equally about the benefits of a budget surplus to deal with inflation—this action would decrease AD at the appropriate time.

Popular opinion about Keynesian economics centers on the mistaken conclusion that Keynes believed that a nation could spend its way to prosperity with deficits as far as the eye could see. This was never his belief. Keynes argued that a deficit was only appropriate for recession situations and a budget surplus was needed for inflation situations and to pay off the previously incurred deficits. For elected officials to follow both sides of the Keynesian theory can require significant political courage.

FINANCING BUDGET DEFICITS

The federal government, as previously mentioned, is in a singularly unique position to influence business cycles. The federal government can spend more than it takes in, for a rather extended period of time. The primary reason for this is that the federal government largely controls our money supply—or at least the ability to refinance indebtedness as stated in the U.S. Constitution, Article I.

The federal government has two methods available to finance deficits. It can borrow the money through the issuance of bonds (a promise to pay), or it can virtually create money through interaction with the Federal Reserve (the United States' central bank). Either process involves the interaction of the U.S. Treasury and the Federal Reserve.

The Treasury has generally chosen to finance deficits through borrowing (issuing bonds). When the borrowed money is spent, it does expand our economy in the Keynesian sense and does not have quite the inflationary risk of money creation. Contrary to some political statements that have been made in the past few years, the debt that is incurred by selling more bonds is real. It is not just numbers on a page—it must be repaid to the person or institution that loaned the government the money. Given the minimal (or even negative) savings rate in this country, it has been necessary to borrow increasing amounts of money from foreign investors and institutions. In recent years, the majority of this lending has come from China, Japan and Europe. See Figure 9.2.

BUDGET PHILOSOPHIES

There is much political discussion about budget deficits and public debt and, not surprisingly, a great deal of confusion on the part of voters. The idea of requiring an annually balanced budget seems reasonable and even mandatory to many people. Some have suggested a constitutional amendment that would dictate that requirement. The problem is that such a requirement would remove fiscal policy as a major tool to combat severe instability. Further, forced balancing of the budget would actually be pro-cyclical. When there is a surplus, government spending would have to increase and when there is a deficit, spending would have to decrease. Required spending to do away with a surplus would likely be inflationary and decreasing spending with a deficit would intensify a recession.

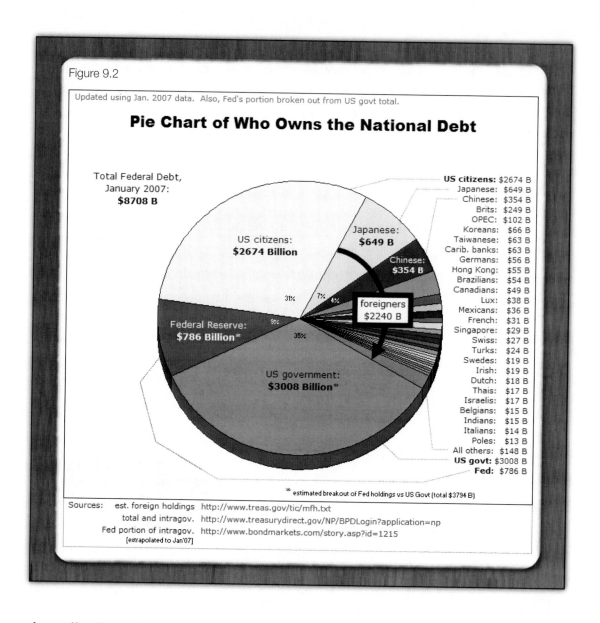

Figure 9.2

Updated using Jan. 2007 data. Also, Fed's portion broken out from US govt total.

Pie Chart of Who Owns the National Debt

Total Federal Debt,
January 2007:
$8708 B

US citizens:
$2674 Billion

Japanese:
$649 B

Chinese:
$354 B

foreigners
$2240 B

31%   7%   4%

9%

Federal Reserve:
$786 Billion*

35%

US government:
$3008 Billion*

US citizens:	$2674 B
Japanese:	$649 B
Chinese:	$354 B
Brits:	$249 B
OPEC:	$102 B
Koreans:	$66 B
Taiwanese:	$63 B
Carib. banks:	$63 B
Germans:	$56 B
Hong Kong:	$55 B
Brazilians:	$54 B
Canadians:	$49 B
Lux:	$38 B
Mexicans:	$36 B
French:	$31 B
Singapore:	$29 B
Swiss:	$27 B
Turks:	$24 B
Swedes:	$19 B
Irish:	$19 B
Dutch:	$18 B
Thais:	$17 B
Israelis:	$17 B
Belgians:	$15 B
Indians:	$15 B
Italians:	$14 B
Poles:	$13 B
All others:	$148 B
US govt:	**$3008 B**
Fed:	$786 B

* estimated breakout of Fed holdings vs US Govt (total $3794 B)

Sources: est. foreign holdings http://www.treas.gov/tic/mfh.txt
total and intragov. http://www.treasurydirect.gov/NP/BPDLogin?application=np
Fed portion of intragov. http://www.bondmarkets.com/story.asp?id=1215
[extrapolated to Jan'07]

A **cyclically balanced budget** would seem more logical than a requirement to balance the budget each and every year—but it can be more difficult to administer. The idea here is to balance the budget over the course of the business cycle, but these cyclical fluctuations are very irregular in length and intensity. A downturn or upswing may last for six months or as much as three or four years. There is no way to know the duration of the cycle until it is completed.

Functional finance is the budgetary philosophy the United States has used since the 1960s. This approach suggests that the federal budget should be managed to focus on the primary objectives of stability, growth and employment—even if this means periodic budget deficits or surpluses. Under this philosophy, balancing the budget is a secondary consideration. This approach does suggest that a deficit is appropriate when the economy is slowing and a surplus is needed when the economy moves toward inflation, but there is difficulty in timing such actions. Functional finance is also difficult because of political realities. Taxpayers generally accept tax cuts or increases in spending in a recession but resist tax increases or decreases in spending in an inflationary situation.

NONDISCRETIONARY FISCAL POLICY

The federal government has created a means of *automatically* countering business cycles through nondiscretionary fiscal policy. What characterizes nondiscretionary policy from other government action is that no legislative action is required—it is already built in. For the most part, these devices are triggered by changes in the level of employment. We know that employment levels go down during recession and go up during inflation. When this happens, tax revenues and government spending will change automatically.

Consider the counter-cyclical influence of **federal income taxes**. Assume that you were out of work for several months last year because of a recession. When you file your tax return, you will find that your tax rate will be lower because your annual income was lower. The result, although small for the individual, is a tax cut, which is appropriate policy for a recession. During an inflationary period, you probably worked all year plus had overtime pay. Now when you file your taxes, your income is up and so is the tax rate—automatically. Appropriate policy for inflation is such a tax increase.

Unemployment insurance is a very similar counter-cyclical policy. During inflation, when more people are working, premiums are paid into the program. During recession, when fewer people are working, the benefits are paid out. We have money (although a relatively small amount) taken out during inflation and then paid out as "unemployment benefits" during a recession—again appropriate policy.

Government subsidy programs have limited impact on actually changing the level of economic activity in a counter-cyclical way. The primary conclusion here is that most of these programs do not automatically adjust very much (in a counter-cyclical way) when economic conditions are changing. Consider Social Security—it puts a tremendous amount of spending into our economy each month. The business cycle may be trending up or down, but these benefits are relatively constant—or possibly *pro-cyclical*.

Advantages of Discretionary Fiscal Policy

There is no question that discretionary fiscal policy is an important and powerful tool to deal with the problem of instability. While we may argue some of the finer points, when it is needed (or not needed) and the particular timing, fiscal policy continues to be used, especially to deal with recession.

Another use of fiscal policy is to target specific groups or different parts of the economy. We may chose to spend our deficit (borrowed money) on defense, health care or training programs or we may choose to cut taxes for specific income groups—lower, middle or upper.

Disadvantages of Fiscal Policy: Timing

Political realities often create a time delay in the passing and implementation of fiscal policy legislation. Our elected officials are obviously concerned about voter's perceptions of a change in policy. In addition, it takes time to accurately identify a change in the cycle—usually at least six months. Also, it takes time to recommend legislative action and actually activate the policy. Finally, it takes time for the economy to realize the effects of changes in taxation or spending. All these delays could postpone the effect of policy actions to well over 18 months. By this time, the natural cyclical adjustments of the market may actually be taking the economy in another direction!

Crowding-Out

The crowding-out effect is another possible problem with fiscal policy. If government borrowing becomes so great that it absorbs most of the savings in the economy, then fiscal policy actions can force interest rates to increase. This can then "crowd-out" private borrowing. This crowding-out lowers business investment spending and may affect our long-run competitiveness and growth.

PUBLIC DEBT—FIGURES 9.3 AND 9.4

The definition for Public Debt is fairly simple. Public Debt includes an accounting of all past deficits and surpluses from previous years. Public debt is past tense. Budget deficits, on the other hand, refer to the current year and measure

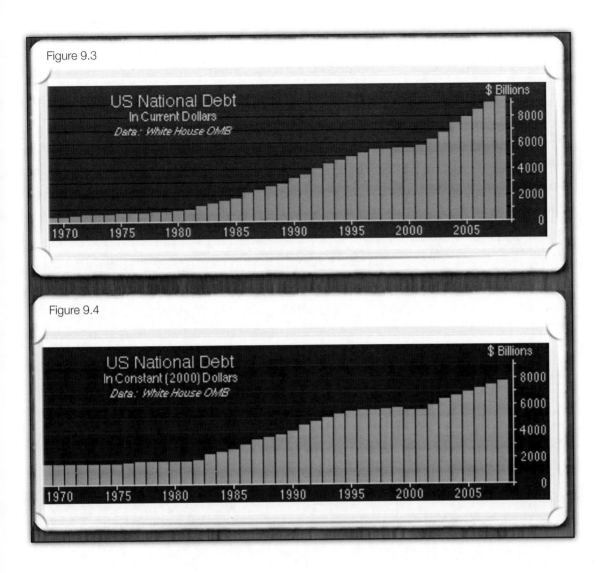

Figure 9.3

US National Debt
In Current Dollars
Data: White House OMB

Figure 9.4

US National Debt
In Constant (2000) Dollars
Data: White House OMB

how much our government spending exceeds the tax revenues—or vice-versa in the case of a budget surplus.

As you can see from Figures 9.3 and 9.4, the data is very straightforward and strictly "positive economics"—no normative judgments. However, it is very difficult to get much further into our analysis without opinion entering the conversation. The questions that immediately come to mind are very direct: Why did debt explode in the early 1980s and why has it continued to grow at such a rapid pace? The political debate that has ensued is similar to many other public issues, with both major political parties blaming each other for the problem.

A HISTORY OF DEFICITS AND SURPLUSES—FIGURES 9.5 AND 9.6

There have been historical periods of rapidly increasing deficits in America's history—particularly those associated with WWII. Since the early 1980s, the increase in budget deficits (and public debt) has been unprecedented. The data is fairly clear, as you can see in Figures 9.5 and 9.6 (Figure 9.5 illustrates Current Dollars and Figure 9.6 shows Constant or Real "Inflation Adjusted" Dollars). These tables do not provide answers as to "why" we have made these political choices nor do they convey the impact that they have had. Remember that the term deficit is always describing the current budget year. We incur a deficit when our federal expenditures are greater than tax revenues. A surplus in the budget occurs when tax revenues are greater than government expenditures, as shown in Figure 9.5 from 1998 to 2001.

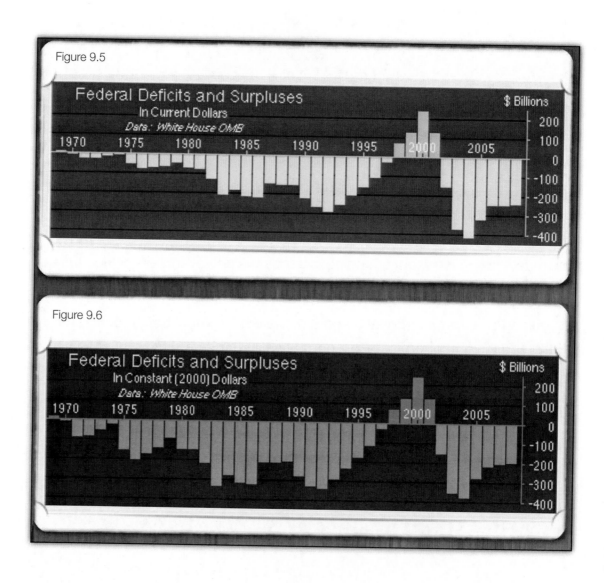

PRESIDENTIAL BUDGETS: DEFICITS AND SURPLUSES—FIGURES 9.7A & B

Even though the "who is responsible" question may be difficult to answer (Congress is very much involved in the budget process), the data in Figure 9.7A does answer the question of "when." The data in the amended table provides an answer as to who was the U.S. president during the relevant time periods. Again, given the lagging effect of sometimes uncontrollable economic events and Congressional involvement, there is still much disagreement about the question of "who is responsible" for deficits and surpluses during each of those administrations.

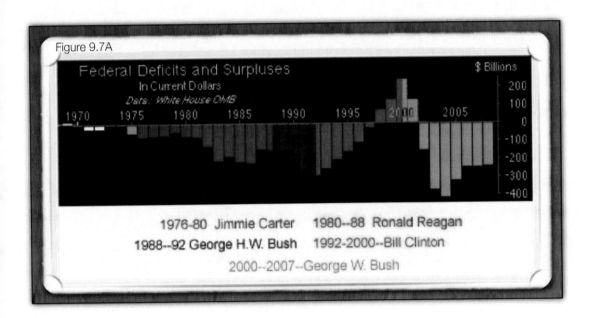

Figure 9.7A

Federal Deficits and Surpluses
In Current Dollars
Data: White House OMB

1976-80 Jimmie Carter   1980--88 Ronald Reagan
1988--92 George H.W. Bush   1992-2000--Bill Clinton
2000--2007--George W. Bush

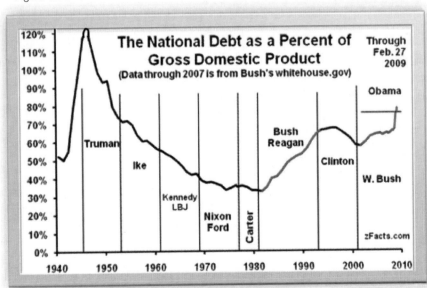

Figure 9.7B

THE BALANCED BUDGET MULTIPLIER

With our total public debt exceeding $11 trillion, it is almost impossible not to be overwhelmed by the immensity of the number. The difficulty of comprehending the magnitude can be overcome by breaking the total down and expressing the debt on a per capita or individual basis. If we divide the total debt by total population in this country, we get *per capita* public debt. This figure is for every man, woman and child in the United States and measures their individual portion of the debt. This is a little easier to understand and can be even more shocking to contemplate. Remember that these are constant dollar figures—the price index has been applied so that we can accurately compare year to year without the effects of inflation.

What we see is that per capita debt has grown from about $3,900 in 1980 to roughly $39,000 today in real terms. The national debt has increased at an average of $3.8 billion per day since September 2007. See Figure 9.8.

Figure 9.8

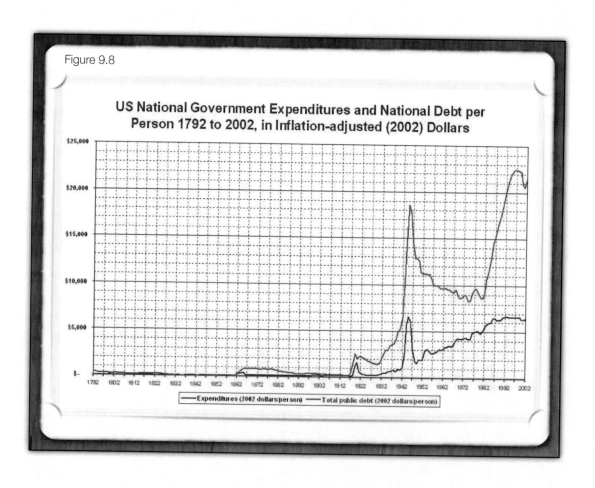

US National Government Expenditures and National Debt per Person 1792 to 2002, in Inflation-adjusted (2002) Dollars

GROWTH IN PUBLIC DEBT—FIGURE 9.9

As we have seen, there are many different opinions about the "why" and "who" questions relative to the debt. It is important that every student and every voter determine their own opinions. Global conflicts have no doubt prompted more government spending, particularly when we are involved in costly wars— (whether a war is justified or not is beyond the scope of the economics, but it is a good example of a normative question). As you should recall from earlier discussion, recessions also have considerable impact on the deficit because a slowing economy reduces the number of jobs and results in lower tax revenues and increases in government transfer payments.

SUPPLY SIDE ECONOMICS

In 1980, Ronald Reagan was elected president and he introduced Supply Side Economics to the nation. This theory was based on classical principles that the supply forces within a nation were primarily responsible for determining

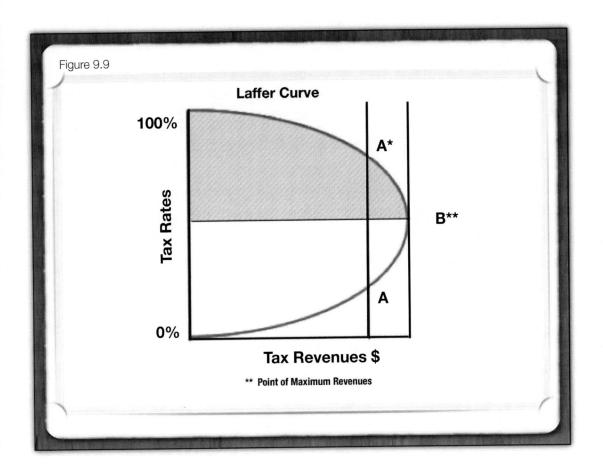

Figure 9.9

employment, output and income. President Reagan introduced legislation to cut taxes and reduce government regulation to encourage increases in productive activity (right shift in the AS). According to Supply Side Economics, increases in aggregate supply would increase output and reduce prices. This effect would multiply through the economy (some would say "lifting all boats" while others would say "trickling down") to lower-income groups through lower prices and increases in employment.

As you look at the impact of Supply Side Economics, most would agree that the tax cuts (without corresponding spending cuts) had significant impact on our increasing debt. The Laffer Curve, shown in Figure 9.9, suggested that tax cuts would increase tax revenue if the tax rate was at A* and moved to B**. Supply Side economists argued that a lower tax rate would encourage people to work more (and work smarter). It was also proposed that more people who had avoided (or even evaded) taxes when rates were high would now pay their taxes with the lower rate.

However, if the nation is at B** on the curve, a movement to A* would actually decrease tax revenues. With the record now available, it appears that the nation may have initially been at B** (not A*) and that cuts in tax rates did, in fact, lower tax revenues. However, the debate continues about the impact of changing tax rates on growth and economic activity.

ECONOMIC GROWTH

The discussion above on increasing or decreasing tax rates does have major implications for changes in the aggregate supply curve as well as the aggregate demand curve. All other things remaining the same, a reduction in tax rates would be associated with increased incentives for production and, therefore, a rightward shift in the AS. This would create an outward growth in the PPF, a "larger" Circular Flow and a sustained (or even increased) upward slope in the Long-Term (Secular) Trend Line for the economy.

Conversely, an increase in tax rates would create a decrease in incentives for production and, therefore, a leftward shift in the AS. At the extreme, this could create an inward shift of the PPF, a "smaller" Circular Flow and a negative slope on the Long-Term Trend Line.

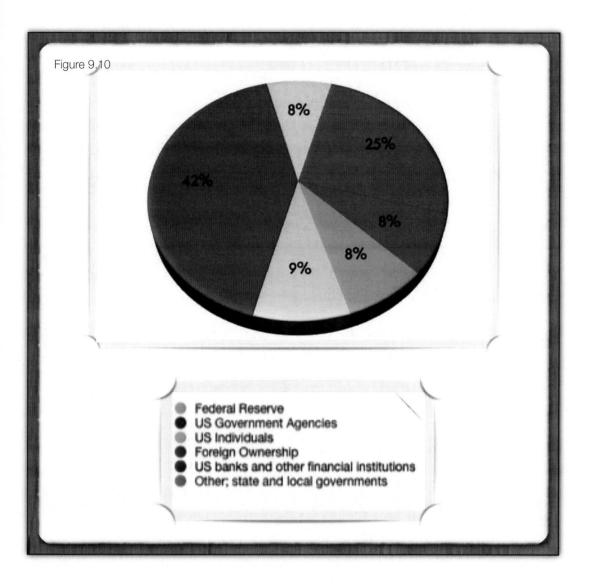

Figure 9.10

Federal Reserve
US Government Agencies
US Individuals
Foreign Ownership
US banks and other financial institutions
Other; state and local governments

WHO OWNS THE PUBLIC DEBT? — FIGURE 9.10

Figure 9.10 illustrates national debt ownership. Even though it is accurate to say that the majority of the debt is money that we owe to ourselves — that is, bondholders who reside in this country — we have seen foreign-held debt escalate dramatically in recent years. Foreign-held debt is money that we owe to someone or some entity outside the country. Domestically held debt is somewhat analogous to a person borrowing money from himself or from his family as compared to money that was borrowed from the bank. Repayment to the bank is somewhat different from repayment to "ourselves."

In Figure 9.10, the debt being held by various government agencies is largely because of tax revenues that are being temporarily invested in government bonds. For example, the Social Security Trust Fund holds surpluses of Social Security tax revenues in U.S. Treasury bonds.

PUBLIC DEBT: MYTHS

We hear frequent statements about public debt (from politicians and others) that may not be entirely true. One often repeated myth is the idea that the **federal government can become bankrupt**. The federal government cannot really go bankrupt because the government largely controls our financial system and can constantly refinance the existing debt (issue new bonds). Of course, the government could mismanage our financial system to the point of financial distress, so the effect could be very similar to "bankruptcy."

Shifting the burden to future generations, another phrase popular with some politicians, is also somewhat inaccurate. The impact of rapidly escalating public debt is generally felt in a shorter time period. For instance, if this (shift to future generations) were completely true, we would still be reeling from the effects of the deficits during World War II—we are the children and grandchildren of that generation. If our resources are employed wisely and economic growth is positive over time, then debt can be managed.

PUBLIC DEBT: TRUE BURDENS

Many of these burdens of the debt have already been discussed. We know that some **crowding-out** takes place with deficit financing as private borrowers find it increasingly difficult to borrow money at higher interest rates. The size of the deficits, other current factors in our economic environment and world affairs all affect the relative magnitude of the crowding-out.

Since the mid- to late 1980s, the amount of **foreign-held debt** has increased dramatically. This has been partially due to the very low savings rate in this country. As the deficits escalated in the 1980s, we were faced with only two alternatives because there was not enough savings to buy up the level of debt being issued by the U.S. Treasury. One alternative was to finance by actually creating money. This is nearly always very inflationary. The second, more politically acceptable option, was to keep interest rates high enough to attract foreign investment. The result has been the growth of debt held by foreign investors (from the example above, this is analogous to money that we owe to the bank rather than to ourselves). Repayment of principle and interest may provide a means for foreign ownership of U.S. assets to increase.

Lastly, some **income and wealth redistribution** has occurred. The majority of debt is held by upper-income groups, both foreign and domestic, while the majority of taxpayers are not part of that group. We do see some wealth being redistributed toward those who hold the debt. However, it is also true that the majority (86 percent) of federal income taxes are paid by taxpayers who are in the top 25 percent of income earners. For further information see: http://www.taxfoundation.org/research/show/250.html.

PUBLIC DEBT AND THE NET EXPORT EFFECT

While most of our discussion has been centered on the impact of deficits and debt on our domestic economy, it is important to realize that our budget deficits have also affected our trade deficits. Budget deficits and net exports are seemingly unrelated, but, since the mid-80s, they have become more "linked."

When budget deficits began to escalate in the early to mid-80s, it became apparent that we could not domestically "buy up" the volume of bonds that were being issued. We faced some unpleasant alternatives. We could "create" the money to buy the bonds and monetize the debt (which is very inflationary) or we could elevate interest rates so that we attracted foreign investors to buy our bonds. We chose the latter.

While we cover the basics of international economics in the micro course, there are many macro considerations when we look at international trade. Why are budget deficits and trade deficits linked so closely? When we began to sell more and more of our debt to foreign investors in the early 1980s, there was an "unintended consequence." The value of our dollar went up dramatically. To purchase U.S. securities, foreign currencies must be converted to U.S. dollars, which meant that more foreign investors wanted to "buy" the U.S. dollars. Since exchange rates are largely a factor of simple supply and demand, the effect was not surprising. The U.S. dollar grew much stronger (higher exchange rate) relative to most all world currencies.

SUMMARY

Isn't a strong dollar better than a weak dollar? The answer to this question would seem to be an automatic yes. But while a strong dollar is good if you are buying foreign goods (they are cheaper), it is not so good if you are trying to sell U.S. goods to foreign markets (our goods became more expensive). The result of this process over the past 25 years has been a dramatically escalating trade deficit. The dollar amount of imports over exports has grown from less than $50 billion in the early 1980s to levels approaching $1 trillion more recently. These trade deficits have affected jobs and income in this country as we have imported increasing amounts of consumer goods.

There is a great deal of debate about the overall implications of globalization and trade in our world today—especially as it relates to employment. Take a moment and review the two different viewpoints in Real-World Economics.

Real-World Economics

OPPOSING VIEWS

Please access links through online E-text.

Annually Balanced Budget: A budget approach that would require that the federal budget be balanced every 12 months—regardless.

Crowding-Out: Excessive government borrowing (usually for deficit financing) that raises interest rates and negatively affects private borrowing needs.

Cyclically Balanced Budget: A budget philosophy that suggests that the budget be balanced in consideration of changes in the business cycle and not just the calendar.

Deficit: Usually associated with the federal government, it is simply the amount by which spending exceeds tax revenues— in a given year.

Discretionary Fiscal Policy: Fiscal policy that requires specific legislative action to change existing federal spending levels or tax codes to stabilize the economy.

Employment Act of 1946: Legislation in that year that established economic objectives for our economy and suggested that fiscal policy could help meet the goals of full employment, price stability and growth.

Fiscal Policy: Using changes in taxation and/or spending to affect aggregate demand to have a counter-cycle affect on the business cycle.

Functional Finance: A budget approach that concludes that the federal budget should be used primarily as a counter-cycle tool and one that attempts to promote employment, stability and growth.

Laffer Curve: A method of comparing tax rates and tax revenues.

Net Export Effect: The effect that rapidly expanding domestic deficits has on our trade deficit as we have to borrow from foreign investors. This causes the dollar to strengthen, making imports cheaper and exports more expensive.

Nondiscretionary Fiscal Policy: Policy that is built into our existing federal budget so that there is some automatic counter-cycle affect when the economy slows or speeds up.

Public Debt: This is the sum of all past Federal deficits and surpluses.

Applied Exercises

Exercise One:

A. Given the Laffer Curve shown below, how would government tax receipts change if tax rates were increased from A?

B. How would they change if tax rates were decreased?

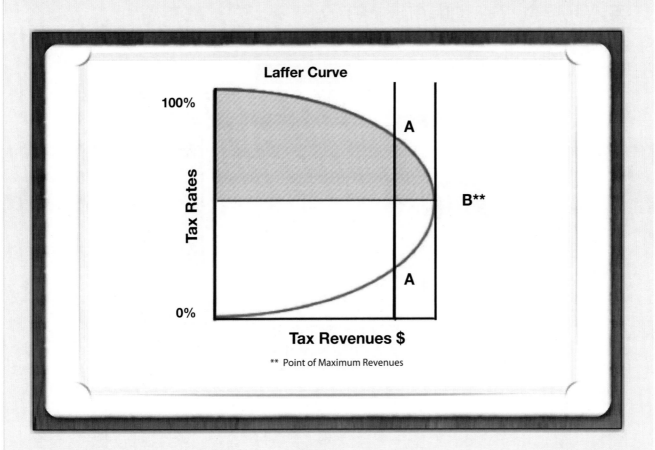

Laffer Curve

** Point of Maximum Revenues

Applied Exercises

Exercise Two:

A. Consider the three stages of the AS curve and describe appropriate fiscal policy in Stage 1. Why is this called the Keynesian range?

B. What would appropriate fiscal policy be in Stage 3?

C. Why is this called the Classical range?

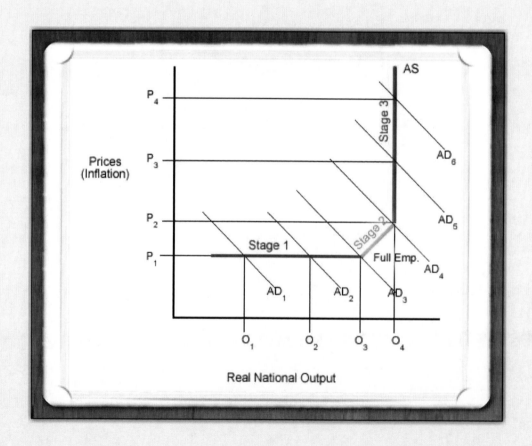

Applied Exercises: Answers

Exercise One:

A. Given the Laffer Curve on page 24, how would government tax receipts change if tax rates were increased from A? **Tax revenue would increase.**

B. How would they change if tax rates were decreased? **Tax revenue would decrease.**

Exercise Two:

A. Consider the three stages of the AS curve and describe appropriate fiscal policy in Stage 1. Why this is called the Keynesian range? **Because Keynes assumed a high level of unused capacity and, therefore, increases in AD would not cause inflation but would increase output.**

B. Why this is called the Classical range? **Because Classical Theorists assumed that an economy was at full employment and therefore the AS curve was vertical.**

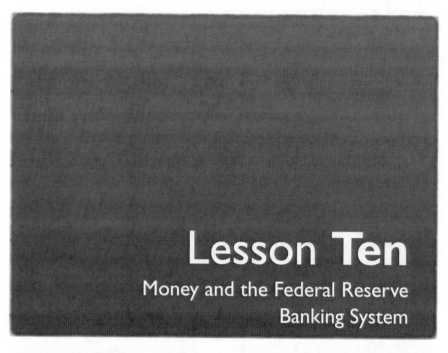

Lesson Ten
Money and the Federal Reserve Banking System

Introduction

Historically, a number of things have been used as money. Not too long ago, most exchange was done through barter (direct trade) so almost any trade-able item was money. We know that barter does allow "buying and selling" transactions but it does have many drawbacks. First, with barter there must be a mutual coincidence of needs. You want something that I own but, for trade to take place, I must want something that you own and be willing to trade with you for my item.

LEARNING OBJECTIVES

Please note the listed objectives. As you will see, the course materials are all objective driven. This provides you with a constant way to direct and monitor your progress throughout the course. Each objective is color-coded and corresponds to that particular section in the text.

OBJECTIVE ONE | 1

Define "money" and explain the three functions of money and its two basic forms.

OBJECTIVE TWO | 2

Describe the components of the Money Supply as determined by the Federal Reserve and list what is NOT considered to be a part of the Money Supply.

OBJECTIVE THREE | 3

Describe the factors that determine the value of money and explain how inflation erodes the value of money.

OBJECTIVE FOUR | 4

What are the three components of Money Demand and explain how the interaction of Money Demand with Money Supply determines interest rates.

OBJECTIVE FIVE | 5

Describe the basic structure of the U.S. Banking System, including commercial banks and Federal Reserve Banks.

INTERACTIVE EXERCISE

Use the Major Economic Models to demonstrate an understanding of the chain reactions resulting from human choices and how they move through an economy. Demonstrate an understanding of the Tradeoffs that result.

WHAT IS MONEY?

This is already complicated but what about establishing exchange value. Is my pig worth one of your cows or is it two pigs? You see the difficulty. Barter, although it does allow economic exchange, is not very efficient and does not facilitate market activity. Consider how difficult it would be if you were forced to exchange the physical goods or services that you produce for everything that you buy. Something that represents value is needed—this creates an emerging role for "money."

THE EVOLUTION OF MONEY

Many of the ancient cultures discovered that it was much easier to forgo bartering and allow something (money) to represent value to make trade more efficient. Money has taken many forms over the years. From animal skins and teeth to seashells and certain rocks, to precious metals such as gold and silver, many items have been used as money. In the colonial period in the United States, some people actually used tobacco as money, and cigarettes were used as money in some locations during World War II.

Although not very convenient, efficient or appealing, all of the things noted above could still work as money today. As long as the three basic functions of money are evident, almost anything can work as money. All of the early forms of money met the functional criteria discussed below.

THE FUNCTIONS OF MONEY

In an economy, money performs three basic functions:

Medium of Exchange

Standard of Value

Store of Value

The most important function of money is as a medium of exchange. Money functions as a medium of exchange when everyone accepts it as being money. This is a very critical point. Money would not be money if it were not universally accepted as a medium of exchange. As noted above, in earlier times money was not always available; therefore, transactions occurred through barter, the direct exchange of physical goods or services.

Money also functions as a standard or unit of value. The value of a particular form of money is established and accepted within an economic community at a specific time. Value is described in monetary units such as dollars. When you ask the price of a new car, the value of the car is described in dollars. If you asked the same question in Germany, the value of the car would be measured in Euros rather than dollars but the concept is the same.

Money functions as a store of value when it is held over a period of time. For money to work effectively, we have to be reasonably sure that the purchasing power or value of the money will not decline while it is in our pocket or in the bank.

The purchasing power (value) of money does decline when there is inflation. Money can be held and used for exchange at a later date, but money is subject to "discounting" by inflation over the time period. People will hold more money when inflation rates are low and less money when inflation rates are high.

TYPES OF MONEY

Money can be present in two forms: commodity money and fiat money. Commodity money, such as gold, is considered to be intrinsically valuable. The exchange value of commodity money is often different than its value as a basic metal. Gold coins melted down into a bar of metal would probably be worth more than the face value on the coins—a person would probably not want to use a $20 gold coin to buy $20 worth of gas (even if the gas station was legally allowed to accept it as money). Through the coining of more modern commodity money (nickels, dimes, quarters, etc.), a nation can gain value because the coins are exchanged for more goods and services than they would be worth as a basic metal. When money is "worth" more than its commodity value, the term **token money** is applied.

On the occasions when the commodity value of money is greater than the token (face) value, the commodity money can be taken out of circulation and hoarded or even melted to be used as a commodity. A principle of money called **Gresham's Law** states that when two forms of money are being used and one is thought to be more highly valued (such as gold compared to copper), the one more prized will be kept by people (hoarded) and the other form of money will be used for transactions and kept in circulation. Some people characterize this situation by saying "bad money drives good money out of circulation."

Fiat money is an item that is declared to have purchasing power value (legal tender) by a government. Such money may have no intrinsic value, but it has value only as dictated by a government. The mere acceptance of fiat money by people gives it value. Fiat money is *"legal tender for debts public and private"* as printed on each American dollar. The term legal tender means that the American dollar is the official unit of money for all transactions within the United States. Payment with such money must be accepted or a debt may no longer accumulate interest from the debtor.

Fiat money is legal tender (declared to be money by the government), exchangeable for goods and services, and is considered to have a relatively stable value for purchasing goods and services. The purchasing power of money is very much determined by government's control over the quantity of money. When the quantity of money grows significantly faster than the quantity of goods and services being produced, then the value of money decreases (inflation occurs).

Money in the United States is, in fact, known as "token money" because the intrinsic value (commodity value) of the metal or paper is less than the face value. In recent times, the zinc in a penny minted after 1981 is worth about $.004. But a penny minted before 1981 is made of cooper and worth about $.017. The metal in the U.S. half-dollar coin (minted after 1971) is worth about $.073 and the quarter (minted after 1965) is worth about $.036. Prior to those dates, those coins were minted with a significant amount of silver and today are worth significantly more than their face value—most have been removed from circulation (Gresham's Law).

Paper money in the United States is actually the circulating debt of the Federal Reserve and has very little intrinsic (commodity) value. Checkable deposits at banks are also considered money but are actually the debts of banks (owed to the depositors) and as such are circulating debt as well.

The Federal Reserve is the primary "money manager" for the nation. The Fed issues coins and paper money. Through the U.S. Mint and the Bureau of Engraving and Printing, the U.S. Treasury actually manufactures the cash, but the Federal Reserve Banks distribute (issue) the money to financial institutions. The supply of paper currency must be continually replenished because paper money deteriorates as it is circulated. The average life of paper currency is only 18 months. The Federal Reserve is charged with supplying and **resupplying** paper money to the economy.

DEFINING MONEY IN THE U. S. ECONOMY

The money supply is defined by the Federal Reserve System in two aggregate forms, M1 and M2. M1 is the "narrow measure of the money supply" and consists of currency held by the public plus the public's checkable deposits. M1 does not include currency or checkable deposits held by the Federal Reserve, U.S. Treasury or currency inside of commercial bank vaults. The calculation by the Fed of the money supply M1 and M2 denotes the amount of liquidity (nearly cash equivalent) nature of money. See Figure 10.1.

M1 = currency + checkable deposits*

(*not including currency or checkable deposits of commercial banks, the U.S. Treasury or the Fed)

Currency consists of coins and paper money (about 54 percent of M1 currency, whereas checkable deposits account for about 46 percent of M1). The current value of currency and checkable deposits is approximately $700 billion each.

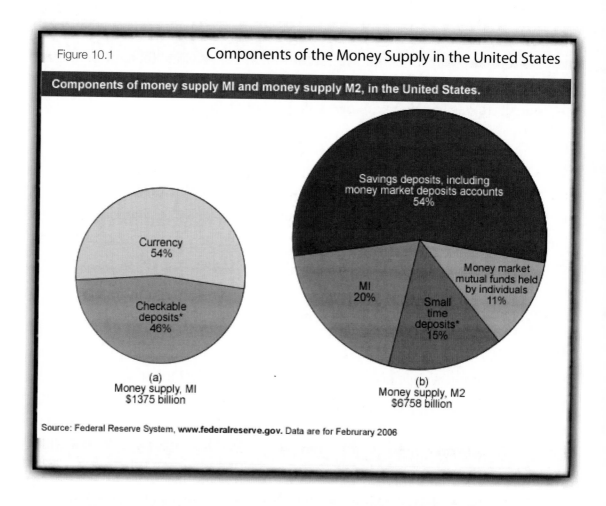

Figure 10.1

Components of the Money Supply in the United States

Components of money supply MI and money supply M2, in the United States.

Savings deposits, including money market deposits accounts
54%

Currency
54%

Checkable deposits*
46%

MI
20%

Money market mutual funds held by individuals
11%

Small time deposits*
15%

(a)
Money supply, MI
$1375 billion

(b)
Money supply, M2
$6758 billion

Source: Federal Reserve System, **www.federalreserve.gov.** Data are for Februrary 2006

M2 = M1 + Small Time Deposits + Money Markets

M2 consists of **M1** *plus* small savings (time) deposits (less than $100,000) + money market deposits + money market mutual funds. M2 includes savings that are easily transferable to cash with a short time delay. M2 is thereby considered to be "near monies."

In general, the more money held by the public, the greater the tendency for people to spend. The public holds more "liquid" money (vs. "savings" money) when interest rates are low. Since the total population of the United States is about 306 million, there is about $4,500 in money (M1) available per person. About half of those funds are in currency and half are in checkable deposits.

Credit cards are not actually "money" according to the Fed's definition because credit cards are actually a means for a consumer to obtain a quick loan. Once the loaned funds enter a retailer's checking account (or the consumer's checking account), then they become "money." The Fed monitors the growth in the money supply (M1 and M2) as well as the relationship between the money supply and the production of goods and services—this is a primary way that the Fed keeps watch on the potential for inflation.

The Fed's definition of money relates to currency that is outside of banks and does not include money in vault cash or on deposit by banks with the Fed. Because of this definition, when a bank spends money or receives an interest payment, the amount of the money supply actually does change. When a bank spends money, the money supply increases (enters the public's hands), but when loan payments are received from borrowers (borrower writes a check to the bank), the money supply actually declines.

WHAT GIVES MONEY VALUE?

Acceptability: we all accept money as "money". Money is our medium of exchange. If we did not have confidence in it and refused to accept it, money would have no value.

Scarcity: if the supply of money were not closely controlled by the Federal Reserve, money would soon have less value.

Legal Tender: if you look at any dollar bill (Federal Reserve Note), is says: "this note is legal tender for all debts public and private" – it must be accepted as a means of re-paying a loan. The government has legally defined what money is in our economy.

The **value of money,** then, is determined by acceptability based on confidence in the money and its relative scarcity. The value of money is basically what you can get for your money. The American dollar is backed by the goods and services produced (GDP), the relative scarcity of the dollars, and by its acceptability compared to other currencies. The value of money also depends very much on the stability of the government that has created it.

The value of money over time has a reciprocal relationship to the price level. The price level can be described by a price index. A price index measures growth in prices (inflation) for a given time period (usually a year) relative to a base year value.

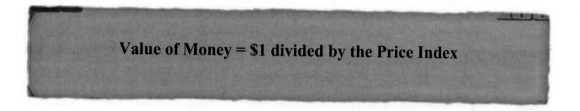

Value of Money = $1 divided by the Price Index

Assume prices increase by 10 percent from a base year in 2010 to 2011. The price index moves from 1.00 to 1.10 and, therefore, 1 divided by 1.10 = $0.909 (or 90.9 cents) for the value of the dollar in 2011 (with base year of 2010).

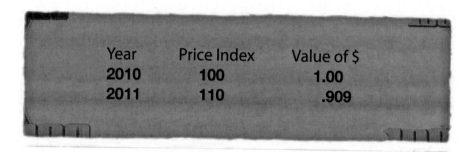

Year	Price Index	Value of $
2010	100	1.00
2011	110	.909

In a nutshell, if the price level (price index) increases due to inflation, the value of money declines. Both the operation of the federal government's fiscal policy and the operation of the Federal Reserve in appropriately controlling the size of the money supply have a major impact on the value of our money.

THE PRICE OF MONEY: INTEREST RATES

The **price of money** is the rate of interest (think "price to rent money") and is determined by <u>both</u> the supply of money and the **total demand for money**. The total demand for money is the sum of (1) <u>transactions</u> demand for money and (2) the <u>asset</u> demand for money. This total demand for money is described graphically by the quantities of money demanded (held in liquid accounts) given the various rates of interest. See Figure 10.2.

Let's look a bit closer at (1) the **transactions demand for money.** At first, you might think that the higher the rate of interest the bank will pay you on a

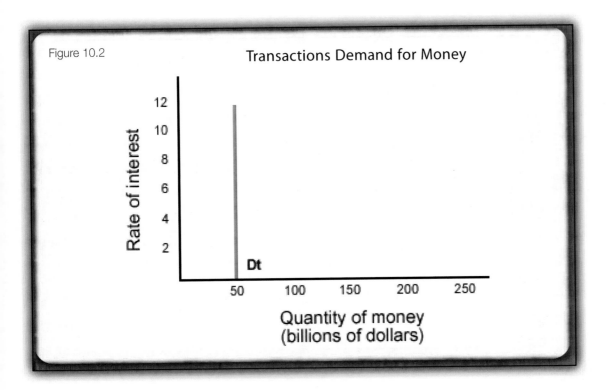

Figure 10.2

Transactions Demand for Money

nonliquid savings account (to "rent" your money), the smaller the amount of money you will tend to keep in your liquid checking account s*pecifically for transactions (paying bills)*—but it turns out that other factors seem to outweigh this initial instinct.

The transactions demand for money is most heavily influenced by the amount of **aggregate economic activity**; that is, it is closely related to the level of nominal GDP. More money is held in liquid checking accounts for transactions when nominal GDP is higher. Since money tends to be held only briefly in checking accounts for transactions (paying bills), there is actually an insensitive relationship to interest rates— the transactions demand for money (Dt) is vertical on our graph. We are assuming, then, that the transactions demand stays the same regardless of the interest rate but will shift right or left as economic

Total Demand for Money = Transactions Demand + Assets Demand

$$Dm = Dt + Da$$

activity (nominal GDP) changes. In summary, people tend to hold the same cash balances for transactions regardless of the interest rate.

The interest rate now comes more into play as we consider the asset demand for money. This is the quantity of money demanded (being held for investment purposes) at various interest rates and it is sensitive to interest rate changes. At a high rate of interest, people will tend to hold less money in their checking accounts and keep more funds "invested" (savings, certificates of deposit, bonds) to obtain the high rate of interest. At a low interest rate, people would hold more funds in their checking accounts, waiting for better opportunities. The opportunity cost of holding those funds as "money" is quite low.

This concept of opportunity cost is applied when cash is held rather than "invested" for interest. The interest payment is foregone and it is, therefore, the opportunity cost of holding "money" in the checking account. If we hold $100 and interest rates are 10 percent, we have incurred a $10 ($100 × 0.10) opportunity cost for holding "money." However, at interest rates of 2 percent, the opportunity cost is only $2 ($100 × 0.02).

This idea (low interest = high money demand, high interest = low money demand) is illustrated in Figures 10.3 and 10.4.

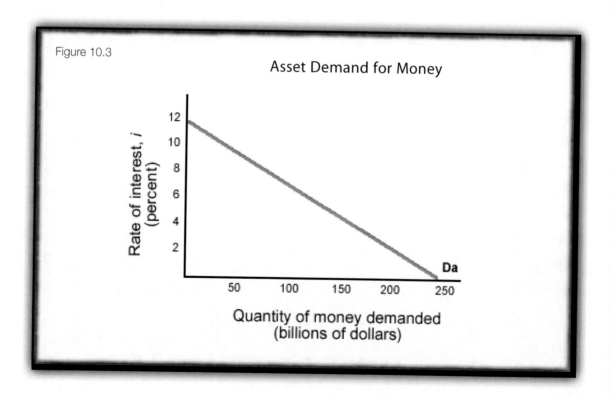

Figure 10.3

Asset Demand for Money

Rate of interest, *i* (percent)

Quantity of money demanded (billions of dollars)

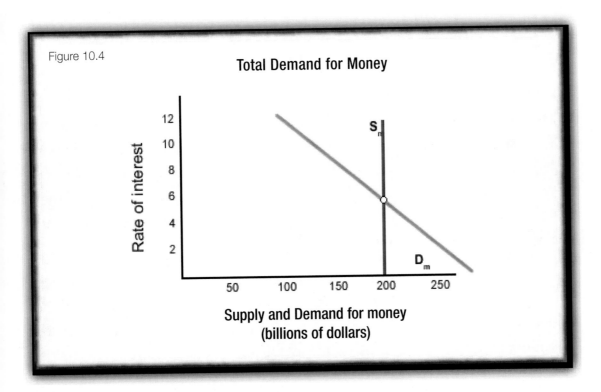

Figure 10.4

Total Demand for Money

Rate of interest

Supply and Demand for money
(billions of dollars)

The actual equilibrium rate of interest is determined by the overall demand for money (Dm = the vertical Dt plus the downward sloping Da) intersecting with the total supply of money (Sm, controlled by the Fed). The equilibrium interest rate, then, is the market price of money (think of the price of "renting" money) and is on the Y-axis (about 6 percent in this example). The equilibrium quantity of money is on the X-axis (about $200 billion in this example).

Overall, then, the supply and demand for money are plotted together in Figure 10.4. The equilibrium rate of interest is established by the total demand for money intersecting with the supply of money determined by the Fed. Increases in the supply of money (a right shift) by the Fed will, all other things being equal, decrease the equilibrium interest rate. Decreases in the money supply (a left shift) will increase that interest rate, all other things being equal.

Disequilibrium between the quantity of money demanded and the quantity supplied can be "corrected" by the buying or selling (exchanging) of financial assets (such as bonds) for the asset known as "money." This is done by the Federal Reserve. If the Fed buys bonds (pays "money" to the public for those bonds), then money supply increases (right shift) and the interest rate goes down. An inverse relationship between market interest rates and bond prices will exist because bond interest payments are set for the life of a bond and do not change as market interest rates go up and down.

Consider a situation where market interest rates are decreasing—with a bond's fixed interest payments, the only way for the market to respond to the general decrease in interest rates is for the price of the bond to increase in the marketplace (the fixed interest payments of the bond are now worth more). Remember that changes in interest rates affect people's willingness to hold money in their checking accounts. Changes in willingness to hold money will restore equilibrium in the money market.

Let's consider a specific example: When a bond is sold at 5 percent yield for 10 years, $50 (.05 x $1,000) is the interest paid each year to the holder of the bond. However, if market interest rates decrease to 4 percent, then the value of the bond is increased to $1,250 (using algebra we can solve for Y, that is, 0.04 times Y = $50 and therefore Y = $1,250). The bondholder gained $125 value because market interest rates decreased. If you are the bondholder, would you be inclined to sell the bond (exchange it for "money")?

Consider the opposite situation where the Fed is driving an increase in market interest rates: If the market interest rate increases to 6 percent, but the existing bond continues to make only $50 interest payments, the value of the bond would decrease to $833 (.06 times Y = 50, Y = $833) and the bondholder loses $167 of value. Increases in interest rates drive bond prices down. If you currently have some extra "money" in your checking account, might you be inclined to purchase this bond while it is available at a discount?

THE U.S. BANKING SYSTEM—THE FEDERAL RESERVE

The U.S. financial system encountered a number of financial panics before 1913 when very little federal intervention or regulation existed. Until that time, there was only a system of national banks with the ability to make or not make loans as individual bankers saw fit during times of distress. In a recession, business loans and loans to households were often "recalled" by the banks (full payment required) as risks of default began to increase. This led to additional decreases in the money supply and extended banking panics. The federal government finally recognized a need for a central bank after several of these bank panics brought devastation to the economy.

In 1913, President Wilson and Congress created a new central banking system to be in charge of the money supply and operate as a bank for banks as well as for the federal government. This new system consisted of a Board of Governors appointed by the president and confirmed by Congress. While the Board was the policymaking body, 12 regional banks also dispersed some of the banking power away from the Eastern banking establishment of the time.

The U.S. Banking System

The individual banking system in the United States is a **dual banking system** with both state and federal bank charters for operation. Federal banks are created through the Comptroller of the Currency and state banks are created through the state banking commission. This arrangement allows for maximum flexibility in the creation of new banks. Commercial banks are chartered either by the federal government or by the state banking commissions (about two-thirds of banks are chartered by the states and one-third by the Comptroller of the Currency).

The Federal Reserve System (the Fed) as an organization is both private and public in nature. The Federal Reserve is quasi-government and quasi-private because private banks own stock in the Fed but the institution reports to Congress and is mandated to operate in the public interest.

The Board of Governors consists of seven members appointed for 14-year terms by the U.S. president and confirmed by the Senate. The president selects the chairperson for a five-year term. The purpose of this arrangement is to make the Board less political so that board members serve under different presidents and different political parties in control of Congress.

The Board of Governors is the policymaking institution and is also responsible for the discount rate (rate of interest charged for bank borrowing) and reserve requirements (the amount of deposits that banks must hold back and not loan or invest).

The Federal Open Market Committee (FOMC) sets open market operations by buying and selling Treasury securities to influence the money supply. This committee is very influential in implementing monetary policy. The FOMC consists of 12 members, including seven members of the Board of Governors, the president of the New York Fed and four rotating Fed bank presidents. The FOMC is the source of many monetary decisions and is closely watched by participants in financial markets and all types of investors.

The Federal Advisory Council consists of private citizens who provide input to the Board of Governors. The role of the council is advisory only but it does provide a means for the public to make their thoughts on economic issues known to the Federal Reserve.

Twelve Federal Reserve Banks serve as central banks by region. The central banking function is jointly held by regional banks, but open market operations are completed by the New York Fed.

Regional banks are quasi-public—owned by commercial banks in their districts but run by the Board of Governors in the public interest. Regional banks are bankers' banks and they hold deposits of the member banks and make loans to those banks to meet reserve requirements. See Figure 10.5.

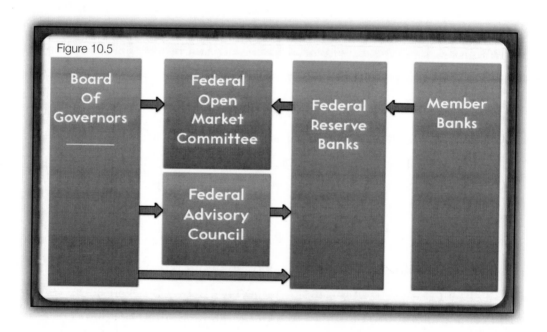

Figure 10.5

FUNCTIONS OF THE FEDERAL RESERVE

The Federal Reserve System performs many economic functions governing the health of our economy. The Fed performs the following functions:

- Issues currency by distributing Federal Reserve Notes through banks. The Fed replaces worn-out currency.

- Controls the money supply through tools of operation.

- Acts as the bankers' bank by holding bank deposits and lending money to banks.

- Provides a check "clearinghouse"—collects checks for banks by making electronic credits and debits on the deposits of the member banks.

- Provides banking services for the federal government as the bank of the federal government. The Fed is the U.S. government's bank.

- Supervises the banks in accordance with banking law.

THE FDIC

Another important quasi-public banking institution is the Federal Depositors Insurance Corporation (FDIC). This organization is essentially an insurance program that insures depositors' accounts in commercial banks in the event of a bank failure. Banks pay an insurance fee into this program and, in turn, depositors' accounts are insured up to $250,000 until December 31, 2009. This level of coverage may return to a value of only $100,000 in 2010 depending on the level of economic recovery following the 2008–2009 crisis.

BANKS AND INTERNATIONAL FINANCE

Our commercial banking system is a very dynamic industry and one that is critical to the overall well-being of our economy. Banks are constantly forced to adjust to global forces using new technology and must accommodate and compete in these new climates. Because of this, banks seek fewer restrictions on their investing and growth. With two-thirds of U.S. dollars actually circulating outside the country, the American banking system is truly global in nature.

SUMMARY APPLICATIONS OF MONETARY POLICY

If the reserve requirement is 10 percent and the Fed buys $100 million in Treasury securities (bonds) from the public, what happen to the money supply immediately and what will be the maximum lending potential change at banks from this action?

> **The money supply will increase by $100 million immediately and by $1 billion ($100 times the money multiplier or $100 times 1/.1 or $100 times 10 = $1,000,000).**

If the reserve requirement is 20 percent and the Fed sells $100 million in Treasury securities to the public, what will happen to the money supply immediately and what will be the maximum leading potential change at banks from this action?

> **The money supply will decrease by $100 million immediately and by $500 million ($100 times the money multiplier or $100 times 1/.2 or $100 times 5 = $500).**

Key Terms

Barter: The act of trading one item for another without the use of money.

Board of Governors: A seven-member board that determines policy for the financial system.

Commodity Money: Something with intrinsic value such as gold or silver.

Federal Depositor Insurance Corporation (FDIC): A quasi-public institution that insures accounts for depositors in commercial banks for up to $100,000.

Federal Advisory Council: A committee made up of private citizens that provides input to the Board of Governors.

Federal Open Market Committee: A committee made up of seven members of the Board of Governors plus five district bank presidents.

Federal Reserve: An entity established by the Federal Reserve Act of 1913 to oversee our financial system and placed under the authority of an appointed Board of Governors. The seven individuals would be appointed for 14-year terms.

Fiat Money: Money that is given value by government decree. All of the U.S. money supply is this type of money.

Legal Tender: Fiat money.

M1: The United States' basic money supply, which includes coins, currency and checkable deposits.

M2: Small-time (savings) deposits plus M1 make up this money measure.

Applied Exercises

Exercise One:

YEAR	NATIONAL MONEY SUPPLY	PRICE INDEX	REAL MONEY SUPPLY
2000	$100 Billion	100	$_____
2001	$125 Billion	110	$_____
2002	$130 Billion	120	$_____
2003	$140 Billion	110	$_____

Exercise Two:

A: What would happen to the money supply if consumers increased their deposits by $100 billion?

B: What would happen to the money supply if consumers increased their borrowing by $100 billion?

C: What would happen to the money supply if consumers paid off $100 billion in loans?

Applied Exercises

Exercise Three:

A: Assume that a $10,000 Treasury bond is issued at an interest rate of 8 percent but two years later the interest rate has increased in the market to require a 10 percent yield. What would be the price of the bond?

B: What would be the price of the bond if the interest rate dropped to 6 percent?

Applied Exercises: Answers

Exercise One:

YEAR	NATIONAL MONEY SUPPLY	PRICE INDEX	REAL MONEY SUPPLY
2000	$100 Billion	100	$100
2001	$125 Billion	110	$114 (125/110)
2002	$130 Billion	120	$108 (130/120)
2003	$140 Billion	110	$127 (140/110)

Exercise Two:

A: What would happen to the money supply if consumers increased their deposits by $100 billion?

There would be no change in M1 because cash put inside a checkable account remains part of the M1.

B: What would happen to the money supply if consumers increased their borrowing by $100 billion?

Increased loans would increase by money supply, potentially by the amount of the excess reserves. This could also be continued throughout the banking system by $100 times the multiplier.

C: What would happen to the money supply if consumers paid off $100 billion in loans?

This would decrease the money supply as money is destroyed.

Applied Exercises: Answers

Exercise Three:

A: Assume that a $10,000 Treasury bond is issued at an interest rate of 8 percent but two years later the interest rate has increased in the market to require a 10 percent yield. What would be the price of the bond?

Using simple algebra, find what is the value of the bond at 10 percent given only an interest payment of $80. .1 X = $80 therefore X = $8,000; the owner has lost $2,000 from his purchase.

B: What would be the price of the bond if the interest rate dropped to 6 percent?

.06 X = $80, therefore X = $1,333; the owner has gained $333 from his purchase.

Lesson **Eleven**
Commercial Banks: The Critical Link

The Goldsmith Principle

Modern-day banking is based on what is now called the gold-smith's principle. In the Middle Ages (1066–1485), goldsmiths held gold and other precious metals to construct elegant dining and serving pieces as well as jewelry for their wealthy patrons. The reason that the goldsmith came to be associated with banking is very simple. The goldsmiths had a safe or vault to store this valuable metal. Because coins minted from precious metals represented most of the money at that point in time, it was a logical connection for people to ask this craftsman to hold any "extra money" in his vault.

LEARNING OBJECTIVES

Please note the listed objectives. As you will see, the course materials are all objective driven. This provides you with a constant way to direct and monitor your progress throughout the course. Each objective is color-coded and corresponds to that particular section in the text.

OBJECTIVE ONE 1

Explain the Goldsmith Principle and the concept of Fractional Reserve Banking.

OBJECTIVE TWO 2

Describe the basic operations and balance sheet of a commercial bank and the role of "legal reserves" in the operations.

OBJECTIVE THREE 3

Explain the process of money creation and the role of "excess reserves" and loans in that process.

OBJECTIVE FOUR 4

Provide a numerical example of the money multiplier process and explain its significance in a dynamic macroeconomy.

OBJECTIVE FIVE 5

Describe the basic concepts of Monetary Policy as implemented by the U.S. Federal Reserve.

INTERACTIVE EXERCISE

Use the Major Economic Models to demonstrate an understanding of the chain reactions resulting from human choices and how they move through an economy. Demonstrate an understanding of the Tradeoffs that result.

The goldsmith's role expanded very rapidly because it dealt with two very important needs: safety and convenience. Coins kept on your person can be lost or stolen and they are heavy. When the coins were deposited with the goldsmith, the problem was solved. When we think about the reasons why we use banks today, the response is almost the same—safety and convenience.

FRACTIONAL RESERVE BANKING

As time passed, goldsmiths began to issue paper receipts to depositors for their gold. These receipts became "exchangeable" as depositors of gold were able to actually use these receipts as exchangeable money. In effect, goldsmiths became the first bankers. Goldsmiths formulated a principle that only 5 percent of the deposits were needed in reserve (actual gold in the vault) at any point in time. The goldsmiths then invested or made loans with the other 95 percent of the deposits that they held. The practice of holding only a small portion of total deposits in actual cash is now called the goldsmith's principle or fractional reserve banking.

A goldsmith could hold some gold in reserve for depositors' withdrawals, but then loan out excess gold (or issue new receipts as "loans") and thereby make a profit from the depositors' funds. Through this process of making a loan, money (an exchangeable receipt) was actually being created. The gold was basically accounted for in the goldsmith's reserves, but new money had also been created.

In the United States, the fractional reserve policy of banking is controlled by the Federal Reserve. Banks, under the direction of the Federal Reserve, are required to hold only a portion of depositors' funds on reserve. These "portions" vary depending on the size of the bank and other factors, but for discussion purposes, 10 percent is a realistic number to use. The Federal Reserve is able to control this process and adjust the "portion" (known as the "reserve requirement") to ensure that the money supply does not grow too rapidly or, in some cases, to actually help the money supply to grow.

In order to control the size of the money supply, government created measures to monitor the quantity of money. M1 is the narrow measure of the money supply and consists of currency in the hands of the public and their checkable deposits (see Lesson 10). Recall that currency includes both paper money and coins. Federal Reserve Notes are the currency printed by the U.S. Bureau of Engraving and coins are produced by the U.S. Mint. Actual changes in the money supply, however, relate mainly to changes in checkable deposits that are determined largely by the Fed and the banking system.

COMMERCIAL BANKS

The business operations of a commercial bank can be illustrated through the changes in its balance sheet. The statement of Assets (accounts of value such as a bank's building and cash in the vault from deposits) and Liabilities (claims on the assets such as the mortgage on the bank's building and the depositors' claims on those deposits in the vault) follow the basic accounting format:

$$Assets = Liabilities + Net\ Worth$$

- Assets or total value of all resources.

- Liabilities or claims by creditors and depositors.

- Net worth or value of investment by stockholders of the bank.

With a double-entry accounting system, the deposits of the bank's customers are both a liability and an asset for the bank. When a customer deposits funds, the cash account (assets) increases in the bank, but the liability of the bank also increases as a balancing factor within the equation.

When a bank deposits funds with the Federal Reserve, the deposits of the bank are an asset of the Fed because its cash has increased, but the deposit is also a liability of the Fed—the Fed "owes" the money to the bank that made the deposit. Likewise, bank deposits with the Fed are assets of the bank making the deposit.

When a customer deposits $100 of currency into her checking account at a commercial bank, there is change within the accounting equation—but no change in M1. The currency circulating outside the bank decreases, but the checkable deposits within the bank increase. In summary, Change in M1 = currency outside banks (−$100) + checkable deposits (+100) = No change.

BANKING OPERATIONS

A single bank's operation is created when a bank is formed through a charter granted by a state or by the U.S. Comptroller of the Currency. Compliance with legal requirements is complex but necessary to assure banking integrity and success.

A discussion on the banking process is provided by the Dallas Federal Reserve in the "Everyday Economics" article. "Banks provide many services, but for most people, banking consists of depositing their salaries into checking accounts and writing checks on that account to buy things and pay the bills." Note: Using a debit card is, in effect, writing a check on your account to buy something or to pay a bill.

People also commonly have savings accounts in which they deposit money they don't need right away or that they are saving for a particular purpose. The bank pays interest (a "rental price") for use of the depositor's money (recall the "goldsmith principle"). Banks will also pay interest on some types of checking accounts and allow you to write limited checks on some types of savings (or "money market") accounts.

A bank becomes a "going concern" (an active business) after meeting all regulatory requirements of the federal and state governments and the Federal Reserve. A bank may then begin operations and accept depositors' funds. Once again, it is a government requirement for maintaining a bank that a specified amount (known as "required reserves") of depositors' funds must be held in the form of "legal reserves" (the bank can then loan or invest the remainder of the depositors' funds).

The **legal reserves** are the particular types of assets that a bank can use to meet the "required reserves" requirement. Legal reserves include only cash in the vault and deposits with the Fed—the bank's building or its company car cannot be used as part of "legal reserves" to meet the "required reserves" requirement.

> Legal Reserves = Cash in vault + Deposits with the Fed

The "Required Reserve" Requirement

Required Reserves are mandated by the Fed to exert control over the amount of depositor funds that banks can loan out. The purpose of Required Reserves is not so much to guarantee the solvency (avoid bankruptcy) of a bank as it is to control the growth of the Money Supply. The Fed is committed to the stability of money and the Financial Markets (the centerpiece of the Circular Flow). This requires that the Money Supply grow fast enough but not too fast.

The reserve requirements actually vary for an individual bank depending on the type of deposit that is made in a bank and the size of the bank. The average reserve requirement (as mentioned earlier) is about 10 percent. The amount of depositors' funds that are above and beyond the Required Reserves are called Excess Reserves and may be loaned out by the bank.

The Equations—Concepts of Fractional Reserve Banking

$$\text{Excess Reserves} = \text{Legal Reserves} - \text{Required Reserves}$$

Recall that:

Legal Reserves of a bank must be in the form of cash in the vault or a deposit with the Fed.

Required Reserves are the minimum amount of funds that must be held in a legal form as a set-aside from customer deposits.

Excess Reserves are reserves held in legal form that are greater than those required and these can be loaned out.

An alternate arrangement of the "Excess Reserves" equation presented above is:

$$\text{Legal Reserves} = \text{Required Reserves} + \text{Excess Reserves}$$

Money Creation

How is money created in our modern banking system? To answer this question, let's assume you deposit $100 of currency into your checking account. If $100 cash is deposited in Bank A with a 10 percent reserve requirement, Bank A must hold $10 ($100 × .10) back in a legal reserve form as a required reserve—but it may loan out $90 ($100 − $10 = $90) to other customers from this $100 deposit.

These money-creating transactions (banks making loans) directly affect the money supply. Simply stated, when banks make loans, banks create money—the money loaned is usually deposited in the customer's checking account. Additional money is created in the loan process because when one bank makes a loan, these loaned funds are spent and then deposited by the recipient at another bank and can be loaned out and deposited in a third bank.

As an example: In Bank A, a loan of $90 is made to a customer to buy clothing; the funds from the customer's loan (when spent) are deposited by the clothing store into its account in Bank B. Bank B can then hold 10 percent of $90 (or $9) and loans $81 to another customer, who spends the funds for shoes with another merchant, which deposits $81 in its shoe store account at Bank C and the process continues.

This process is well described by the previously cited article "Everyday Economics" by the Dallas Federal Reserve: "Banks actually create money when they lend it. Here's how it works: Most of a bank's loans are made to its own customers and are deposited in their checking accounts. Because the loan becomes a new deposit, just like a paycheck does, the bank once again holds a small percentage of that new amount in reserve and again lends the remainder to someone else, repeating the money-creation process many times." For more information on money and banking, see the Dallas Federal Reserve site at http://dallasfed.org/educate/everyday/ev9.html.

When a check is drawn (cashed) against a customer's account at a bank, not only are the Legal Reserves (cash) decreased but also the bank's liability for the deposit. Each bank is responsible to the Fed to report their Legal Reserves as well as their deposit liabilities (depositors' funds) on a frequent basis.

Commercial banks also create new money when they buy government securities such as Treasury bonds from the public. The bank gives funds to the individual bondholder and these funds are then part of M1, or cash outside of the bank's vault. Also, the money supply decreases when a commercial bank sells securities to the public. When a bank takes in money from the public (out of depositor accounts and into the bank vault), there is less money available outside of banks.

Money also can be destroyed by banks. Money is destroyed when a customer repays a loan. When a loan is repaid, there are fewer funds available in the money system. However, this is a dynamic process with new loans being made as old loans are repaid. The difference is often an expanding value of loans outstanding in a growing economy.

Because banks are required to maintain a reserve (or set aside) for checkable and many other types of customer deposits, the higher this reserve requirement, the lower bank profits will be because these funds (required reserves) cannot be invested or loaned to customers.

DEPOSIT EXPANSION MULTIPLIER

The **Money Multiplier**—the commercial banking system as a whole can lend by a multiple of its excess reserves because the banking <u>system</u> as a whole does not lose reserves (although individual banks can lose reserves to other banks). When Bank A makes a loan, the funds are deposited into the customer's account at Bank A. The customer then spends the funds at Business Q, which results in the funds being transferred to Bank B (where Business Q has an account). Bank B can now loan the funds again (except for the Required Reserve). This process of money creation within the system results in a multiple expansion of the Money Supply (M1).

The multiple by which the banking system can lend on the basis of each dollar of excess reserves is the reciprocal of the reserve ratio. This multiple credit expansion process is also reversible (a contraction) when loans are repaid.

Money Multiplier = 1 / Reserve Requirement

Total Expansion of Money = Excess Reserves x Money Multiplier

Consider the following example of the money multiplier concept: Assume $1,000 of currency is deposited in a checkable account by Mr. X in Bank A. Assume further that the reserve requirement is 0.10, meaning that Bank A must hold back at least $100 ($1,000 times 0.1 or $100) but can loan out the excess ($1,000 − 100 or $900). The total amount of money that can be created in the banking system by this excess reserve at Bank A is the $900 excess times the money multiplier.

Remember that the money multiplier is 1/reserve requirement or $1/0.1 = 10$. Therefore, $900 times 10 equals a total of $9,000 that might be created through the system by this excess once it is set in motion.

LIMITS OF DEPOSIT EXPANSION

The multiplier process is limited by leaks of currency as individuals may hold ("keep out") some of the cash from their loan or banks may not "fully loan out." Banks often maintain a safety margin. Especially during recessions, banks may not be willing to lend all their excess reserves or borrowers may not be willing to borrow. Any of these conditions will limit the amount of expansion experienced through the money multiplier—the amount of expansion can be substantially less than the maximum.

Let's consider a more complete example: If we assume a required reserve of 20 percent, $r = 0.2$, and further assume a person deposits $100 of currency into First Bank, then First Bank must hold back $20 but has excess reserves of $80 ($100 \times 0.2 = $20 required reserve). The excess reserve is $100 − $20 = $80. If First Bank lends out the $80, which is deposited in Second Bank, then Second Bank is required to hold $16 but has excess of $64 to lend. The loan of $64 gets deposited into Third Bank, which lends out $51.20 and the process continues. The total amount of increase in the money supply is the excess from the first transaction times the money multiplier, or $80 \times 1/0.2 = $80 \times 5 = $400 in this example.

A modification and extension of an earlier example is illustrated in Figure 11.1. Assume a 10 percent reserve requirement with a $100 cash deposit into Bank A.

Figure 11.1

Bank	Reserves Gain	Req. Res	Excess Res	Money Created
A	$100.00	$10.00	$ 90.00	$ 90.00
B	90.00	9.00	81.00	81.00
C	81.00	8.10	72.90	72.90
D	72.90	7.29	65.81	65.81
E	65.81	6.58	59.23	59.23
All Other	--	--	--	471.17
Money Created:				$ 900.00

The maximum money created is the money multiplier times the excess reserves. With $100 deposited in Bank A, $90 in excess reserves exists times the money multiplier (1/reserve requirement = 1/0.1=10), resulting in $90 times 10 = $900 in new maximum money created.

This same process works in reverse when a loan is repaid because fewer funds are available and the amount of money that is destroyed is equal to the loan repayment times the money multiplier.

The amount of money creation (and sometimes "contraction") is monitored carefully by the Fed because it is the Federal Reserve's responsibility to maintain a stable money supply and promote growth. The process of controlling the money supply is a "tremendous responsibility" because the health of the economy is at stake. Recall that the Fed was created by Congress to be independent so that political considerations would not drive its actions.

MONETARY POLICY

The money control process is called **monetary policy.** Monetary policy consists of several tools to influence the growth of the money supply. An active involvement by the Fed in the money creation (or destruction) process is often needed to promote a healthy economy.

Monetary policy is considered to be "**easy**" when the money supply is increasing *rapidly*, but it is considered "**tight**" when the money supply is increasing *slowly*. During periods of recession, an easy money policy is appropriate to encourage business expansion with low interest rates. During a period of inflation, a tight money policy is recommended to control excessive expansion of the money supply that causes inflation. The balancing of these efforts is difficult because the economy is constantly changing and each action by the Fed has a lag effect as well as an interactive effect on related variables (i.e., the value of the dollar in the currency markets). Overall, there must be a healthy balance between maintaining banking stability for the nation and allowing banks to operate profitably and provide necessary liquidity for borrowers.

Banks assume a very important role in the economy by providing funds for credit markets and allowing savers a channel for their funds to be deposited and held safely. A strong banking system facilitates the savings and investment process that is highlighted in the Circular Flow Animations—this is essential for the economic stability and growth of any society.

The entire banking system in the United States depends on the trust and confidence of the public. The public must have confidence in both the commercial banks and the Fed's commitment to protect their deposits as well as the purchasing power of their money. The proper implementation of monetary policy by the Fed is very important in this process, but so too is the operation of the federal government in fiscal policy.

Our economy is a flow of goods and services created and consumed by individuals and businesses. These flows are enabled by a strong banking and financial system as well as by appropriate government policy. The proper role of the Fed and the federal government is to facilitate the "flow" and ensure its viability.

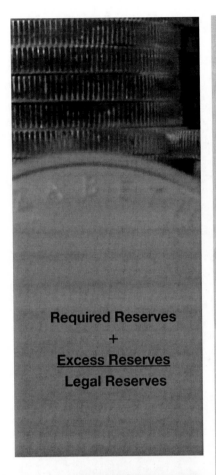

Required Reserves
+
Excess Reserves
Legal Reserves

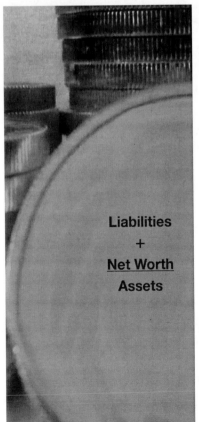

Liabilities
+
Net Worth
Assets

Lesson Summary and Application

Banking has a long history emanating from the Middle Ages, when goldsmiths issued receipts for gold deposits and thus created the first "paper money."

Goldsmiths found they could maintain a reserve on deposits of only 5 percent and loan or invest 95 percent, thereby gaining interest or profits. This process created money within the society as gold receipts began to circulate and loans were made to create and purchase even more goods.

The goldsmiths' principle became known in modern banking as the fractional reserve system. Banks today maintain a reserve on their customers' deposits but loan or invest most of those funds, holding only that fractional reserve.

Money creation today is largely determined through the bank loan process. Because banks must hold back required reserves (cash in the vault or deposits with the Federal Reserve), this allows the Federal Reserve to control the quantity of money being created.

The important formula for **Bank Reserves** is:

Legal Reserves = Required Reserves + Excess Reserves

Overall, banks account for their funds through the **bookkeeping equation**:

Assets = Liabilities + Net Worth

Net worth (the value of the investment made by stockholders into a bank) *plus*

Liabilities (largely composed of the bank customers' deposits) *equals*

Assets (primarily composed of the loans and investments a bank has made with its depositors' funds).

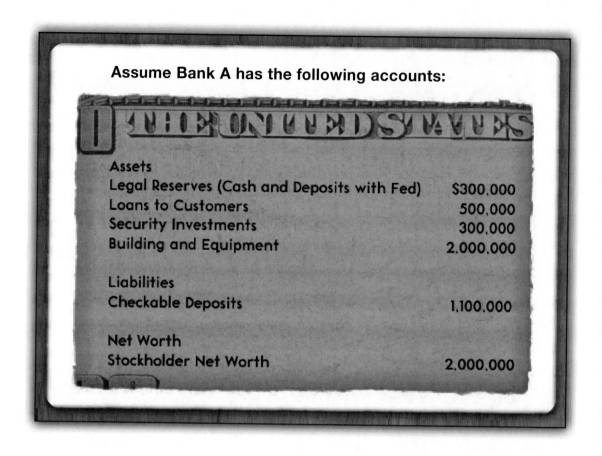

Assume Bank A has the following accounts:

THE UNITED STATES

Assets
Legal Reserves (Cash and Deposits with Fed)	$300,000
Loans to Customers	500,000
Security Investments	300,000
Building and Equipment	2,000,000

Liabilities
Checkable Deposits	1,100,000

Net Worth
Stockholder Net Worth	2,000,000

If Bank A must hold required reserve of 20 percent of checkable deposits, how much is available for loans (excess reserves)?

Given the information above, we know that deposits are $1,100,000 and Bank A must hold back a required reserve of 20 percent or $1,100,000 times .2 = $220,000 but there is a legal reserve of $300,000, therefore, $300,000 – $220,000 leaves an excess reserve of $80,000 that can be loaned.

The amount of money creation is constrained by an individual bank to the amount of excess reserves. This is the maximum amount that an individual bank may loan, however, the banking system as a whole can increase the money supply by the amount of the excess reserve times the money multiplier. This is possible because as a bank makes a loan, these funds are transferred to another bank that can loan the excess from the deposit transferred from the other bank. The maximum amount of possible expansion in funds is limited to the money multiplier times the excess reserves.

The Money Multiplier = 1/Required Reserve = 1/.2 = 5

The Excess Reserve is $80,000 times 5 = a maximum expansion of $400,000 if all banks receiving transfers are fully loaned out.

The banking process allows for both money creation and money destruction. When a loan is made, money is created and when a loan is repaid, money is destroyed. The expansion or contraction is multiplied by the money multiplier in either direction. The process is highly dynamic within the banking system as loans are made and repaid continually but the net difference is the effect on the money system. The money multiplier is the maximum multiplier to the creation or contraction of the net money position.

The process of expansion or contraction is limited by both consumers and banks. If consumers do not spend all the borrowed funds or banks do not fully loan out all the excess funds transferred, then the amount of the multiple change is lessened. In periods of economic growth, banks will hold fewer excess reserves; in recessionary times, banks will hold more excess reserves.

Finally, apply money and banking applications to your banking activity. Consider that you put $100 into Bank X that has a 20 percent required reserve. How much can Bank X loan to other customers? Because Bank X must keep back $20, it can loan out $80 and this can be expanded within the banking system to $80 times the multiplier of 5 (1/.2) or $400 maximum.

What would happen if the next day you wrote a check for $40 on your account within Bank X? Bank X now has only $60 of your money and can only lend out $48 because it must hold back $12. The banking system now can only expand from your deposit by $48 times 5 or $240.

Real-World Economics

Please access links through online E-text.

Key Terms

Commercial Bank: A profit-centered entity chartered and regulated by either the state or the Federal Reserve.

Demand of Checkable Deposits: Money that is deposited in a bank must be returned to the depositor when it is demanded (i.e., when a check is written).

Deposit Expansion Multiplier: The process of money creation as one bank loan is spent, redeposited in another bank and so on. Fractional reserve banking allows this process to create new money by a multiple of the reserve.

Excess Reserves: Deposits that are in excess of the required reserve and made to be loaned out.

Federal Reserve: A quasi-public body established by the Federal Reserve Act or 1913, which gave this entity regulatory authority over our commercial banking system.

Fractional Reserve Banking: Under our commercial banking system, banks are only required to keep a fraction of total deposits on reserve. The remaining balance can then be loaned to someone else.

Goldsmith Principle: The historical beginning of fractional reserve banking as local craftsmen allowed the deposit of coins.

Legal Reserves: Bank monies that must be held with the Fed or kept as vault cash at the bank.

Monetary Policy: Actions taken by the Federal Reserve (and directed to banks) to influence the availability and cost of the bank credit. This may result in either a tight or easy money policy depending on the business cycle.

Required Reserves: Bank monies that must be held and legally set aside from other deposits.

Vault Cash: Money kept in the bank vault in the form of cash.

Applied Exercises

Exercise One:

Given the following Bank Y balance sheet, complete the questions below.

Bank X

Assets		Liabilities	
Reserves	$120,000	Deposits	$300,000
Investments	180,000	Net Worth	500,000
Property	500,000		

A: If the required reserve is 20 percent, how much are the required reserves?

B: Given the Reserves above, what is the maximum that Bank Y can increase loans?

C: If the required reserve was changed to 15 percent, how much could loans be increased?

Exercise Two:

Calculate the money multiplier given the following required reserves:

Required Reserve	Money Multiplier
10 percent	_____
20 percent	_____
25 percent	_____

Applied Exercises

Exercise Three:

Given the following balance sheet, for the banking system with a 30 percent reserve requirement, complete the questions below.

Assets		Liabilities	
Reserves	$100	Deposits	$150
Investments	100	Net Worth	170
Property	120		

A: How much excess reserves are in the system?

B: How much can the system expand the supply of money?

C: How much would excess reserves be if the system makes loans to its maximum?

Applied Exercises: Answers

Exercise One:

A: If the required reserve is 20 percent, how much are the required reserves? **.2 times $300 = $60.**

B: Given the Reserves above, what is the maximum that Bank X can increase loans? **$120−$60 = $60**

C: If the required reserve was changed to 15 percent, how much could loans be increased? **.15 times $300 = $45 required and $120 in reserve so $120 − $45 = $75.**

Exercise Two:

Calculate the money multiplier given the following required reserves:

Required Reserve	Money Multiplier
10 percent	_____ 1/.1 = 10
20 percent	_____ 1/.2 = 5
25 percent	_____ 1/.25 = 4

Exercise Three:

A: How much excess reserves are in the system? **.2 times $140 = $28 required with $22 excess ($50 − $28 =)**

B: How much can the system expand the supply of money? **The money multiplier = 1/reserve requirement = 1/.2 = 5. Excess reserves times the money multiplier = maximum expansion = 5 times $22 = $110**

C: How much would excess reserves be if the system makes loans to its maximum? **If the system has reached its maximum, there could be no immediate loan increase. There would be no ability to expand if there were no excess reserves present.**

Lesson **Twelve**
The Federal Reserve and Monetary Policy

Monetary Policy

Monetary policy is the management of the money supply by the Federal Reserve to best achieve price stability, full employment and economic growth. Most of the Fed's policy is directed toward commercial banks and attempts to influence the banks' lending ability by making money (M1) either more or less available to borrowers. The cost of credit or the "rental price" of money is the interest rate. Monetary policy is determined by the Fed but still must be coordinated with the federal government (fiscal policy) through U.S. Treasury operations. Monetary policy is an essential counter-cycle tool.

LEARNING OBJECTIVES

Please note the listed objectives. As you will see, the course materials are all objective driven. This provides you with a constant way to direct and monitor your progress throughout the course. Each objective is color-coded and corresponds to that particular section in the text.

OBJECTIVE ONE | 1

Provide a basic definition of Monetary Policy and describe the primary and secondary tools of Monetary Policy.

OBJECTIVE TWO | 2

Explain the advantages and disadvantages of Monetary Policy and the concept of "easy money" and "tight money."

OBJECTIVE THREE | 3

Describe the minor controls of Monetary Policy.

OBJECTIVE FOUR | 4

Demonstrate an understanding of the "Equation of Exchange" and provide a numerical example.

OBJECTIVE FIVE | 5

Describe the Quantity Theory of Money and describe the ongoing debate between Monetarists and Keynesians regarding government involvement in the macro-economy.

INTERACTIVE EXERCISE

Use the Major Economic Models to demonstrate an understanding of the chain reactions resulting from human choices and how they move through an economy. Demonstrate an understanding of the Tradeoffs that result.

THE OBJECTIVES OF MONETARY POLICY

If you remember the objectives of fiscal policy from Lesson 9, then you have a good start here in Lesson 12. The objectives of monetary policy are basically the same but the "tools" (introduced in Lesson 11) are different. The Federal Reserve is attempting to promote a growing economy with more and better jobs within a stable (noninflationary) environment. Although the tools are different, the intent is basically the same as fiscal policy.

THE TOOLS OF MONETARY POLICY

The Fed regulates the money supply by using its major or quantitative tools of operation. As the term "major" implies, these are the primary tools used to meet Fed objectives. All of these primary tools will affect the availability and cost (interest rates) of bank credit. These tools can indirectly affect the lending ability of financial institutions to create checkbook money through loans as well as directly affecting the supply of money through the buying and selling of government securities. The level of required reserves (depositor funds that banks "hold back") is also very important.

The Major Fed Tools are:

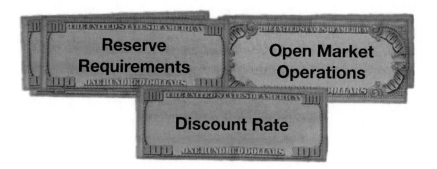

The Fed's most powerful tool is the control of reserve requirements. The Fed sets the minimum percentage of depositor funds that must be retained by commercial banks in legal reserves (cash in the vault or deposits with the Fed). The reserve requirement varies according to the size of the financial institution and the type of deposit. Changing this percentage not only changes the availability of excess reserves, but it also changes the money multiplier. With this "double impact," this tool is obviously very powerful and is, therefore, used infrequently by the Fed, which prefers a more gradual approach when possible.

The **discount rate** is the interest rate charged to commercial banks when they borrow from the Fed to meet reserve requirements. The discount rate is set monthly and is a highly visible tool of Fed operations. The Fed is known as the "lender of last resort" for commercial banks. A financial institution with a loss of deposits can usually (but not automatically) borrow from the Fed, if it cannot borrow elsewhere, to maintain its required reserves.

The **Federal Open Market Committee (FOMC)** directs the buying and selling of securities (usually U.S. Treasury securities) to influence the nation's money supply. The open market operations of the FOMC are the most frequently used tool of the Fed because they are effective in changing reserves in a gradual manner.

Open Market Operations

In a recession, the money supply can be increased when the Fed buys securities. Through this purchase of Treasury securities, the Fed sends money into the bank's or public's hands and the bank or public sends the securities to the Fed. When the Fed sends the money to the seller's bank account, the bank itself then holds more funds (excess reserves) from which it can make loans. Purchase of securities directly from a bank results in an increase in the bank's legal reserves and also results in more "excess reserves" and, therefore, the potential for new loans for increases in the supply of money (M1).

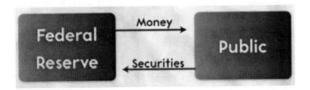

In an inflationary period, the money supply can be restrained (or even contracted) by the Fed selling securities. The above process is reversed when the Fed sells securities to the banks (or the public). When the Fed sells securities, banks have fewer excess reserves to make available for loans

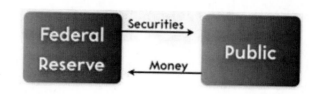

and the public has less money in their checking accounts, therefore, M1 has declined.

Open market operations (OMO) as described above take place through buy/sell agreements coordinated by the Fed with the Treasury. Each action is targeted for its impact on interest rates and the growth in the money supply. The following quote from the New York Federal Reserve explains the key concepts of OMO.

Open Market Operations: Key Concepts

- "Temporary open market operations involve repurchase and reverse repurchase agreements that are designed to temporarily add or drain reserves available to the banking system.

- Permanent open market operations involve the buying and selling of securities outright to permanently add or drain reserves available to the banking system.

- The federal funds rate is the interest rate at which depository institutions lend their balances at the Federal Reserve to other depository institutions overnight."

Source: New York Federal Reserve

You notice from the information above that open market operations involve short-term interventions in the financial market to smooth interest rates and also longer-term "permanent open market operations" to change the long-term money supply.

The Fed as a Bank

An understanding of the basic accounts of financial institutions and the Fed is important to grasp the process of monetary policy. Recall from Lesson 11 that the balance sheet equation of bookkeeping is Assets = Liabilities + Net Worth. The Fed, like all financial institutions, has assets that it obtains from stockholders, lenders to the bank or depositors.

Balance Sheet of the Federal Reserve* (in millions) 2009

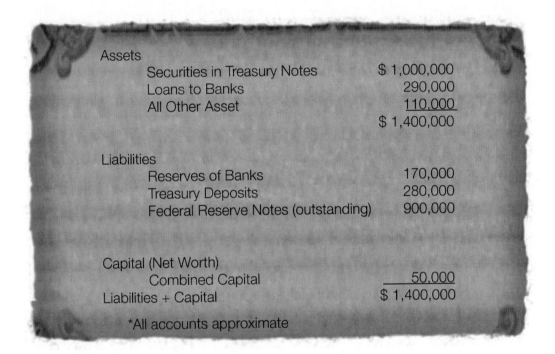

Assets	
Securities in Treasury Notes	$ 1,000,000
Loans to Banks	290,000
All Other Asset	110,000
	$ 1,400,000
Liabilities	
Reserves of Banks	170,000
Treasury Deposits	280,000
Federal Reserve Notes (outstanding)	900,000
Capital (Net Worth)	
Combined Capital	50,000
Liabilities + Capital	$ 1,400,000
*All accounts approximate	

The assets of the Fed include investments in U.S. Treasury bills, bonds, notes, loans (at the discount rate) to banks and selected other necessary operating assets. Liabilities include the funds deposited by banks into the Fed, the checking account balance of the U.S. Treasury and the Federal Reserve Notes outstanding. Federal Reserve Notes are the paper money issued by the Fed that is the currency in circulation. The capital account (net worth) includes the investment that the commercial banks are required to make in the Fed as a corporation.

The actions of the Fed were dramatic in 2008 and 2009 as reflected by major changes in the Federal Reserve Balance Sheet. These changes caused the

Federal Reserve to issue a statement explaining the positions on the balance sheet at that time. The following statement was released by the Federal Reserve on April 3, 2009 from Chairman Ben S. Bernanke:

The Federal Reserve's Balance Sheet

In ordinary financial and economic times, my topic, "The Federal Reserve's Balance Sheet," might not be considered a "grabber." But these are far from ordinary times. To address the current crisis, the Federal Reserve has taken a number of aggressive and creative policy actions, many of which are reflected in the size and composition of the Fed's balance sheet. So, I thought that a brief guided tour of our balance sheet might be an instructive way to discuss the Fed's policy strategy and some related issues. As I will discuss, we no longer live in a world in which central bank policies are confined to adjusting the short-term interest rate. Instead, by using their balance sheets, the Federal Reserve and other central banks are developing new tools to ease financial conditions and support economic growth." See the Fed statement at:

http://www.federalreserve.gov/newsevents/speech/bernanke20090403a.htm

This statement notes the role of the Fed's balance sheet in reflecting the dramatic changes in monetary policy that were used in an attempt to resist a major recession/depression. The role of the Fed is critical when the economy experiences a financial crisis as it did beginning in 2007. The traditional tools of the Fed together with fiscal policy are used in an attempt to counter downward forces in the economy. There is further discussion on this topic at the end of this Lesson.

EASY MONEY AND TIGHT MONEY

Fed tools are used to control the money supply in various ways. As discussed above, when the Fed wants to increase the money supply (easy money), it buys Treasury securities. The securities held by the public are exchanged for cash (the transfer of funds from the Fed to the bank). These funds are held by banks that can then extend more loans and this increases the money supply by a multiple of the original amount.

The money supply is also expanded when a commercial bank purchases securities from the public because the funds move from the commercial bank "vault" into the public's hands. Remember that only depositor funds (not the bank's funds) are counted as part of the money supply.

The money supply decreases (tight money) when bank reserves decrease. Once again, when the Fed sells Treasury securities or when a bank sells Treasury securities, the reserves will decrease. The public decreases checking account balances in order to buy the Treasury securities.

The Reserve Ratio

As noted at the start of this Lesson, the money supply is affected through changes in the reserve ratio. When the Fed decreases reserve requirements, banks are required to "hold back" less legal reserve on depositors' accounts and can, therefore, make more loans. Once again, as more loans are made, the money supply expands by a multiple amount. Increasing the reserve ratio decreases the ability of banks to create money (make loans) and also dec

The Discount Rate

The Discount Rate, as noted above, is the interest rate that the Fed charges banks to borrow funds to meet the reserve requirement. The discount rate is, in effect, the "wholesale cost" of funds. A higher discount rate tends to decrease bank reserves because the price of loans increases. Higher interest rates result in less borrowing as fewer projects become viable for a business profit. Conversely, a lower discount rate tends to increase bank reserves and encourages business expansion.

Enacting Monetary Policy

Basic concepts of the Fed's use of tools:

> 1. Easy money (money is readily available)
>   - a. Federal Reserve buys securities
>   - b. Reserve ratio could be reduced
>   - c. Discount rate could be reduced

"Easy" money (expansionary) chain reaction:

Fed buys securities and/or decreases reserve ratio and/or decreases the discount rate, which:

- Causes an increase in the money supply

- Results in a decrease in interest rates

- Causing an increase in aggregate demand because business investment increases

- Causing an increase in employment, output and income

> 2. Tight money (money is not readily available)
>   - a. Federal Reserve sells securities
>   - b. Reserve ratio could be raised
>   - c. Discount rate could be raised

Fed sells securities and/or increases reserve ratio and/or increases the discount rate, which:

- Causes a decrease in the money supply

- Results in an increase in interest rates

- Causing a decrease in aggregate demand because business investment decreases

- Causing a decrease in employment, output and income

POLICY TOOLS IMPACT

Each of the major tools of the Fed varies in the amount of its use and its impact. Open market operations are the most important because they are used most frequently and most effectively. The effectiveness of a change in the discount rate depends on commercial banks' reaction to the change. Banks may or may not change their lending practices in reaction to a change in the discount rate. The reserve ratio is too powerful to be changed very often because even a small change can be magnified in a large way throughout the banking system.

MINOR CONTROLS

The Federal Reserve has other tools that are less influential than the three major tools.

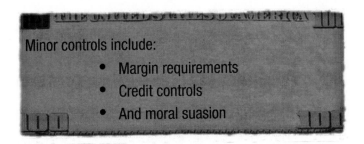

Minor controls include:
- Margin requirements
- Credit controls
- And moral suasion

Margin requirements set the <u>minimum</u> amount of a buyer's own cash that must be invested to purchase securities. The margin requirement as of this writing is 50 percent. The purpose of margin requirements is to lessen speculation in the securities markets. If you purchase Ford Motor Company stock today, you would be required to have at least half of the funds in cash. If you purchase $10,000 of stock, you must have at least $5,000 of your own funds invested, but you could borrow up to $5,000 from a broker or bank to complete the purchase.

The Fed also has **credit controls** that set the length of time <u>and</u> the amount of down payment on consumer credit purchases. During a recession, the amount of time allowed to repay a loan can be extended and the amount of the down payment decreased to encourage consumer purchases. During an inflationary period the amount of time allowed to repay a loan can be decreased and the amount of the down payment increased to discourage consumer purchases.

Finally, the Fed can <u>suggest</u> bank loan funding that would benefit the national economy. The activity is called **moral suasion** and is the application of "positive influence" and not force to encourage banks to increase or decrease loan activity as is appropriate for the national economy. In periods of inflation, restraint on loans is encouraged, whereas in periods of recession, loan growth might be encouraged. Banks are normally reluctant to increase loans in a recession because of increased risk of non-payment by consumers/businesses and are more likely to increase loans in inflationary periods because of increased business activity/profits. A "suggestion" from the Fed can help move things along in a better direction.

The Advantages and Disadvantages of Monetary Policy

Monetary policy is a powerful tool that has a direct effect on the equilibrium level of GDP as well as Net Domestic Product (NDP) and on the aggregate price level. The financial markets can be strongly influenced by the Fed, but ultimately it is these markets that determine interest rates. In turn, these interest rates are critical in determining the amount of business investment because of their effect on costs and, therefore, profits. The level of GDP/NDP is directly affected by the amount of aggregate demand that includes business investment. Interest rates are obviously a critical link in this economic process.

When there is an **easy money policy** (expansion), the Fed helps increase the money supply, and interest rates are reduced. Business investment increases because the cost of doing business is reduced. This in turn increases aggregate demand as well as GDP/NDP.

When there is a **tight money policy** (contraction), the economic relationships work in the opposite direction. A reduction in the money supply growth increases interest rates, which decreases business investment. This in turn decreases aggregate demand and increases GDP/NDP.

Advantages of Monetary Policy:

Speed and Flexibility

Isolation from Political Pressure

Equal Impact

ADVANTAGES (BENEFITS) OF MONETARY POLICY

The effectiveness of monetary policy is widely believed to be very significant because of three basic advantages:

SPEED AND FLEXIBILITY

The ability of the Fed to react very quickly to influence economic conditions is a major advantage. This phenomenon was witnessed on several occasions but especially with the attack in New York on 9/11/01. The Federal Reserve immediately intervened to reverse the dramatic loss of funds from the money supply caused by the panic within the financial markets. If you recall, speed of implementation was a major disadvantage with fiscal policy.

ISOLATED FROM POLITICAL PRESSURE

Second, monetary policy is considered effective because it is largely isolated from political pressure. The members of the Board of Governors do not have to answer directly to the President or Congress. This was one of the reasons for structuring the Fed with some level of independence. The Fed was created by Congress and must periodically report back to Congress, but it maintains its independence on a day-to-day basis.

EQUAL IMPACT

Finally, monetary policy is thought by many to be effective because its operations equally impact all citizens without regard to income, location or politics, but this may not be the case with fiscal policy.

Disadvantages of Monetary Policy (Costs, Risks and Limitations)

As with all economic activities, the implementation of monetary policy does have some costs and risks as well as its critics.

Recession

Critics argue that monetary policy is more effective in controlling inflation, but it is ineffective in moving the economy from recession to growth. Clearly the impact of monetary policy is greater in reducing inflation by increasing interest rates, but it is less successful at inducing businesses to expand in a recession. It might be more accurate to say that in a recession, the Fed can induce businesses to contract less than they would have had the Fed not intervened.

Contractionary Monetary Policy

Another criticism is that implementation of contractionary monetary policy can result in a reduction in the private sector through the crowding-out effect. Contractionary monetary policy with higher interest rates can actually expand government relative to the private sector.

Unequal Impact

Some critics also argue that monetary policy does not impact all individuals equally because real estate and construction (for instance) are significantly more affected by interest rate changes than other areas of the economy.

Disadvantages of Monetary Policy:

Recession

Contractionary Monetary Policy

Unequal Impact

VELOCITY DEBATE

A final problem of monetary policy is the difficulty in controlling the velocity of money (velocity is the average number of times a dollar is spent during a year). With the complexity of economic activity, the turnover (velocity) of money is not directly controlled by the Fed. The speed of money turnover is determined by spending pressure in the economy.

As you would expect with a relatively fixed supply of money, during periods of growing GDP, the velocity of money increases as money is spent more rapidly. In a recession, velocity will slow down.

MONEY SUPPLY GROWTH TARGETS

Monetary policy is often targeted on a particular variable as a guide for monitoring the effects of policy changes. In the past, the Fed has specifically targeted the growth in M1 and M2—at other times, it has targeted changes in specific interest rates. Although money supply growth ultimately affects interest rates, each target is somewhat different. At the time of this writing, the Fed was actually targeting the federal funds rate (interest rates banks charge each other on overnight loans to meet reserve requirements). The Fed funds rate is highly sensitive to money market factors and well exemplifies the interaction of supply and demand for banking funds. The prime rate (the rate banks charge their best customers) tends to follow the Fed funds rate. See Figures 12.1 and 12.2 on the following page.

The Federal Open Market Committee (FOMC) usually directs its open market operations to target the federal funds rate. The effectiveness of the Fed operations is then measured by its effect on the federal funds rate. In 2009, the target for federal funds was 0.25 percent for most of the year. This rate is very low in nominal terms—and even a negative number in "real" (inflation-adjusted) terms. This was a very "easy money" (expansionary) position for monetary policy. As mentioned previously, the actual implementation of OMO occurs through the Federal Reserve Bank of New York with its close proximity (geographic and virtual) to the major financial markets.

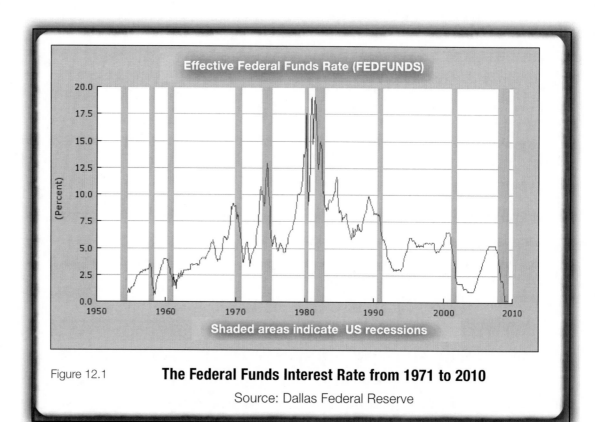

Figure 12.1   **The Federal Funds Interest Rate from 1971 to 2010**

Source: Dallas Federal Reserve

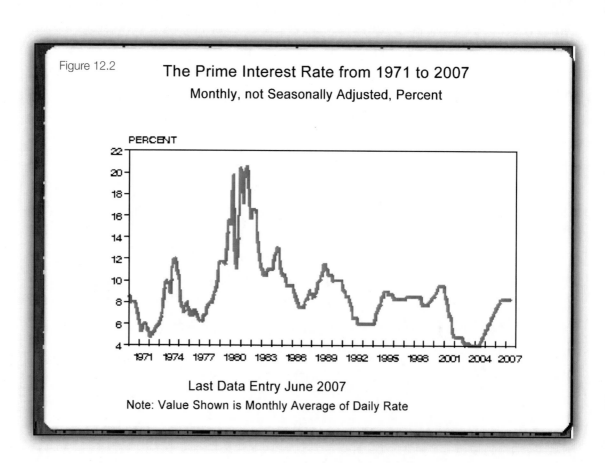

Figure 12.2

The Prime Interest Rate from 1971 to 2007
Monthly, not Seasonally Adjusted, Percent

Last Data Entry June 2007

Note: Value Shown is Monthly Average of Daily Rate

MONETARY POLICY AND GLOBAL ECONOMICS

The implementation of monetary policy is made additionally complex by the international position of the U.S. dollar. The dollar is widely used throughout the world and, in a closely related matter, the United States currently has a substantial deficit between exports and imports. This creates an outflow of American money to pay for the greater amount of imports. The net outflow of dollars is often returned to the United States for purchase of Treasury bonds that pay an attractive market interest rate (to a foreign investor) with low risk. The challenge is this: If interest rates are low, American firms are more likely to expand—but if interest rates are low, foreign investors also will trade dollars gained through trade for investments in other nations (instead of the United States), forcing down the value of the dollar. In order to balance these factors, the Fed must consider a higher interest rate to attract foreign investors to U.S. debt instruments (Treasury bonds)—but such a rate may slow the American economy.

An easy money policy (low interest rates) will decrease the value of the dollar and increase exports from the United States, but reduced interest rates will also discourage foreigners from investing in America. A tight money policy (high interest rates) will increase the value of the dollar, reduce exports and slow the American economy, but it also will attract a return of American dollars spent for imports. There is a podcast discussion of international trade at http://dallasfed.org/video/index.html with various global titles.

EQUATION OF EXCHANGE

For more than 200 years, economists have studied the relationship of money supply to inflation. In early economic history, John Stuart Mill recognized the importance of the money supply to prices, although at that time national income data were not available to accurately quantify the relationship. However, Irving Fisher formulated the equation of exchange in mathematical terms using modern national income data created during the 1940s. In modern economics, his equation is shortened to:

$$M \times V = P \times Q$$

$$M \times V = P \times Q$$

M is the average amount in circulation

V is the velocity of the money that is described as the annual frequency with which a dollar is spent

P is the average price level

Q is the quantity purchased (or produced)

This formula is a truism, meaning that the values are true by definition. If you multiply the number of dollars in circulation by the average number of times that each one is spent during a year, the result will equal the average price of an item times the quantity of items purchased (or produced). Another view of this relationship is that the amount of money times the number of times it is spent is equal to GDP (P times Q).

THE QUANTITY THEORY OF MONEY

The **quantity theory of money** is based on the equation of exchange. This theory assumes that V and Q tend to be relatively stable during a year. Therefore, there is a strong relationship between the quantity of money and the price level. The new Classical Theory discussed in Lesson 7 began with this Monetarist Theory. The Monetarist school of economics (not to be confused with Monetary Policy) uses the quantity theory of money (equation of exchange) as a basis of theory. Monetarists emphasize changes in the money supply as the most important determinant of employment, output and prices. According to this theory, the money supply is a critical causal force yielding the nominal GDP.

Critics of the Monetarist Theory, such as Keynesians, argue that V and Q are not stable. Keynesians further assume that the velocity of money varies directly with the interest rate. The unstable nature of V (in their view) can cause a significant effect on GDP. The view of some critics of the Monetarist Theory is that changes in the level of prices <u>correlate</u> to changes in the money supply, but they are <u>not caused</u> by changes in the money supply. Having a full moon the night before may correlate with your favorite team winning its game the next day but it may not cause the team to win (then again maybe it does—these are interesting questions).

There are many debates between Monetarists and Keynesians over the use of monetary policy. Monetarists argue that fiscal policy is weak due to the crowding-out effect. Keynesians believe that there is only a small amount of crowding-out.

Monetarists argue that requiring the Fed to operate with a "monetary rule" (money growth at the same rate as potential increases in real GDP) is wise. Such a rule, according to Fiscalists (Keynesians), would be very constraining for the Fed and would only increase the severity of business cycles.

The debate continues between these different schools of thought. While the approaches vary, the basic goals for the economy are the same. The Monetarist school was influential during the Reagan administration and continues to be an important part of monetary considerations. A presentation of this view is well documented by the Dallas Federal Reserve in the discussion with Economics Nobel Laureate Milton Friedman at http://www.dallasfed.org?video?index. html. Under the Economic Education tab, you will find videos with a recording titled "Cooperatives not Competitors" and "Trading Freely."

Monetarist Theory, the Supply Side Theory and Keynesian (Fiscalist) Theory are all widely held (and widely debated) today and each is slowly evolving. The fundamental relationships previously described have held, with some "evolution," since the 1930s. All three schools actually provide analytical frameworks for helping to understand the nature of our economy today and in the future. Most credible discussions of our economy will include some elements of all three theories.

ECONOMIC GROWTH

It is very important to remember (as you saw in Lessons 6, 8 and 9) that "real growth" in the economy depends on relatively slow, evolving rightward shifts in the aggregate supply. As your instincts might tell you, the presence of a steady (but not too rapid) expansion in the supply of money is very important to the real growth of the economy. On the opposite side of the coin, the lack of a balanced expansion in the money supply can certainly inhibit real growth and result in a stagnant (or even backsliding) AS curve.

It is critical for the health of an economy that expansion of the money supply (as well as long-term savings) be well balanced with the potential for rightward shifts in aggregate supply and the resulting expansion of production capacity (growth in the PPF). The Federal Reserve faces many challenging choices and trade-offs in trying to provide a balanced approach that considers the short-term health of the U.-S. economy as well as its long-term growth.

Regarding "challenging choices" and the expansion of the AS and PPF, we should not forget what ultimately underlies our material standard of living. As long as our legitimate creativity, innovation and productivity as individuals and as a society continues to expand, then we can continue to grow in a sustainable way—and a strong standard of living can be shared by all. It really is about trying to make those good choices. If each of us individually, in our own microeconomy, can follow such an approach, then as a community (and as a larger society) we can all share in a strong standard of living—and a good quality of life.

SUMMARY

The Federal Reserve is responsible for monetary policy and working with the federal government to facilitate (assist) economic growth, stability and full employment (but remember that it cannot actually create those conditions—this can only be done at the "micro" level). The Federal Reserve uses both major and minor tools to assist in the pursuit of our economic goals. The Fed's major (or quantitative) tools include open market operations, the discount rate and reserve requirements. The minor tools include moral suasion, consumer credit controls and margin requirements.

Additional Thoughts on "Growth" and the AS/AD Model

There is some mutual ground on the topic of "economic growth" among the views noted above (the "schools of thought"). Each view does acknowledge the AS/AD model and its relevance to growth. In each of these views, a rightward shift in both the AS and AD curves represents growth in employment, output and income. The means of facilitating these shifts may center on the supply side forces of capitalism and lower taxation and regulation or on the demand side forces with increased access to education and training. Some economists advocate increasing AS by decreasing government spending while others advocate increasing government spending for education and training; changes in government spending are eventually tied to changes in government taxing. In our economic future, we will most likely see an emphasis on a number of different approaches to facilitate the "rightward shifts" of both AS and AD.

A Postscript:

Theory vs. Reality—Our Recent Economic Problems

Dealing with the recession of 2008–2009 was an interesting experiment in the use of both monetary and fiscal policy to counter business cycles. This recession began with a mortgage debt crisis that resulted from poorly collateralized real estate loans and speculation in mortgage-backed securities and the insurance products generated for these securities. Risky loans were made for houses (called subprime mortgages) with the assumption that housing prices would continuously increase and, therefore, even if a borrower did have a problem, he could always sell the property to cover the loan.

The U.S. economy, however, entered a recession. This was initially driven by a financial crisis that was generated by those same mortgage-backed securities and their derivatives mentioned above. The price of housing in many markets began to fall significantly. This forced buyers into foreclosure and banks took possession of houses valued at less than the balance on their mortgage loans. These houses were often unsaleable in the short term. The mortgages were often insured, but due to the large scale of the defaults, insurance firms were not able to provide the funds.

With the slump of the housing and insurance industries, the financial markets continued to encounter problems because they were part of the structure of securities backing the original mortgages. As a number of banks as well as insurance and financial firms faced bankruptcy, President Bush requested a "bailout" for these institutions. Their collapse would potentially have caused a problem for the entire U.S. economy as well as many international banks holding U.S. mortgage-backed securities. Eventually Congress approved and the president signed a bill authorizing funds for banks as well as several insurance and financial firms. This represented an unprecedented modern use of fiscal policy on the part of the U.S. government.

In order to facilitate movement away from the risk of an even larger recession, the Federal Reserve began expanding its loan operations. The Fed made funds available for credit markets through extensive loan increases and nominal interest rates were reduced to almost zero. The Federal government, through the U.S. Treasury, bought stock in many banks and financial institutions in a coordinated effort with the Fed.

President Obama continued the federal bailout movement by purchasing controlling interest in Chrysler (Fiat) and General Motors. A second stimulus package was passed by Congress and signed by President Obama to use fiscal means to bolster the economy through tax cuts and increasing government funding for projects across the nation. This was intended to provide a major stimulus to aggregate demand.

These are very extraordinary actions within both fiscal and monetary policy. There are many arguments both for and against such government and Federal Reserve action. However, most economists agree that the recession of 2008–2009 was potentially the worst threat since the Depression in the 1930s.

Conclusion

A fundamental knowledge of economics would seem to be crucial to survival and prosperity in today's world. Most economists agree on the basic principles that you have studied in this course. There are, however, a number of different perspectives on the policy actions that can be taken by the federal government and the Federal Reserve (recall "normative economics"). You should now be well aware that the Classical, Monetarist and Keynesian views often differ on "what to do and when to do it."

Real-World Economics

Please access links through online E-text.

Monetary Policy: Actions taken by the Federal Reserve to influence the availability and cost of bank credit in order to promote economic stability.

Reserve Requirement: The percentage of a bank's deposits that must be retained by the bank or deposited with the Federal Reserve.

Discount Rate: The interest rate paid by a commercial bank if it borrows from the Federal Reserve.

Open Market Operations: The buying and selling of government securities in the open market to influence bank reserves.

Tight Money Policy: If the Fed restricts the money supply (M1), usually in response to inflationary pressure, it is called tight money.

Easy Money Policy: If the Fed makes more money available (M1) for lending, usually in response to recessionary pressure, it is called easy money.

Margin Requirement: The amount of down payment required when you buy stock. Currently 50 percent of the total purchase must be paid when you complete the transaction.

Moral Suasion: The informal influence associated with the importance of the Federal Reserve.

Credit Controls: A seldom-used Fed control device, but it gives the Fed the authority to dictate any interest rate of terms of any loan.

Velocity: The speed at which money is spent.

Federal Funds Rate: The rate that banks charge each other for short-term (usually overnight) loans.

Prime Rate: The interest rate banks charge their best (usually corporate) customers. It is the benchmark for most other loans.

Monetarist Theory: One of the major schools of contemporary economics which asserts that controlling the money supply is the key to maintaining a stable economy. Monetarists are usually associated to a more conservative political viewpoint.

Equation of Exchange: This equation (MV=PQ) is a way of analyzing not only the growth of the money supply but also the speed at which money is turning over in our economy and the effects that follow.

Keynesian Theory: Sometimes called Neo-Keynesian economics, this school of thought is based on the aggregate demand/aggregate supply theory first developed by John Maynard Keynes. It sees the control of the money supply of secondary importance to Fiscal Policy. Keynesians are typically associated with a more liberal political viewpoint.

Applied Exercises

Exercise One:

COMMERCIAL BANKING SYSTEM

Assets		Liabilities and Net Worth	
Reserves	$80	Deposits	$300
Investments	$120	Loans from Fed	4
Loans	$60		

FEDERAL RESERVE BANKS

Assets		Liabilities and Net Worth	
Securities	$326	Reserves of Banks	$80
Loans to Bank	4	Treasury Deposits	50
		Federal Reserve Notes	$200

A. From the information above, how much do banks have in excess reserve?

B. How much is the maximum quantity of money that could be created?

C. If the Federal Reserve buys $2 in securities from the public and it is deposited in checking accounts in banks, how will the supply of money change?

D. If the Federal Reserve sells $2 in securities to the public and it is taken from checking accounts in banks, how will the supply of money change?

Applied Exercises

Exercise Two:

The quantity theory of money argues that the long-run price levels move in proportion to changes in the money supply. Answer the following questions based on that assumption.

A. Money Supply (M) $2,000

   Price Level (P)   10

   Quantity (Y)   500

Calculate the velocity of money given the above information.

B. Based on the quantity theory of money assumptions, what would happen if the money supply increased to $2,200?

Applied Exercises: Answers

Exercise One:

A. Reserves = $80 and Loans = $60, therefore, there is excess reserve of $20.

B. The excess reserves are $20 times the money multiplier = money creation maximum. The money multiplier is 1/reserve requirement. Loans are 60/300 or .2 and excess reserves are $20, therefore 5 times 20 = $100.

C. The direct impact immediately would be $2 increase in reserves with an excess of .8 times $2 or $1.6 times 5 = $8.

D. A decrease in money creation potential of $10 ($2 times money multiplier).

Exercise Two:

A. MV = PQ, therefore $2,000 times V = 10 times 500, resulting in a V = 2.5.

B. MV = PQ, therefore $2,200 times 2.5 = $5,500, therefore the market cost of the economy has increased by 10 percent from $5,000 to $5,500.